Without Regard to Good Manners

Frontispiece: Portrait of Gilbert Stuart by John Donaldson.
(Reproduced with permission of John Murray.)

Without Regard to Good Manners

A Biography of
Gilbert Stuart 1743–1786

WILLIAM ZACHS

EDINBURGH UNIVERSITY PRESS

© William Zachs, 1992

Edinburgh University Press
22 George Square, Edinburgh

Typeset in Linotron Palatino
by Koinonia Ltd., Bury, and
printed in Great Britain by
Hartnolls Ltd, Bodmin ____

The publisher acknowledges subsidy
from the Scottish Arts Council
towards the publication of this volume.

British Library Cataloguing
 in Publication Data
Zachs, William
 "Without regard to good manners":
 A biography of Gilbert Stuart 1743–1786.
 I. Title
 820.9
 ISBN   0 7846 0319 0

Contents

Acknowledgements vii

Abbreviations and References ix

Introduction xi

1. Academic Beginnings 1743–1768   1
2. Living to Write and Writing to Live 1769–1773   39
3. *The Edinburgh Magazine and Review*: Redefining the Limits of Criticism 1773–1776   63
4. Conjectures on Society 1776–1779   96
5. Scottish Narrative History: A Reformation in Historical Writing 1780–1782   131
6. Acrimonious Endings 1783–1786   172

Notes 189

Bibliography of Works by Gilbert Stuart 216

Index 221

Acknowledgements

'The author is conscious of the little force and ability with which he has been able to conceive and express his sentiments; and he delivers them to the public with fears and wishes' (EC, vi). So wrote Gilbert Stuart at the start of his first book. Without intending too close an association with my subject, I would like to add to similar 'fears and wishes' what is more important: acknowledgement of those institutions and individuals who helped to make this book a reality. Among the former are included the Edinburgh University Library, the National Library of Scotland, the British Library and the Manx Museum, at Douglas.

I owe a special debt of gratitude to the British Academy for awarding me a post-doctoral fellowship from 1989–92.

My greatest individual debt is to Virginia Murray, the archivist at the publisher John Murray. This long-established London house originally published many of Stuart's works and their founder was his close friend. They hold the largest collection of manuscript material relating to Stuart, and each time I visited something new was brought to my attention, whether it was a series of letters or the original drawing of Stuart reproduced as the frontispiece to this biography. A glance at the Notes shows the extent of my obligation to the Murrays, with whose permission so much material is quoted.

A number of people were kind enough to read this work in part or in full at various stages of preparation: H. T. Dickinson, Michael Lynch, Richard Sher, Nicholas Phillipson, John Price, David Shuttleton, Alan Rankin, Nigel Beanland, Geoffrey Carnall and particularly Michael Barfoot. I thank them for many constructive comments which have made this a much better book than it otherwise would have been. At the same time I take full responsibility for the errors and inadequacies which remain.

I offer thanks to my family and to Martin Adam for their continued encouragement.

Without the support and ideas of Martin Spencer, Secretary to Edinburgh University Press 1987–90, Gilbert Stuart would have remained in oblivion. I am grateful to him for believing in both of us and am deeply saddened by his untimely death.

Abbreviations and References

Stuart's Writings

CO   *Critical Observations concerning the Scottish Historians Hume, Stuart, and Robertson: including an Idea of the Reign of Mary Queen of Scots, as a Portion of History; Specimens of the Histories of this Princess, by Dr. Stuart and Dr. Robertson; and a Comparative View of the Merits of these Rival Historians: with A Literary Picture of Dr. Robertson, In a contrasted Opposition with the celebrated Mr. Hume*. London, 1782. In text: *Critical Observations*.

EC   *An Historical Dissertation concerning the Antiquity of the English Constitution*, second edition. London, 1770. In text: *English Constitution*

EMR   *The Edinburgh Magazine and Review*, 5 vols. Edinburgh, 1773–6

ER   *The English Review, or an Abstract of English and Foreign Literature*, 20 vols. London, 1783–93

FD   *Faction Displayed or, A Genuine Relation of the Representation of the Trades, and of the late Political Contentions in the City of Edinburgh.* [Edinburgh, 1778]

HRS   *The History the Establishment of the Reformation of Religion in Scotland.* London, 1780. In text: *History of the Reformation in Scotland*

MQS   *The History of Scotland, from the Establishment of the Reformation, till the Death of Queen Mary*, 2 vols, second edition. London, 1783–4. In text: *History of Mary Queen of Scots*

PH   *The Political Herald, and Review; or, a Survey of Domestic and Foreign Politics; and a Critical Account of Political and Historical Publications*, 3 vols. London, 1785–86

PLS   *Observations concerning the Public Law, and the Constitutional History of Scotland: with Occasional Remarks concerning English Antiquity*. Edinburgh, 1779. In text: *Public Law of Scotland*

VS   *A View of Society in Europe, in its Progress from Rudeness to Refinement: or, Inquiries concerning the History of Law, Government, and Manners*, second edition. London, 1782. In text: *View of Society*

Manuscript Collections

EUL	Edinburgh University Library
Hughenden Papers	Letters of Gilbert Stuart to the publisher John Murray in the Bodleian Library, MS Disraeli Deposit, G/1/904–44
Murray Archive	Letters received by John Murray. These are catalogued alphabetically and are located at John Murray, 50 Albemarle Street, London.
Murray's Copybooks	Copies of letters written by Murray between 1765 and 1793 and entered into a set of bound volumes. The correspondence is in chronological order, and as such is referenced by the date of the letter. They are located at John Murray.
NLS	National Library of Scotland

Introduction

Who is that Drawcansir?

Why Sir, a fierce Hero, that ... does what he will, without regard to good manners, justice, or numbers.

George Villiers, *The Rehearsal* (London,1672), IV, i

When Gilbert Stuart is mentioned it is most often unfavourably. Typical of the dismissive regard with which he has been held is Austin Allibone's remark in the *Critical Dictionary of English Literature* (1870) that 'more than most readers will care to know about such a sot, grumbler, scold and literary Ishmaelite will be found in the authorities cited below'.[1] In the *Calamities of Authors* (1812) Isaac D'Israeli described him as a 'literary assassin' who 'derived the last consolations of life from an obscure corner of a Burton alehouse' and added no more favourably that 'his historical works possess the show, without the solidity, of research'.[2] More recently Ernest Mossner, the biographer of David Hume, characterised Stuart as a 'malevolent genius' who 'hated everything Scottish and endeavoured to work off his literary spleen through literary vituperation'.[3] These men have exposed one side of Stuart's life and writings, but in doing so they have obscured other more important ones.

Rather than defend him from the aspersions of critics, I intend to examine the conditions which contributed to his development. Stuart's life is characterised more by his encounters, adventures and difficulties than by his ideas and innovations. The intensity of his polemics has tended to obscure the issues on which they were based. Stuart fought against adversaries whom he had little hope of defeating, yet he persisted in the belief that his principles were just and he could overcome anything. William Godwin, the author of *An Enquiry concerning Political Justice* (1793), was one of the few who publicly defended the integrity of Stuart's creed. Shortly after

Stuart's death, he wrote the following remarks in the *Political Herald*, a radical periodical which Stuart edited and to which Godwin regularly contributed:

> If ever any man defended or opposed measures from the genuine sentiments of his heart, it was doctor Stuart ... Among all the characters that ever adorned literature, among all the inhabitants of this island, perhaps there will not be found one, whose pleadings were so generous, so constant and so unalterable for the rights of mankind (PH, III, 281).[4]

Godwin's hyperbolic comments were among the few to support the conduct of his fellow journalist. Censure rather than praise was to follow; or, what is worse, complete disregard.

Stuart was well known in his day. Students of eighteenth-century Scottish culture know him as the editor of the *Edinburgh Magazine and Review* (1773–6). This periodical promised to be a perceptive and entertaining journal, but before long it became too contentious for polite Scottish society and too provincial for the wider English and international market. Journalism was Stuart's main source of income, and he was a skilful critic. But historical writing was the genuine calling of his heart.

He was the son of a professor and grew up at the centre of Edinburgh's academic community among the ministers, doctors and lawyers who ran the University and dominated the life of the town. In some respects he followed the successful examples of Hume and William Robertson as historians, though at times he wrote with the intention of undermining their political sentiments and literary methods. Hume was an obvious target for an aspiring writer with a contentious nature. Robertson was the Principal of Edinburgh University and the leader of the powerful Moderate party of the Presbyterian Scottish church. Stuart rested many hopes on the patronage of Robertson and actively supported him at the start of his own career. When the law chair he expected to gain was denied him in 1778, he turned against the Principal and the establishment he led.

Stuart sought literary fame and the financial rewards that came with it. However, he gained public recognition as an historical writer only near the end of his short career with the publication of his *History of Mary Queen of Scots*. In this vindication of the queen he challenged the opinions not only of Robertson, whose account of Mary had been the most popular of its kind since its appearance twenty-five years before, but also those of Hume, who devoted a portion of his *History of England* to the reign of Mary. The victory he obtained over these men in the name of historical truth was considerable in England, but in Scotland his views were hardly noticed.

Stuart's appointment as the editor of the *Political Herald* in 1785 placed him in an enviable and powerful position. He was in regular contact with Edmund Burke, Richard Brinsley Sheridan and Charles James Fox, the leaders of the Opposition who backed this journal against the government of William Pitt and his Scottish minister Henry Dundas. One year later illness brought a halt to his rising prospects. Stuart had gradually undermined his health by drinking to excess. His death at the age of forty-two was lamented by friends and family, but not by the targets of his criticisms.

I am not suggesting that Stuart's writings should become part of an eighteenth-century literary canon. The embattled context in which he wrote make them useful to those interested in the literary and political worlds of late eighteenth-century Britain. Stuart and his works were held in such ill repute during his life and afterwards that his innovative literary contributions were hastily discounted along with his often unsavoury character. To dismiss Stuart because of the acrimony of his personality and the satirical and controversial features of his writings is to miss the opportunity of discovering an unusual individual who wrote prolifically in response to his times.

Stuart's writings are the basic materials for this book. They are supplemented by an extant correspondence of about 150 letters and a range of secondary sources. The first chapter moves from biographical information about Stuart and his family to how he came to write his first book, the *English Constitution*. I have introduced a critique of this work with definitions of the two historical genres in which he wrote: conjectural and narrative history.

Chapter 2 considers Stuart venturing upon a career as a professional writer in London. The variety of people he met there and the diverse activities in which he was engaged as a reviewer, hack writer, historian and translator show the range of his literary interests.

Stuart returned to Edinburgh in 1773 to establish his own periodical, the *Edinburgh Magazine and Review*, which is the subject of Chapter 3. In the context of the Scottish periodical tradition of the late eighteenth and early nineteenth century, it provides an indicator of the religious and political climate of the period.

Stuart's flair for journalism did not prevent him returning to his historical pursuits. After the dissolution of his periodical in 1776, he remained in Scotland and published in consecutive years the *View of Society* and the *Public Law of Scotland*. These works of conjectural history dealt with many of the same themes as the *English Constitution*. Although Stuart's general subject was feudal society, readers did not miss pointed allusions to contemporary events.

The fifth chapter takes up Stuart's accounts of the Scottish Reformation and of the reign of Mary Queen of Scots, considering both the literary dimensions of the texts and the ways in which he differed from fellow historians.

The final chapter summarises the last years of his life. The main writings of this period are his contributions to the *English Review* and the *Political Herald*, two London-based periodicals in which he was actively involved.

A remark of James Boswell, who knew Stuart well, may serve as a useful guide for this biography: 'His bluntness did not please me, though his strong mind did.'[5] This 'strong mind' and the works it produced together with the 'bluntness' of his character merit examination – at a distance of over two hundred years the vitriolic and alcoholic life he led may be more an object of interest than a cause for moral indignation.

1

Academic Beginnings 1743–1768

They that found absolute monarchy upon the title of the
sword, make their heroes ... arrant Drawcansirs ... We are
told by some, that the English monarchy is founded in the
Norman conquest, and that our princes have thereby a title to
absolute dominion: which if it were true, (as by the history it
appears otherwise) and that William had a right to make war
on this island; yet his dominion by conquest could reach no
farther than to the Saxons and Britons, that were then inhabitants of this country.

John Locke, *Two Treatises of Government*, (London, 1690), II,
xvi, 177

It was an academic beginning. On 9 November 1743 Gilbert Stuart
was born in the old college buildings of Edinburgh University , or
Town's College as it was then called. He was the first child of
George Stuart, Professor of Humanity (Latin) at the College and
Jean Duncanson Stuart. When Gilbert was a few days old the
Reverend Patrick Cumming, a divinity professor, baptised him
into the Presbyterian faith. The registration of his birth was witnessed by Thomas and Walter Ruddiman, printers at Edinburgh.[1]
Gilbert was the eldest of six children: two died in infancy, and the
other three (Walter, Mary and Anne) were born between May 1746
and October 1750.[2]

What little is known of the family on the Stuart and Duncanson
sides hardly merits note. The ties with the Ruddimans were far
more significant. George Stuart described his relationship with
Thomas as one 'both in blood and friendship'.[3] He was a father
figure for George and a man with whom the family 'had lived long
in intimacy'.[4] The influence he exerted on Gilbert's thought and
writing was considerable.

Thomas Ruddiman (1674–1757), a scholar, printer, and keeper
of the Advocates' Library, was an important figure in Scottish
literary society. He was the author of the most popular Latin
grammar books in eighteenth-century Britain (if not Europe), the

editor of the vernacular Scots *Eneados* (1710) by Gavin Douglas
and the works of William Drummond of Hawthornden (1711)
and, with his brother, the publisher of the popular Edinburgh
newspaper, the *Caledonian Mercury*.[5] Ruddiman's most ambitious
and controversial undertaking was his 1715 edition of the works
of George Buchanan, the Reformation poet and historian who was
the tutor to James VI and the enemy of Mary Queen of Scots.
Ruddiman transmitted to Gilbert Stuart, indeed to post-Union
Scotland, a tradition of Scottish humanist scholarship which went
back to Buchanan and had persisted in Scotland during the late
seventeenth and early eighteenth centuries in the ideas of such
men as Archibald Pitcairne and Robert Sibbald. His classical learning and extensive publications, his passionate defence of Mary
Queen of Scots, his ardent Jacobitism, and his respected position
in Edinburgh society struck young Gilbert with awe and provided
him with a model worthy of emulation.

In some respects Ruddiman's contentious approach to politics
and literature was contrary to the politeness and moderation
which characterise the Scottish Enlightenment. But he was most
active in the period before the intellectual ascendancy of Hume
and Smith, when the 'hotbed of genius', as Smollett called it in his
novel *Humphry Clinker* (1771), had not yet come to fruition. Stuart
grew up in the generation which saw Scotland's rise to prominence in European intellectual culture, and Ruddiman's example
provided him with a diverse view of the purposes of scholarship
and literature. His death in 1757 did not put an end to his influence
upon Gilbert. This national and family inheritance was transmitted by George Stuart.

In almost every case, Gilbert's literary productions benefited
from the thoughtful attention of his father. The elder Stuart had
himself uncommon scholarly discernment and literary taste. For
both his son and a generation of Edinburgh University students he
brought together the humanist legacy of Ruddiman with an ap-
preciation of what Joseph Addison described in the *Tatler* as 'the
sense and soul of an author'.[6]

George Stuart was born in August 1711 in the parish of Forglen
in Banffshire, not far from where the Ruddimans originated.[7] He
was educated at the local grammar school and probably took
courses at a Scottish university.[8] Through the influence of
Ruddiman he found employment in June 1736 with Gilbert Elliot
(Lord Minto of the Court of Session). He oversaw various improvements on the Minto estate and acted as tutor to Elliot's eldest

son Gilbert, who rose to occupy important governmental posts, and to patronise a circle of respected literary and civic-minded men which included Hume and Robertson. In a society where social and financial advancement largely depended on receiving patronage from the landed classes, George Stuart made a good start in life by nurturing his connection with the Elliots. Lord and Lady Minto were genuinely fond of him and always concerned themselves with the welfare of his growing family.[9]

When Gilbert Elliot went to Edinburgh to attend the University, Stuart was engaged as a tutor to the son of another prominent legal figure, Robert Dundas (Lord Arniston). His position at the family home in Dalkeith was shortlived, because the young boy died while under Stuart's care. Dundas bore some resentment towards him, a situation which Stuart found worrying.

Shortly after this unfortunate incident Stuart moved to Edinburgh where he put himself forward as a candidate for the chair of Humanity at the University. Although qualified for the post, he was concerned that Dundas might use his influence against him. Stuart therefore requested that Charles Mackie, the Professor of Universal Civil History, 'obviate any prejudice his L[ord]s[hi]p may have conceived against me'.[10] Ultimately, his fears proved to be unfounded. On 16 December 1741 the Edinburgh Town Council, who largely managed the University, appointed him to the professorship and provided him with lodgings in college buildings.[11] Stuart's successful candidacy was largely due to the influence of Lord Minto and the support of Thomas Ruddiman. What better man to recommend him to the post than Ruddiman, the author of the prestigious Latin grammar? The event, Mackie explained to Lord Bolgonie, 'made a great deal of noise, as little things always do in a narrow Town'.[12] A ballad was even written in the course of the contest which made clear the importance of Elliot's patronage in gaining the appointment.[13]

The careers of George and Gilbert Stuart are marked by the success or failure of their efforts to gain the patronage of superiors. Despite complaints to the contrary, George attained a moderate level of social status and financial security through the interest of Ruddiman and the Elliot family. Persistent and calculating, he employed whatever information and influence he had to the advantage of his patrons.[14] The fact that he owned land near Selkirk (at Midlem) and was eligible to cast a vote for the Elliot interest is one of several reasons why that family concerned itself with the affairs of the Stuarts. In 1772 George sold this property to the

Elliots and with the proceeds purchased the home at Fisherrow, where he retired in 1775. Upon the sale he wrote to Elliot that 'whatever he who is your own man of business thinks a reasonable price, I most heartily agree to'.[15] Here was George Stuart in an uncharacteristic mood of fiscal generosity. More often he was a prudent and parsimonious manager of his funds, who complained of having little, yet when he died in 1793, at the age of eighty-one, he left a sizeable estate of over £5,000 carefully divided among his grandchildren. Although financially comfortable, in his last years he was left 'disconsolate and forlorn' by the loss not only of his wife but of three of his four children, including his favourite, Gibbie.[16]

George's loyalty to patrons was not so strongly developed in his son. Gilbert too could be patient and obsequious, but ultimately he did not obtain the preferment he sought, either in the form of a university chair or a government post. When the patronage of Elliot proved ineffectual, others were enlisted, including David Hume, Lord Mansfield, the Duke of Atholl, Laurence Dundas, Lord North, Henry Dundas, Lord Hailes and the Earl of Buchan. None of these men, however, brought Gilbert the financial security which his father and indeed the generation following Gilbert Stuart found in the Elliots of Minto.[17]

Less than a year after George Stuart was appointed to the Humanity chair he married Jean Duncanson at Edinburgh on 31 October 1742. She was born in Dunbartonshire in May 1712 and was the third of seven children born to James Duncanson of Gearsheath and Janet Mason. The family probably had ties of kinship with the Smolletts of Bonhill. The exact relationship to the novelist is uncertain, but when Tobias Smollett died in 1771, Gilbert Stuart was promised access to literary and family papers 'to write the history of his hero' and afterwards received a substantial legacy from Smollett's wealthy cousin, James Smollett of Cameron House.[18]

George Stuart's income as a professor, collected by subscription from each student, rarely amounted to more than £40 per annum, a sum barely sufficient to maintain his growing family. University matriculation rolls during Stuart's tenure show that the Humanity class was nearly as well subscribed as the other arts classes (Greek, logic and metaphysics and natural philosophy), but while many professorships had substantial salaries attached to them, that of Humanity did not. Most young men who elected to fulfil the requirements of the arts course attended Stuart's lectures. Among his students, James Boswell is the most notable.[19] Gilbert is listed in his father's class roll for the 1757–58 academic year, when he was fourteen years old, the age when most students began their university education.[20] By the time students entered the higher level Humanity class they possessed a thorough knowledge of the Latin language. John Ramsay of Ochtertyre explained that it was George Stuart's 'great object' to acquaint his students 'with the beauties of the writers of the Augustan Age. In short, he wished rather to improve their taste than to play the part of a school master.'[21] Stuart published an outline of his advanced Latin course under the title *Heads of Lectures for the Use of the Highest Class of Students in Humanity in the University of Edinburgh* (1780). This was his only publication, which is surprising when one considers that fellow professors were making substantial sums by publishing their lectures. Rather more pedantic and less ambitious, George spent his scholarly hours compiling a Latin dictionary, which remained unpublished partly because he demanded a higher price than any bookseller was willing to offer.[22]

To supplement his meagre salary, George Stuart enlisted the patronage of the Duke of Atholl and was appointed College Librarian in 1747. Although strictly a Town Council appointment, the Duke had control of this post.[23] Initially, Stuart's brother Alexander (later minister of Edinburgh's West Kirk) was brought in to assist him in the Library. In the late 1750s, when Gilbert was a teenager, he assumed the role of assistant. This privileged and formative experience gave him a sense of the value of the printed word and encouraged the desire to contribute his own ideas to the storehouse of knowledge which surrounded him.

At the time of his father's appointment the Library was in a very disordered state. George's first duty was to compile two catalogues: one alphabetical by author; the other of the books as they appeared on the shelves. He followed a plan similar to that used by Ruddiman in his *Catalogue of the Advocates' Library* of 1742. Accounts of the Library's history (with the exception of Stuart's own), however, suggest that his efforts did little to put the library in better order.[24] But by the spring of 1748, he had produced a three-volume alphabetical catalogue, though he complained that it had been at 'great expense to his health'.[25] In recompense for this service, and those he would continue to perform, he successfully applied to the Town Council for additional chambers in the college buildings 'to be fitted up at his own expense both for the conveniency of their service as Library Keeper and to enable him to be more extensively useful as he proposed to employ it for the benefit of Education in accommodating Gentlemen's Sons who were sent into the university.'[26] Among the most notable students to reside with the Stuart family were the two teenage sons of Gilbert Elliot. The boys reported upon arrival in October 1766 that 'we are perfectly pleased with our Rooms' and added 'our eating is better than we could have expected'.[27] The boys attended lectures given by Edinburgh's eminent professors and in the afternoons received lessons in drawing, fencing and other activities which would prepare them for careers in public service. George Stuart also gave them private Latin tuition. It was with pride that he later saw them assume important political and military posts.

There were times when Gilbert found his parents preoccupied with caring for their important charges and he was no doubt envious of the expensive extra-curricular activities of which he heard enthusiastic reports but was largely denied himself. Yet from these experiences he learned not only to value more highly the time his father and mother could spend with him, but also began to understand the meaning of the distinction of ranks in society, a theme to which he gave considerable attention in his published works. If socially inferior to lodgers such as the Elliots, he gained confidence by equalling or surpassing them in intellectual ability.

George Stuart's duties as professor, librarian and guardian to 'Gentlemen's sons' may have limited his attendance upon the needs of his own children, but he did not neglect the education of his boys. He knew from personal experience that a cultivated intelligence could be a passport to success. At an early age Gilbert enrolled at the grammar school of James Mundell in Edinburgh's West Bow, the same school that Boswell had attended a few years before. He also studied French and Italian under the direction of John Murdoch at Caruthers Close in the High Street. His proficiency in French is evident in his later English translations of French texts. At the age of eleven he moved on to the popular Edinburgh High School. In his youth Gilbert is said to have been 'remarkable for dullness and an apparent want of comprehension'. But his patient father was 'the first who discovered the strength and solidity of his understanding ... and prophesied, that his son would one day rise to considerable eminence'.[28] He was a temperamental child, putting all his energy into the subjects he liked, and was doubtless a problem for the master whose subject did not interest him. After two years at the High School he enrolled in classes at the University. As he lived in college buildings and was known to the professors, he probably attended some without paying fees. After completing his father's lectures he attended Adam Ferguson's moral philosophy class for 1764 and William Wallace's municipal law class for 1766.[29] His eight-year university education was twice the normal period, but his circumstances clearly differed from the ordinary student. However, like the majority who enrolled (apart from those in the Medical and Divinity Faculties), Stuart did not take a degree.

Scottish university education in the mid-eighteenth century was on the whole a less structured system than its English or continental counterparts. In Edinburgh there were also many 'extramural' educational opportunities available. In the summer of 1761 Stuart may have heard the popular course of lectures given by the actor Thomas Sheridan on 'Elocution and on the English Tongue'. His preoccupation with correctly written English suggests that Sheridan's lectures or perhaps reading them influenced him, as they did many Scots of the day.[30]

Educating his sons and the future leaders of the British Empire did not entirely satisfy George Stuart. He wanted to free himself from the drudgery of teaching and to find a lucrative government post. In 1757 he wrote to Gilbert Elliot of his 'fondness of exchanging business' and implored, 'my whole dependence is upon you'.[31] Whenever a position arose which Stuart believed might be obtained with Elliot's influence, a letter was duly written. As Gilbert and Walter grew to manhood they were included in their father's schemes. In 1762 George Stuart conceived a plan to publish a thrice-weekly newspaper to be called the *Edinburgh Advertiser*. The intention was to promote the policies of the Earl of Bute, then the Prime Minister. As proprietor, Stuart requested that he be granted a royal patent for the privilege of sending the paper to post towns and Royal Burghs, by which income from regular subscriptions would be guaranteed. Gilbert's literary talents were already evident, and he welcomed the prospect of writing for the public. Unfortunately, the idea did not meet with government support.[32] When Gilbert established the *Edinburgh Magazine and Review* in 1773, it was in a way the vicarious realisation of his father's unfulfilled ambition to be an editor.

Sometimes George Stuart's tireless efforts to improve his family's situation put stress on his friendship with Elliot, who had numerous requests of the kind to cope with. On one occasion Stuart apologetically told his patron that his concern about set-

tling Gilbert in employment 'made me write perhaps with too
much heat for which I humbly ask pardon'.[33] John Mackenzie of
Delvine, a legal advisor to Elliot, shared with him a benevolent yet
cautious response to George Stuart's request for favours. Mackenzie agreed that Gilbert was well qualified for the post of Keeper of
the Court of Session Minute Book, which had become vacant, but
implored George not to be surprised if the post could not be
obtained. 'The professor', he reported to Elliot, 'imagines you can
overcome all obstacles & I shall be very Glad that it prove so.'[34] In
this case the post was not within the reach of Mackenzie or Elliot.

With no job immediately available, George decided to prepare
Gilbert for a career as a lawyer, and was able to obtain an apprenticeship at Mackenzie's law office in the Horse Wynd off the High
Street. Henry Mackenzie, who was also an apprentice there, offered a rather unfavourable account of his co-worker. Each morning their employer provided a breakfast for his apprentices, 'but
Gilbert sat up too late, and drank too much to be often there'.
Remarking of Stuart's 'seeming stupidity', he mentioned the comment of a visitor to the University Library who 'thought it was put
on ... to change his father's design of making a lawyer of him'.[35]
The *Encyclopaedia Perthensis* wrote of Gilbert's short career as a
lawyer: 'for that profession he has been represented as unqualified
by indolence; by a passion which at a very early period he displayed for general literature; or by boundless dissipation.'[36] In an
anonymous article in the *Monthly Review* in 1772 Stuart explained
why a profession which offered financial security and social
standing would have proved intellectually stifling and ultimately
unfulfilling:

> The memory of a lawyer is perpetually and fully employed;
> but he is rarely induced to exercise judgement ... To compre-
> hend the spirit of laws is no object of his care ... In one word,
> the branch of knowledge which he ventures to profess, he
> has not studied as a science.
>
> The law, in this aspect, cannot fail of giving disgust and
> inquietude to the student. His ingenuity is never exerted; his
> curiosity is never inflamed. He labours, but without pleas-
> ure; and in the sordid prospect of future gain, he alone can
> find a consolation for the fatigue he suffers.[37]

Towards the end of 1766 Stuart completed his apprenticeship. His
retrospective comments indicate that it was tedious work which
did not appeal to him. All the litigation of the Outer Court (the
court in which causes were first heard) was written down, an

arduous task which was assigned to the apprentice. Such a system led Boswell to comment that 'ours is a court of *papers*. We are never seriously engaged but when we write.'[38] Where Boswell submitted to paternal influence (his father was a Court of Session judge) and began to practise law, Stuart convinced his father that he could succeed in another sphere where, as he wrote in the same review, 'the law, when traced historically from its earliest condition to its more cultivated state, becomes a rational occupation'.[39]

As a young man living at the University, Stuart witnessed the gradual establishment of Edinburgh as a literary and scientific centre. He was impressed by the fame and financial successes of Hume, Robertson, Hugh Blair and others, and intrigued by the blend of history, law and philosophy in the writings of Montesquieu, Lord Kames, and John Dalrymple. Works by Lafitau and Charlevoix brought before him the manners of primitive societies in the Americas. Seventeenth-century antiquaries taught him the complexity and dignity of Scottish and English jurisprudence. The works of Ruddiman were a source of pride and a model for emulation. Classical writers, so important a part of his father's scholarly interests, imparted to him a sense of the value and power of literature. He wrote:

> The true historian will unite, as far as it is in his power, the simplicity of Herodotus and Caesar, the majesty of Thucydides, the elegance of Xenophon and Sallust, the knowledge and penetration of Tacitus, the spirit and fire of Livy.   (EMR, V, 35).

He was intimidated by the knowledge he had begun to acquire, yet, inherently ambitious, he was encouraged to test his own capacity as an author. In the course of his legal training Stuart began to study and write. Even if he did retire to the taverns of Edinburgh to forget the drudgery of an unhappy apprenticeship, it is clear that he also went to the Library to pursue a systematic study of jurisprudence and constitutional history. His obituary in the *Daily Universal Register* referred to this early ardour for legal study: 'To Voet and Vinnius he applied as to a necessary useful task; but to Montesquieu and Hume his mind turned spontaneously, with the glow of enthusiasm, and the congeniality of taste.'[40]

As a former assistant in the Library, Stuart was familiar with the collection, and the proximity of his home made access easy. His extensive borrowing is recorded in the Library's registers. Most readers were required to leave a substantial deposit on books and to return them within a fortnight. But Stuart, retaining privileged borrowing rights, merely marked the register 'to be returned on demand'.[41]

By November 1767 he had organised his reading into a well-formed essay, and his proud and hopeful father told Gilbert Elliot that 'the work has been in the hands of some of our people here, Robertson, Ferguson &c. & is highly approved'.[42] He asked if Elliot would accept the dedication, but the patron preferred not to associate himself so closely with the work and its author. Neither a dedication nor even Stuart's name appeared in the first edition. In June 1768 the Edinburgh booksellers Alexander Kincaid and John Bell published the work under the title *An Historical Dissertation concerning the Antiquity of the English Constitution*, priced at five shillings in boards. The London marketing was handled by William Sandby, but the more well known booksellers – Dodsley, Dilly and Cadell – purchased enough copies to gain a place in the imprint.

On the surface the work is a summary history of England, beginning with its first inhabitants, the Britons, continuing with the Roman period, then the Saxon times and concluding with the Norman period. It is not merely an account, or annal, of monarchs and battles, but a discourse on the nature of political liberty through these periods. By liberty Stuart meant the freedom of a nation to govern itself and to resist the absolute authority of a monarch. The English constitution, he believed, guaranteed these rights at all periods, down to the present. His purpose was to show that the anomalous English government called the constitution originated with the ancient Germanic tribes. One of these tribes, the Saxons, introduced their institutions and manners when they conquered Britain.

In the Advertisement to the *English Constitution* Stuart explained that 'a peculiarity, which he had occasion to observe concerning property among the Germans, suggested to him the leading sentiments that he has employed in this essay' (EC, v), namely that in the era following the fall of Rome land was considered the property of nations. It was only in the later stages of feudal society (Norman times) that it came to be vested in leaders and subsequently devolved upon individuals. On this premise Stuart based his original contribution to the history of political liberty and set himself against those authors who, 'not attending to the history of mankind, have perhaps failed to describe it [land] with precision' (EC, 28–9).

In the first part of the work he outlined the free and virtuous state in which the early tribes lived. In the next four parts he compared respectively 'The State of Land', 'The Orders of Men', 'The Judicial Arrangements' and 'The Great Council, or Parliament' in ancient Germany with the equivalent in England. This was the basic plan of the *English Constitution*. Stuart's aim was to show that those who traced political liberty to the people were right, while those who ascribed it to concessions of the monarchy were wrong. But he went about it in a different way from the numerous writers who had preceded his effort. While continuing a centuries old debate, this work was the product of a new and distinctively Scottish historical approach through which Stuart hoped to shift the balance of opinion permanently in favour of his own view.

To understand what this approach was, it will be helpful to clarify the different types of historical writing Stuart produced and consider their place in the historiography of the Enlightenment.[43] This cultural period in Scotland, as elsewhere, was prolific in philosophical and historical writing. David Hume, a leading figure in both fields, remarked to his bookseller William Strahan, 'I believe this is the historical Age and this the historical Nation.'[44] Much of the best historical writing of the day, and Hume's in particular, is characterised by its philosophical quality, that is by its manner of seeking after knowledge, truth and morality. Bolingbroke's comment that 'history is philosophy teaching by examples' is indicative of a central theme in histories written in the second half of the eighteenth century.[45]

There are a number of terms used to describe one important category of these philosophically-minded historical works, of which the *English Constitution* is an example. They are: philosophical history, theoretical history, and conjectural history. The first term is the most general and, for the purposes of differentiating types of writing, can be ambiguous. The second is misleading as it suggests that facts and experience are not important. The last term is the one I prefer to use because it best describes the way Stuart speculated, ordered facts and ideas and drew conclusions about the distant past.

Dugald Stewart first introduced the phrase 'theoretical or conjectural history' in his biography of Adam Smith to describe Smith's *Dissertation on the Origin of Language* (1767). This type of inquiry, according to Stewart, attempted to answer the question 'by what gradual steps the transition has been made from the first simple efforts of uncultivated nature, to a state of things so won-

derfully artificial and complicated'.[46] He viewed conjectural history as something 'entirely of modern origin'.[47] But Scottish writers of the mid-eighteenth century were in fact developing their
ideas within a tradition of inquiry that had roots in the classical
writings of Aristotle (*Politics*), Lucretius (*De Rerum Natura*) and,
particularly in Gilbert Stuart's case, Tacitus (*Germania*).[48] Political
and military institutions, jurisprudence, property, manners, the
division of labour, the orders of men, the influence of climate and
situation, and the roles of the sexes are typical of the kind of
subjects which occupy the conjectural writers. Stuart's works in
this category include the *English Constitution*, the *View of Society*
and the *Public Law of Scotland*. Well known among the conjectural
works of his contemporaries are Hume's *Natural History of Religion*
(1757), Adam Ferguson's *Essay on the History of Civil Society* (1767),
John Millar's *Observations concerning the Distinctions of Ranks in
Society* (1771), Lord Kames' *Sketches of the History of Man* (1774),
Lord Monboddo's *Of the Origin and Progress of Language* (1773-92)
and Adam Smith's *Inquiry into the Nature and Causes of the Wealth of
Nations* (1776). The impact of these and other works of the kind on
the minds of contemporary readers and of subsequent generations
was considerable, even though most are no longer known or read.
Jeremy Bentham, J. S. Mill, Karl Marx and other thinkers were
influenced by Scottish conjectural writing. Moreover, it could be
said that modern academic disciplines such as sociology, anthro-
pology, and linguistics have their origins in this literature.

Another type of philosophical historical writing was also produced at this time, which I find most useful to label 'narrative
history'. Whereas a conjectural approach examined the history of
man and his society in general developmental terms, narrative
history looked more to the sequence of past events in the history of
nations. The evolution of social systems and the general progress
of society were recurring topics for the conjectural historian. The
reigns of monarchs and dramatic occurrences such as wars and
rebellions, were the typical subjects of the narrative approach. The
aim of the latter, however, was not merely to present a chronicle,
or annal, of events (this was history without philosophy). Instead,
the narrative historian sought to relate these events to other periods, especially contemporary times. By this process it was thought
possible to discover general principles of historical and political
change, even of human nature. Typically, conjectural history dealt
with times for which few and often uncertain records were available, while narrative history, though also interpretive, was based

on surviving primary documents and existing secondary material.

Francis Jeffrey, founder of the *Edinburgh Review* in 1802, further clarified the distinction between the two types of historical writing when he remarked that the period after 1603, when the crowns of Scotland and England were united, was 'a fitter object for particular [i.e. narrative] history, but a less suitable one for general philosophical dissertation [i.e conjectural history]'.[49] The publisher John Murray described the narrative genre in terms of its audience and potential for profit:

> To make a saleable work it should be addressed to the Mob of Readers, to literary Amateurs, & to Smatterers in taste. Hume, Gibbon, Robertson and now Ferguson have derived most part of their success & reputation ... by adapting their History to Slender as well as to profound capacities. If you are able to entertain the ladies your business is done.[50]

Conjectural writing was geared towards a more scholarly audience and could bring the author and his bookseller only modest returns. Narrative works, by contrast, could produce substantial profits. Hume's *History of England* (1754–62), William Robertson's *History of Scotland* (1759), Edward Gibbon's *Decline and Fall of the Roman Empire* (1776–88) and Adam Ferguson's *History of the Roman Republic* (1783) are examples of this type of writing, as are Stuart's unpublished 'Memoirs of the Isle of Man', his *History of the Reformation in Scotland* and his *History of Mary Queen of Scots*.

In an anonymous pamphlet written shortly after the publication of this last work, Stuart revealed himself as a narrative historian of a different kind from his contemporaries. In the *Critical Observations on the Scottish Historians: Hume, Stuart, and Robertson*, he defined his approach this way: the historian, 'by uniting the interests of truth and humanity and reconciling the judgment of the understanding to the feelings of the heart ... renders ... history as pleasing and pathetic as it is interesting and important' (CO, 12). Stuart believed that a more sentimental and evocative rendering of history could facilitate understanding and yet could co-exist with the pursuit of historical truth. His historical approach emphasised the personal, the immediate and the intentional. Robertson, Hume and others, by contrast, emphasised the systematic, the rational and the pragmatic. Stuart transcended the fundamental ironic and sceptical elements of Enlightenment historical writing, and, by his rejection of a belief in the possibility of progress and indifference to what Hayden White terms the idea that 'all effects had to be presumed to have both necessary and sufficient causes',[51] he opened a new direction for the historical genre. The subject of Mary provided the materials for what emerged as a type of 'Tragic historiography' composed of 'existential paradox' and 'dialectical contradiction'.[52]

The *Critical Observations* set out other related principles on which he wrote narrative history. Employing the language of utility and thereby reminding his audience of their responsibility to the community, and borrowing the general principle from Bolingbroke, he explained the relevance of Mary's reign for his own day:

> When we trace the connection between the present and the past and mark the openings of a scene in which we ourselves bear a part, a period of greater interest appears, and historical studies come home to mankind. Down to that era we ought to read history as scholars; from that era we ought to study it as citizens.   (CO, 5)

Reminiscent of Francis Jeffrey's comment, Stuart set the date slightly earlier to include Mary's reign.

Both conjectural and narrative historical writing were literary by-products of intellectual developments which took place in the British Isles and on the Continent through the seventeenth century. In the *Advancement of Learning* (1605) and other works, Francis Bacon outlined principles for the systematic classification of knowledge and nature. This was to be achieved by careful observation, beginning with specific facts and advancing to general principles. Newton further popularised a model of experimental enquiry which culminated in the discovery of general laws of nature.[53] Others, including Hume, attempted to apply the same method to the nature of the mind, morality and society. Montesquieu, in *L'Esprit des Loix* (1748) was the first to analyse systematically the political institutions of Europe; and Adam Smith applied to this the organising idea of a progress of society.[54] Lord Kames and John Dalrymple, amongst others, had also engaged in this activity. Smith himself remarked of the conjectural approach that 'we must every one of us acknowledge Kames for our master'.[55] It was primarily the appearance of Kames' *Historical Law Tracts* (1758) which prompted this praise. The originality of this work led Hume to remark to Smith that 'a man might as well think of making a fine sauce by a mixture of wormwood and aloes, as an agreeable composition by joining metaphysics and Scottish law'.[56] Producing variations on this diet of philosophy and law (the *English Constitution* is one example) became the scholarly fashion.

Gilbert Stuart praised Montesquieu above fellow Scottish writers. He regarded John Dalrymple of Cranstoun rather than Kames, whose *Historical Law Tracts* he had studied ardently, but with whom he disagreed on several historical points, to be the first British writer to apply accurately Montesquieu's systematic approach. Dalrymple's important work in this context was an *Essay toward a General History of Feudal Property in Great Britain* (1757). According to Stuart this work was 'replete with great views, and original genius', and he added more generally that 'there is no improvement ... more important or valuable than the introduction of philosophy into law and jurisprudence' (EMR, III, 314).[57] Montesquieu and Dalrymple provided Stuart with a model for the type of conjectural history he wrote in the *English Constitution*. But the *Germania* of Tacitus, a monograph on the origin, geography and institutions of the German tribes, was his primary source book and inspiration. 'Antiquity,' he wrote of this classical work, 'has not given to the kingdoms of Europe a present more valuable' (VS, 2). Edward Gibbon extended similar thoughts on Tacitus to Scottish historians like Stuart. He observed that Tacitus, writing about the primitive state and independence of the Germans, was

> the first of historians who applied the science of philosophy to the study of facts. The expressive conciseness of his descriptions has deserved to exercise the diligence of innumerable antiquarians, and to excite the genius and penetration of the philosophic historians of our own times.[58]

Stuart placed himself at the centre of this tradition when he took a quotation from *L'Esprit des Loix* for the title page epigram of the *English Constitution*. It translates: 'If one is going to read the admirable work of Tacitus on the manners of the Germans, then one will see that it is from them that the English have taken the idea of their political government. This fine system has its origin in the woods'. Montesquieu stated further that England was the 'one nation ... in the world that has for the direct end of its constitution political Liberty'.[59] The Frenchman, however, had investigated the system of English government rather superficially in his great work. Thus for Stuart Montesquieu was both a source of reference and a point of departure.

Stuart was not a pioneer in constitutional or jurisprudential studies like his mentor Montesquieu. Rather he followed a complex tradition of European thought that also included such figures from the Continent as Hugo Grotius and Samuel Pufendorf; in England, Edward Coke, Henry Spelman, John Selden, Robert

Brady and John Locke; and in Scotland, Thomas Craig, George
Mackenzie, Dalrymple, Kames, Hume and others. Stuart borrowed selectively from the constitutional writers and political
theorists of the seventeenth and eighteenth centuries. In some
cases he praised and elaborated their models, in others criticised
them. The choice was largely determined by the political views of
the writer. Stuart's brand of conjectural history was more politicised than his contemporaries.

The *English Constitution* occupies a minor place in the long
tradition of British political and antiquarian writing. Numerous
works were added to it throughout the eighteenth century by
advocates of all political ideologies. In his first work Stuart joined
together the conjectural historian and political commentator and
presented a Whig view of English government. The formulation of
something approaching a science of history enabled him to employ a factual study of social progress which could give credibility
to the expression of a political ideology. Stuart certainly did not
write in an antiquarian vacuum. The *English Constitution* was not
only the product of a rich scholarly tradition but also a response to
recent political events.

The British political scene after the 1745 Rebellion was very
turbulent. The once powerful Whig oligarchy of Walpole and
Pelham had fallen in the early 1760s and a new period of political
instability began. After a succession of ministries in the 1760s,
Lord North established control of affairs for twelve years (1770–
1782). During his ministry resurgences of political tensions and of
constitutional issues were beginning to trouble government and
society. The Treaty of Paris in 1763, ending the Seven Years' War,
had done little to resolve continental affairs or to settle economic
problems at home. The conflict in North America which began
soon afterwards was the dominant political event of Stuart's adult
life. This, together with John Wilkes' moves to reform government
and other radical events brought the public ever more into the
political arena. Extra-parliamentary groups were beginning to
exert influence on government. Metropolitan organisations, such
as the Society of the Supporters of the Bill of Rights and the Society
for Constitutional Information; provincial organisations such as
the Reverend Christopher Wyvill's Yorkshire Association; and
religious groups such as Lord George Gordon's Protestant Association marked the beginnings of an age of radicalism and popular
agitation in which Stuart was very much involved. The public and
the press were becoming formative political influences in society.

As a contributor to newspapers and periodicals, Stuart was at the forefront of these developments. He was even regarded by some to have been the author of the popular 'Letters of Junius', radical attacks on the government to promote constitutional reform.[60]

Despite being sceptical about the extent to which lessons could be learned from the past, Stuart believed it was incumbent upon the historian to pursue this objective. As a historian he endeavoured to use the lessons of history. As a citizen he defended the rights of mankind and opposed policies which increased the power of the Court. In this sense he was a Whig and a writer of whiggish history. But further clarification of such terms is necessary. It is true that after 1746, both government and opposition sides in parliament were whiggish in that they supported the 1688-90 Revolution, the Union and the Hanoverian succession. At the time the *English Constitution* appeared, however, domestic and foreign political turmoil had generated a new set of constitutional arguments. Political labels, such as 'defenders of prerogative' and 'friends of liberty', came into use. The notion of public opinion, that is the voice of the people, likewise took on greater significance.

In his first work Stuart clarified generally what he meant by 'the people'. Historically, it referred to soldiers of merit who had been allotted a portion of land and who attended the national assembly. In contemporary terms this meant a man of independent means, such as a freeholder.[61] He mentioned only briefly the unfranchised landless labourers in the *English Constitution*. Although he ascribed to them no right to political power, nevertheless, 'a road was ... opened for the meanest in the community to attain to its honours' (EC, 186).

In writing about the politics of Stuart's time, labels such as Whig and Tory, Country and Court, should be used with caution. At different times they mean different things. Dr Johnson borrowed a definition of 'whiggish' from Jonathan Swift to remind his readers of the ambiguity of the terms in his own day:

> She'll prove herself a tory plain,
> From principles the whigs maintain;
> And, to defend the whiggish cause,
> Her topics from the tories draws.[62]

Today the term whig, or whiggish, history refers to something quite different from the idea that Stuart presented. It refers to a type of historical fallacy, or misapplication of method, by judging a former period in terms of current values and knowledge.

Stuart's whiggery did not have this pejorative sense. He advocated a political ideology which asserted that the foundation of government was public utility rather than authority. He therefore criticised historians who saw English liberty arising out of monarchical concessions (such as the Magna Charta), rather than as the original free condition of the people before monarchs rose to hold extensive power.

David Hume was one writer whom Stuart challenged on these grounds. The volumes Hume had written in the 1740s and early 1750s on moral, literary and political subjects and the *Enquiry concerning the Principles of Human Understanding* (1748) had shown him to be a formidable philosopher. Stuart admired and, it would seem, understood Hume's important philosophical contributions.[63] In the 1741 essay 'Of the Parties of Great Britain' Hume sketched the characteristics of the two opposing political groups in a telling manner: 'Those of mild tempers, who love peace and order ... will always entertain more favourable sentiments of monarchy, than men of bold and generous spirits, who are passionate lovers of liberty'.[64]

Hume further refined his political thinking when he took to writing as a historian. In 1754 he published the first volume of what was to be a comprehensive history of England. After this account of the reigns of James I and Charles I, he produced a second volume in 1757 on the Commonwealth and the reigns of Charles II and James II. Next he turned back in time to the Tudors and, moving further back, concluded the work with an account of events from Roman times to the accession of Henry VII. The effort of nearly a decade was completed in 1762 in six quarto volumes, and it brought Hume the fame and fortune he had always wished for.

Paradoxically, Hume's work was not only immensely popular but also immensely unsettling to politicians and political theorists alike. For Hume made historical inquiry a relativist rather than absolute exercise of the understanding, by making the study of human nature, not the study of the facts of history, the focus of attention.[65] He thereby undermined ideological claims to authority on all sides, political as well as religious. No longer could one appeal to the idea of a divine guide to the nation's progress or to the antiquity of constitutional liberty. Hume showed that the laws and customs, religion and culture of the age determined political behaviour.[66] The emphasis in Hume's writings on preserving the *status quo* and protecting the individual rights associated with property led many (Stuart among them) to regard Hume as a Tory. Innovation may be necessary, but violent innovation is to be avoided. Too much liberty led to anarchy; therefore even a tyrannic government, he believed, was better than none at all. In the *History of England* Hume showed the 'passionate lovers of liberty' the folly of their ideology.

> Those who, from a pretended respect to antiquity, appeal at every turn to an original plan of the constitution, only cover their turbulent spirit and their private ambition under the appearance of venerable forms; and whatever period they pitch on for their model, they may still be carried back to a more ancient period, where they will find the measures of power entirely different, and where every circumstance, by reason of the greater barbarity of the times, will appear still less worthy of imitation.[67]

There was no easy or decisive response to this new historical approach. One had almost to discover a new theory of human nature more convincing than Hume's to rewrite English history. Stuart, faced with that unenviable task, opted for a number of more realistic strategies in the *English Constitution*. First, he saw that two weaknesses of Hume's *History* were the number of factual inaccuracies and the too frequent dependence on secondary sources. If he could collect these errors and show from primary documentation that Hume was wrong, this evidence might carry some weight. Second, Stuart presented himself as a scholarly inquirer into the nature of early society, where Hume had covered the period before the Roman's arrival in Britain only in general terms and with no pretence of antiquarian scholarship. This was narrative rather than conjectural history as Hume's initial remarks indicate.

> We shall briefly run over the events, which attended the conquest made by that empire, as belonging more to Roman than British story: We shall hasten through the obscure and uninteresting period of Saxon annals: And shall reserve a more full narration for those times, when the truth is both so well ascertained and so complete, as to promise entertainment and instruction to the reader.[68]

In response to this approach the scholar-antiquary, who drew a detailed picture of the past, could gain ground on the philosopher-historian who sketched broadly. Finally, Stuart challenged Hume on conventional party lines by aiming his artillery at the parts of the *History* which tended to show the author as a monarchist. He added to this a fulsome volley of passionate whig rhetoric. Having attacked forcefully, he qualified his criticisms with such remarks as: 'If so great a man has been mistaken, into how many errors must I have fallen?' (EC, 170n). But in the *View of Society*, published in 1778, two years after Hume's death, Stuart intensified his attack. Further study had confirmed him in his views.

> To give completeness to the spirit of my present volume, it is sufficient for me to assert the antiquity of the commons, in opposition to an opinion of their late rise, which a modern historian, of great reputation, has inculcated, with that hardiness which he displays in all his writings, but with little of that power of thought and of reasoning which does honour to his philosophical works ...
>
> His history, from its beginning to its conclusion, is chiefly to be regarded as a plausible defence of prerogative. As an elegant and spirited composition, it merits every commendation. But no friend to humanity, and to the freedom of this kingdom, will consider his constitutional inquiries, with their effect on his narrative, and compare them with the antient and venerable monuments of our story, without feeling a lively surprise, and a patriot indignation. (VS, 327–8)

When the *English Constitution* was published, Stuart sent a copy to Hume. In a carefully composed letter which accompanied it he exhibited a mixture of humility and self-confidence not unlike that which characterises the work itself. He acknowledged that 'the public has profited very much from the learned and masterly reflections you have communicated concerning' English constitutional history, but he stated more emphatically that 'I have presumed to take a different road from that which you have followed, and if I have taken the liberty to differ from you in several particulars, it has been alwise with the greatest deference and respect.'[69] Stuart was extremely anxious for the reply, which is lost, but another which Hume wrote to Gilbert Elliot is sufficiently revealing of his opinion:

> I send you my Letter enclosed to Mr Stewart, which I hope is calculated to encourage a young Man of Merit, without overstraining the Compliment. It were better, however, for him, and for every body, to pursue, in Preference to the idle Trade of Writing, some other lawful Occupation, such as Cheating like an Attorney, Quacking like a Physician, Canting & Hypocrising like a Parson &c &c &c. It is for very

little Purpose to go out of the common Track. Does he expect to make Men wiser? A very pretty Expectation truly![70] Stuart was probably unaware of the good-natured cynicism with which Hume looked back upon his own literary career and upon the prospect of his ideas being fully understood. The young man, for his part, was encouraged by the attention, however guarded, of such a great man.

In political terms the *English Constitution* was a bold response to Hume's revolutionary contribution to historical writing. In other ways it shows many aims and assumptions common to Hume and other Scottish writers. Stuart's argument about the sources of political liberty were set within a model that divided cultural evolution into four stages: hunting, pastoral, agricultural and commercial. By 1768 much of the groundwork for such an historical view of progress had been laid by Kames, Smith and Ferguson. An outline of the theory is found in Aristotle's *Politics*, a text Stuart had on loan from the College Library while writing the *English Constitution*. However, Lord Kames reworked the stadial model of social progress far more systematically in the *Historical Law Tracts*. For the Scottish writers generally property was the central feature of their social analysis. To illustrate how it was regarded during the early stages of society, Stuart referred to passages from classical and biblical texts. What these sources reveal about manners and institutions developing around property contributes to a celebratory picture of romantic primitivism in early history. It is an image of the barbarian which recalls Rousseau's Noble Savage, and this standpoint enabled Stuart to criticise implicitly the corruption of his own country's institutions. The unspoiled condition of the early Britons was thus contrasted with contemporary decline:

> Vice, in those simple and virtuous times, had not lifted her head in triumph over innocence. Ambition had not intruded into the place of modesty; nor were the poor crushed under the proud oppression of the rich. A wasteful expence had not put to shame a temperate frugality: a jarring of interests had not opposed itself to concord and union: nor was a precarious justice to be bought from the corrupted tribunals of judges. The ignorance of crime was a firmer preservative to their manners, than to other nations – the strictness of law, and the knowledge of virtue.   (EC, 24)

When compared with the civility of Rome, or with modern commercial society, the so-called barbarians may have seemed primitive. Yet Stuart contended that if the exact nature of their political liberty was examined, the resultant picture refuted a conception of the Germans and their institutions as barbarous. The nostalgic contrast Stuart drew between this former period and mid-eighteenth-century Britain is similar to Tacitus' comparison in the *Germania* between the same courageous and community minded Germanic tribes and the decadent Romans of his own day. The passage also reflects the influence of an Ossianic ideal, then fresh in the minds of his readers after the publication of James MacPherson's *Fingal* (1762) and *Temora* (1763). These works were purported to be lost epic poems, translated from the Gaelic, which described the freedom and courage of the ancient inhabitants of Scotland. They were the subject of a heated and extended controversy over authenticity that went to the heart of Scottish cultural, political and literary identity.[71] Stuart followed Hugh Blair and others in believing them to be genuine. Hume, Dr Johnson, Gibbon and others 'of mild tempers' knew them to be the recent compositions of MacPherson. In a way the Ossian affair was a post-Union cultural rebellion, in that it compelled Scots of the day to consider the nature of their identity.

From the start of the *English Constitution* Stuart pointedly referred to 'our laws', 'our constitution' and 'our historians', by which he meant British rather than English or Scottish. At the outset he affirmed that 'there is no subject more interesting to a native of Great Britain, and none that leads to discoveries more curious and important, than an inquiry concerning the antiquity of our laws and constitution' (EC, iii). Stuart wrote some sixty years after the Union of 1707 and less than a generation after the 1745 Rebellion. Implicit in his use of the pronoun 'our' was the idea that Scotland shared in the advantages of a previously English, but now British, constitution. To enjoy its benefits the Scots must know its origins, and thus the history of English liberty was important to Scotland. Hume was the first Scotsman to write a comprehensive narrative history of Britain, and Stuart saw himself continuing the tradition in the conjectural field by writing a new history of the English constitution.

The Union was among the most important constitutional events of the eighteenth century. In its immediate aftermath Scotland's human and economic resources reached a low point. Through the 1750s and 1760s, however, Scottish society gradually revitalised itself and became a European centre for intellectual advancement. Through its educational institutions, its church, its legal system and more generally through its enterprising people, Scotland became an integral partner in the Union and an influential contributor to world culture. As a boy, Stuart witnessed this progress; as a young man he set out to contribute to it. When he grew older, he came to question its value and consequently sought to change its direction. In the *English Constitution* he laid an historical foundation justifying and explaining the advantages of the Union. The assertion of a progressive brand of British nationalism did not replace the patriotic Scottish feeling which is also evident in the work; nevertheless, his work cannot be seen as an appeal for political independence. Scottish patriotism and British unionism were part of a general growth of national consciousness from the middle part of the century onwards and this, to some extent, explains Stuart's enhanced interest in local and national politics.[72]

Stuart's regard for Scottish culture and history is apparent in the critical manner in which he dealt with other writers (especially Scots) who minimised differences between the two nations or who suggested that Scotland was inferior to England. Lord Kames, the 'learned judge', is one who came under attack for following the erroneous conjectures of previous scholars. Stuart countered his assertion that the early laws of England were taken up by the Scots: 'The matter is doubtless important: for to judge by their dates, the *Regia Majestas* [the Scottish law code] preceded the *Glanvil* [the English code]; and the English must have borrowed from the Scots the model, or the expression, of their law' (EC, 124n). Clearly there were similarities between the early laws, as there were with jurisprudential developments in many European countries, but in principle Kames' idea was contrary to Stuart's patriotic ideals and shown to be wrong by scholarly inquiry. It was important for the Scots to take an interest in what was now 'our constitution', but they must not go so far as to forsake their national distinctiveness. For Stuart, more than for many Scottish writers of the day, Scotland was a primary concern. In the *English Constitution,* he more readily adopted the conciliatory Anglo-Scottish position shared by much of the Scottish establishment. In later writings he became more outspoken against assimilation and English political control. Those Scottish politicians who subscribed to policies he considered detrimental to Scotland, and those writers whose works served to justify such men, met with Stuart's determined antagonism.

One of Stuart's main historical endeavours was to correct the errors of his predecessors. It was inevitable that he address controversial issues, but it was necessary for him to do so without compromising the appearance of impartiality or the integrity of the main narrative. Primarily for these reasons, the footnote (and end note) became an important feature of his work. A examination of this subtext reveals much about his historiographical method and social and political concerns.[73] Here too the polarity of his approach is apparent. On the one hand he substantiated his ideas with a rigorous scholarly apparatus; on the other he would introduce a reference with such a casual phrase as, 'I forget my authorities; but I have read somewhere ... ' (EC, 35n).[74] In the *English Constitution* 370 notes supplement 290 pages of text. They are an integral part of the literary whole, where Stuart freely expressed views that were more pedantic, speculative or controversial than might be acceptable in the text itself. Furthermore, they set a leisurely pace to the reading of the work and enabled him to engage his audience at a more intimate level. In the *View of Society* and the *Public Law of Scotland* he placed even more emphasis on the notes; they became far more substantial than the main text and were moved from the bottom of the page to the end of the main text.

There are two basic types of notes in the *English Constitution*. The first, which I have called reference notes, simply cite sources for support. The second, the critical notes, contain more interesting commentary. Stuart's reference notes, largely taken from classical sources, show the particular influence of Tacitus' *Germania* and Caesar's *De Bello Gallico*. He cites these works on nearly every page of the first half of the book and at times his narrative is little more than a reworded translation of them. 'The short, but comprehensive and sentimental, work of Tacitus', he wrote, 'is the key to the Institutions ... of the barbarians: yet how seldom is it appealed to?' (EC, 108n).[75] References to Ovid, Virgil, Homer and Sophocles appear as well, primarily for their observations about manners in former times.

In the second half of the *English Constitution* references to the legal documents of early nations and of English kings take over from classical references and serve as irrefutable proofs for Stuart's ideas about the nature of feudal society, more persuasive than any appeal to abstract political concepts.[76] He took many of these legal citations from the works of seventeenth-century antiquaries, whose compendious and often politicised writings served both as scholarly resources and objects of disputation. He also included references to more recent writers – Montesquieu,

Hume, Kames and Adam Ferguson – whose ideas he expanded upon in some critical notes. Occasionally Stuart referred to himself; even in this first work he rather self-confidently cited previous sections to substantiate his argument. The critical notes illustrate his polemical approach to scholarly dissertation. Although his comments are usually balanced with respect for the utility of the divergent corpus of scholarship, a moralistic aside is occasionally added to the corrective. After establishing a detailed philological point Stuart stated:

This leads me to remark a practice which is common to antiquaries. When they have found, with much industry, the age of a particular word, they invariably conclude, that the ceremony, or incident denoted by it, was not known till that period. They have no conception that the *thing* could prevail before the *name*. They act as philologers, while they should attend to the force of history, and the spirit of ages.

(EC, 104n)

Other authors with whose fundamental reasoning Stuart disagreed, he argued, drew conclusions from their political or religious prejudices rather than from the vantage point of an impartial historian who systematically gathered facts and synthesised them according to established principles. The distinction Stuart made between the deductive methods of his adversaries and his own *a posteriori* reasoning is largely rhetorical. On the subject of a divinely appointed monarch, for example, he criticised the Tory historians, or, as he called them, the 'advocates for tyranny'.

It is observable, that the advocates for tyranny call in religion to their aid, when they find, that the testimony and informations of history are too strong for their arts and disguises. They trace back, with an impious zeal the rise of government to the Deity ... But in all this they talk not the language of reason; they discover their illiberal minds, and show that they were unworthy to enjoy the privileges of a free administration. Their arguments carry their refutation along with them; and few men can listen to them without indignation.

(EC, 141–2n)

According to Stuart, writers such as Robert Brady in the seventeenth century and Hume in the eighteenth century saw English liberty as arising from a series of monarchical concessions after the Norman conquest, and overlooked the earlier history of the Anglo-Saxon period when monarchical power was limited and a republican spirit prevailed. As a result they 'ascribe to these

monarchs prerogatives which were not known till posterior ages'
(EC, 150).

Stuart reiterated this view of British history so many times in
the *English Constitution* and subsequently that it won him a place
in William Hayley's poem, *An Essay on History* (1780) as 'a living
author, who has lately vindicated the ancient constitution'.[77] In
1785 John Pinkerton, the miscellaneous writer, placed Stuart's
whiggery in an Anglo-Scottish context: 'I know not how it is that
the whole late Scot[t]ish writers of any eminence have been on
the tyrannic side, if we except Dr. Stuart, a man of real abilities,
but strangely misapplied in pulling down those of others.'[78]
William Godwin noted in rather more sympathetic terms that
Stuart was a minority voice in Scotland against the authority of
government.

> It has been too generally the description of the Scottish
> nation, that they are the friends of power, that they side with
> the court, whoever may be in place, and that their concep-
> tions of liberty are weak, narrow and uncertain. To this
> maxim doctor Stuart forms the most illustrious exception.
> From earliest life he breathed the soul of liberty.(PH, III,
> 281)[79]

Stuart erected the rhetoric of liberty on a foundation of solid legal
scholarship. The concept of law, like property, is central to the
English Constitution. He explained how alterations to legal institutions corrupted simple judicial arrangements. Jurisdiction, once
'the consequence of virtue and ability, was now annexed to the
possession of land' (EC, 227). In the context of Montesquieu's
assertion that the British legal system had political liberty as its
direct end, Stuart explained the relativism of his own approach in
comments which show the extent of his intellectual debt to Hume.

> In the judgements pronounced concerning men, we are gen-
> erally guided by the manners to which we have been accus-
> tomed. We forget, that the human mind is conscious of a
> progress, and that mankind are ever exhibiting different
> manners, and a new way of thinking. The good-natured
> moralist may fancy, that in every age the mind of the indi-
> vidual is sensible of right and wrong ... But no sentiment is
> more contradictory to the history of mankind. (EC, 216-17)

According to Stuart, historians often made two errors regarding
the nature of justice and the evolution of legal systems. First, there
were those who thought laws arose spontaneously. Second, there
were those who saw in the progress of law a supreme design

guiding society from barbarism to civilisation. Stuart largely rejected both these ideas. In his view it was 'by circumstance and accident that rules are discovered for the conduct of men; and society must have subsisted for ages, and its different appearances must have been often unfolded, before the wisdom of individuals could plan or project the arrangements of nations' (EC, 223). Like Hume and Adam Ferguson, Stuart maintained that the risk of corruption was as great as the possibility of improvement. He also shared the view expressed by Ferguson in his *Essay on the History of Civil Society* that 'we are apt to exaggerate the misery of barbarous times, by an imagination of what we ourselves should suffer in a situation to which we are not accustomed. But every age hath its consolations, as well as its sufferings.'[80]

Stuart's account of the first stages of society follows the lines of the second part of Ferguson's book, 'Of the History of Rude Nations'. When there was no idea of property, there was accordingly no idea of law. Morality and natural justice existed, but on a level detached from objects and possessions and grounded in virtue and compassion. As social interaction increased, a limited legal system evolved. Stuart offered examples in support of his argument: to steal the sheep of a neighbour was a crime of the highest magnitude; to steal that of your enemy, a virtuous act (EC, 26–7). Following this principle he argued that some writers wrongly rejected the existence of justice in primitive times when indeed a strict, though crude system by eighteenth-century standards was in practice.

With this relativist principle established, Stuart turned to consider the influence of the Roman Empire upon Britain. At one point he described the benefits of its civilisation and at another implied rather pessimistically that as a consequence of its presence 'our deluded progenitors ... yielding to the Roman manners ... forgot the value of liberty, and stooped in a tame subjection to the will of kings' (EC, 56). Here, the narrative shifts to the present tense and a journalistic style like a foreign news report from an eighteenth-century newspaper is introduced. Stuart did this to pass rapidly over centuries of history and bring his reader to the time when the original Britons, having imported the Saxons to assist them in defeating the Picts and the Scots, found themselves conquered by their allies. The observation that 'there is not a single *British* word in our language' (EC, 59n) was an attempt to substantiate his view of a complete Saxon conquest, by implication more complete than the subsequent Norman one.[81] From a series of rhetorical questions, suggestive of a Roman oration, concerning the nature of the Saxon conquest, Stuart reiterated the main thesis he had traced in historians from Tacitus to Montesquieu.

> Proud from victory ... would they [the Saxons] surrender their liberties to a private man [William of Normandy]? Would temporary leaders ... ever think to usurp an authority over warriors, who considered themselves as their equals ... The conquerors of Britain retained their independence; and this island saw itself again in that free state in which the Roman arms had discovered it ...
>
> In the woods of Germany shall we find the principles which directed the state of land in the different kingdoms of Europe; and there shall we find the foundations of those ranks of men and those civil arrangements which the barbarians every where established and which the English alone have the good fortune, or the spirit, to preserve. (EC, 59–61)

In this optimistic tone Stuart concluded Book I, having brought into perspective a millenium of events. It was not wholly an exercise in antiquarianism, but a political discourse grounded in the observations of Tacitus and Caesar, guided by a selective use of seventeenth-century scholarship, inspired by Montesquieu and conceived in opposition to those writers who 'guided only by prejudice, have asserted, that the first government of the Britains was regal and despotic' (EC, 52–3).

Stuart complemented his enthusiastic descriptions of the Germans and their British counterparts with philosophical reasoning about the causes of the gradual change in society. As men came to scatter themselves through the country and to turn to the improvement of their property, the bonds of public interest, fostered by communal war, gradually weakened (EC, 108–9). As private and commercial interests grew, property became distanced from the needs of the community. A spirit of commercialism was growing, but adequate laws were lacking to preserve the foundations of political liberty on which it rested.

> The enlarging experience of men is ever altering their manners: the present still improves on the past: and those customs and attachments which one age adopts, and pursues with pleasure, the next renounces, and avoids as oppressive and grievous. Constant alone in the changes they exhibit, men are ever furnishing the materials of those motley pictures which compose their history.   (EC, 111)

Later Stuart returned to the question of why change came about.

He speculated on how property gradually assumed dominance in the organisation of a community. His reasoning followed commonplace notions of social progress. First, a natural attachment arose between the individual and the land he cultivated; then nations which at one time had divided the year equally between conquest and cultivation, came to prefer the latter. Distinctions of rank, divisions of labour and the spirit of commerce emerged and complicated peoples' ideas about property. By necessity rather than design

> men have learned to provide for the future, and conceive a kind of property in the stores they have hoarded; and when instructed of their weakness in the savage and solitary state, they have united into bodies: it is in such a situation that the virtue of justice is discovered.   (EC, 218)

> Society must have subsisted for ages, and its different appearances must have been often unfolded, before the wisdom of individuals could plan or project the arrangements of nations.   (EC, 223)

To illustrate the process by which men compromised their original liberty and show the principles which enabled them to regain it, Stuart described the origin, rise and decline of various social institutions in feudal times. He organised his analysis around a simple idea: through much of the Saxon period these institutions were expressions of a mutually beneficial association between the king and his nobility and between the nobleman and his subjects. But during the height of the Norman rule they became obligatory and oppressive. This theory led him to argue that the notion of an all powerful leader only emerged in the post-Saxon period, when, for example, monarchical consent for legislation became a requirement. Likewise, it was only upon the invasion of the Normans and the advent of hereditary fiefs that succession began to descend within the family of the king. Again Stuart asserted of the early English kings:

> The prejudice of authors has taught them to ascribe to these monarchs prerogatives which were not known till posterior ages ... Struck with the glare of their condition [of monarchs in a cultivated age], the bulk of men are deceived into the highest admiration; and, forgetful of their natural rights, and of the privileges of citizens, they would bind themselves over to slavery and oppression.   (EC, 149–50)

He scrutinised the theory advanced by the 'writers for prerogative' that the Norman kings alone secured constitutional freedoms and, in return, were obeyed by the people. This suggested a society ignorant of its original liberty. However, he qualified his polemic with remarks acknowledging the benefits derived from the Normans. To their invasion (he refused to call it a conquest) 'are we indebted for our first advances to art and civility. Lands ... were made hereditary and perpetual ... and the feudal law in its more enlarged condition, spread itself over England' (EC, 122–3).

Stuart's comparative account of the early inhabitants of England is a secular one. Nevertheless it would not be complete without considering one of the most formidable 'orders of men' in feudal times: the clergy. He contended that in the earliest times superstition, 'which takes so durable a hold of the human mind, had not force to make them think with respect of their deities' (EC, 17). But in the course of time the clergy were able to manipulate superstitious sentiments and consequently to obtain a large share of political dominion. Although Stuart acknowledged the potential good of religious teaching, he placed more emphasis on the destructive features of clerical power. The clergy separated themselves from society, contrary to civic spirit, and displayed their authority in war and peace both by manipulating the superstitious disposition of the people and by administering justice. Moreover, their dominion was not limited to man's condition on earth.

> Do we turn over the ecclesiastical annals of almost every nation, and of every age? we shall still be presented with the same picture. The priests of almost every religion have been alike ambitious, and alike successful in their encroachments on the civil rights, and the common understanding of men. Nor has the history of human affairs a cause to offer more subversive of the progress of refinement than the ghostly practices of priestly power. They poison and confine the mind of the barbarian, when, impelled by hope and ambition, he looks forward ... to better his condition, and enlarge his views; and in the most cultivated ages, they have erected their standard, and are able to support their dominion by the ignorance they establish.   (EC, 214–5)

In tone these criticisms recall Hume's comments on the sixteenth-century reformers in the Tudor volumes of the *History of England*.[82] Stuart's anti-clericism was a censure of fanaticism, more of Catholicism than of Protestantism, and implicitly more of orthodox groups in the Scottish church than of Moderates with whom he associated at the University. He qualified such remarks by noting that 'the observations in this section refer to the Saxon times. They will not apply, and I desire they may not be extended, to the present clergy in England. There is not perhaps in the world an order of priesthood more respectable' (EC, 211n). In subsequent writings Stuart was less apologetic. He challenged the clergy for advancing their 'temporal emolument', 'an end, which is at all times more important to them than the interests of religion and virtue' (VS, 290). He also remarked: 'Religion, which must ever mix in human affairs, is oftner to debase than to enlighten. It is, for the most part, a mass of superstitions, which encourage the weaknesses of mankind' (VS, 144).

In the closing parts of the *English Constitution* Stuart assumed a more confident tone. Like an advocate before a jury, he drew together the main arguments of his work: the state of land, the orders of men, the judicial arrangements, and the legislative assembly together compose the English Constitution. He then returned to the phrase 'our constitution' to remind his Scottish audience of the political benefits they shared with England. This was an assertion of a progressive nationalism of which he was genuinely proud. Finally, he re-established the modest tone with which the work began and recalled his debt to Tacitus and Montesquieu:

> If I have made it appear, that the parts which compose our constitution arose more immediately from the forests of Germany, I have answered my intention. Those who have more learning and capacity may penetrate farther, and delineate, with a happier pencil, the plan of our government.(EC, 290)

The public reception of the *English Constitution* was mixed. Contemporary critics did not completely understand the nature of Stuart's innovations. A writer for the *Critical Review* denied him any degree of original thought: 'Like a Monmouth-street saleshop, we are here presented with second-hand clothing of all kinds, and some of them ... *the worse for the wear*.'[83] The *Monthly Review* was more sympathetic to Stuart's whiggish politics and praised 'so agreeable a specimen of his ingenuity and learning'.[84] Both reviews contained extensive excerpts from the work and made very few substantial remarks.

In 1779 the book was translated into German, and in 1794 into French by Antoine Marie Henri Boulard.[85] The German publication shows the success of this early attempt to establish a nexus between English and Germanic cultures.[86] Describing these Anglo-Germanic parallels became a preoccupation a generation after Stuart with writers such as Coleridge and Thomas Carlyle.

Stuart's small contribution to the long and complex tradition of constitutional inquiry was overshadowed by the eclecticism of his approach. The *English Constitution* was a youthful display of considerable but as yet imperfectly channelled ability. It attempted to synthesize the conjectural approach of Hume and Kames with the controversialism of Ruddiman, and adapt the legal scholarship of Montesquieu and Dalrymple to the needs of contemporary politics. This combination, the result of diverse, though less than systematic reading, produced a style which Stuart would continue to develop in the *View of Society* and the *Public Law of Scotland*.

The *English Constitution* also represents an attempt to ingratiate Stuart as a political writer with those who might offer patronage. The men to whom he presented copies indicates the literary and political spheres in which he sought to make himself known. The list includes Hume, Gilbert Elliot, George Lyttleton and Charles Jenkinson.[87] After two years the work was reprinted with minor corrections.

This second edition, with a London imprint and the author's name, appeared in 1770 and was reissued in 1771. Stuart looked to the favour of Lord Mansfield, the Lord Chief Justice, by dedicating the new edition to him. If a book was not ambitious enough to be dedicated to the king, the leading legal figure in Britain (and a Scotsman) was a useful alternative for an aspiring writer. In the Dedication, Stuart described how Mansfield's office in a constitutional monarchy 'teach[es] government to restrain its force and the people to respect it. You perceive ... what belongs to prerogative and to liberty: the former you allow not to grow into tyranny, nor the latter to degenerate into licentiousness.' (EC, iii–iv.) From Mansfield, he received 'thanks and his Dinner, with a promise of further Countenance', as his former employer John Mackenzie put it.[88] Apart from this one evening with the judge, Stuart gained nothing tangible in the way of patronage. If he could boast to friends and family of the honour of meeting those of such superior standing, he was also beginning to learn the same lesson as his father about placing too great a dependence on such men. He realised that his own efforts would best produce the ends he desired. In the *English Constitution* he had written of the Saxons that 'no artificial differences of place, or of rank, being known, the only distinctions among men were their personal qualities'(EC, 41). Stuart lived in a more complex, a more corrupted age. Nevertheless, he believed his talents could win him fame, and he was ambitious enough to meet this challenge.

With a publication to his credit, Stuart still had no prospect of employment. During a visit to the Minto estate after the work first appeared, George Stuart put forward a new suggestion for his son's future: might he not succeed to the professorship of Public Law and the Law of Nature and Nations at Edinburgh University? This post was a Crown appointment and formally under the patronage of the Lord Advocate of Scotland, James Montgomery of Stanhope. It was then a sinecure, and usually reserved for a member of the Faculty of Advocates, but in practice was bought and sold at the discretion of the incumbent professor. James Balfour of Pilrig took the chair in 1764 when he resigned his moral philosophy professorship to Adam Ferguson,[89] who revitalised the key philosophy chair and gave the Moderates a firmer control in the University.[90] George Stuart saw no reason why a similar arrangement could not be made for the law chair.

The purchase price at £1200 was expensive to say the least. But the substantial annual salary of £300 was assured so that over a number of years the original outlay could be repaid. George Stuart was hopeful of winning this post for his son. Unable to restrain his fatherly pride, he reminded Gilbert Elliot of the intellectual potential displayed in the *English Constitution*. He also offered to obtain a letter of recommendation from Principal Robertson, 'who says that he will get great honour by his present work. If you cou'd procure the reversion of this, it can do no sort of harm to the present incumbent & will train up one fit for properly discharging the office.'[91] To prepare his son for the post, George Stuart contemplated sending him abroad to study law at Leyden or Utrecht, where many Scotsmen then received part of their legal training. He also indicated that he would advance the young man's patrimony to defray part of the purchase price. Reflecting on his own position, he added pleadingly:

> You was so good as to write to me often that tho' you found it difficult to alter my situation in life, that you would take care of my sons, that's all I ask; 'tis all I live for, 'tis all I wish ... And you'll always find that serving one in this way not only adds to your interest here but to your consequence above.[92]

This was a plea from the paternal heart. George Stuart knew that opportunities in Edinburgh were few and that, like so many enterprising young Scotsmen, his son would look to London for better prospects. More than anything he wanted Gilbert to have the lucrative post he could not obtain for himself. Gilbert naturally shared these hopes.

Once again George Stuart was unable to win a place in the Edinburgh establishment for his son. Elliot's chief interest lay elsewhere and Balfour was probably unwilling to relinquish a lucrative sinecure. It was perhaps overly ambitious to expect that a twenty-three-year-old could obtain the highest paid professorship in the University. Yet the power of patronage was such that this prospect was not entirely unrealistic were Elliot and Robertson willing to support the nomination. Ten years later Gilbert Stuart sought the chair of Public Law again, but he was again unsuccessful. This second time, however, he could discover no rational motive for his failure after he had been promised the post by Principal Robertson and Henry Dundas, the Lord Advocate.

In 1768 the only form of preferment that could be extracted from the University was an honorary Doctor of Laws degree.[93] Stuart's published work on jurisprudence had earned him this honour, although with the fee of twelve guineas such a degree was easily obtained for the son of a professor. Subsequently, he was referred to as Dr Stuart. But the title provided little solace for a major career disappointment.

Characteristic patterns in Gilbert's personality were already discernable. Periods of happiness and vigorous study were followed by bouts of despondency and drinking. George Stuart privately described his son as 'a young man of the greatest parts pining away in misery that he has nothing to do'.[94] Another description printed during his own lifetime elucidates this distinctive aspect of his character: 'His countenance is modest and expressive; sometimes glowing with sentiments of friendship, of which he is very susceptible, and at others darting that satire and indignation at folly and vice which appear in some of his writings.'[95] Stuart felt the extremes of emotion more than most, and his polarity of feeling was also a marked feature of his writings. It was apparent in the youthful *English Constitution* and brought to refinement in the *History of Mary Queen of Scots*. At one moment he observes and judges with detached philosophical calm – whether it be a new acquaintance or an historical event – at another he is caustic and passionately emotional.

Stuart was an extremely social and gregarious individual. His closest friend in Edinburgh was William Smellie, who trained as a printer, and whose literary and scientific abilities were considerable. Robert Kerr's *Life of Smellie* (1811) is the best source of information about Gilbert Stuart and shows the extent to which the two men worked together and made their way in Edinburgh society.

When Smellie began to edit and prepare articles for the first edition of the *Encyclopaedia Britannica*, he probably called in Stuart to assist him. This ambitious project was issued in one hundred parts from 1768 to 1771. Many of the entries were compiled from standard contemporary sources (listed in the work's Preface), some of which correspond to books that Stuart borrowed from the Library during this period.

Dr John Brown was also good friends with Smellie and Stuart. He was then promoting the controversial 'Brunonian' theory of medicine and, like his associates, hoped to obtain a professorship at the University.[96] Stuart was enthusiastic about Brown's ideas and offered advice about the best way to market the Doctor's new 'exciting pill'. According to Brown's son, Stuart 'assured him, that such was the rage for these arcana, that he might get 10,000 L. for the receipt, but much more in proportion, annually, by keeping it in his own hands'. As it turned out, this venture did not prove profitable.[97] Both Brown and Stuart found it difficult to earn as much as they spent;[98] both lived for the moment and the immediate gratification of their needs and pleasures.

Evenings of drinking and illicit sexual activity enticed Stuart especially. Whether or not he produced illegitimate offspring, as did Boswell and other 'gentlemen', is not recorded. Stuart did not marry, and little is known of his love life apart from rather obscure references in his correspondence to unrequited affairs and the occasional reflective comment in his works on such subjects as 'the metaphysic of love' (VS, 12) and 'those tender connections which please and agitate' (EC, 199). Generally, he acknowledged that man 'cannot but be drawn by beauty; he must know a preference in the objects of his affections and must feel ... that bewitching intercourse, and those delightful agitations, which constitute the greatest charm of cultivated life' (VS, 12–13). Though no stranger to physical love, there is no mention of any lasting romantic attachment. In the *English Constitution* Stuart compared marriage in ancient times with the present, and was led to remark pessimistically:

> More guided by sentiment than the savage and the barbarian, the member of a polished age finds a thousand charms, and a thousand obstacles, to incite and obstruct his passions: more guided also by interest, he oftener debases his affections to a sordid and ignoble traffick: and these motives joined their influence against the *incident of marriage*.
>
> (EC, 110)

Stuart's interest in prostitution, a 'sordid and ignoble traffic', was both a matter of personal experience and scholarly conjecture. In the *View of Society* he examined this social institution from the perspective of a conjectural historian and offered reasons for its legalisation in Britain.

> It has frequently been a subject of inquiry among politicians, whether public stews, under proper regulations, with a view to the health of individuals, and the peace of society, be not an advantageous institution. In some states in Europe, a tolerated or authorized prostitution is known at this day ... I avoid, however, to enter into a question of such infinite delicacy. It is dangerous in a state to give the slightest stab to morality. Yet, I cannot but observe, that, in most cultivated nations, there are laws and regulations which wound morality more severely than could be done by an authorized prostitution, and with less of utility to mankind. (VS, 406–7)

Stuart's libertarian point of view is part of a commonplace eighteenth-century discourse founded upon the notion that masturbation is more of an evil than prostitution and therefore encounters of the type he had had in Hyde Park (a favourite London rendezvous) or in Edinburgh's brothels were a preferred form of sexual release for men. Stuart referred to European and Hindu sources to justify his opinion. Contemporary readers were also likely to recall Bernard Mandeville's *Modest Defence of Publick Stews* (1724) or the Scottish poet John Armstrong's advice in the *Oeconomy of Love* (1736) for young men to 'Banish from thy Shades/Th' ungenerous, selfish, solitary Joy' and 'hie To Bagnio lewd or Tavern, nightly where / Venereal Rites are done'.[99] Stuart (and even Boswell) remained silent on the subject of 'solitary Joy', but of his experience of Scotland's 'public stews' there is a humorous record.

One evening, after such a visit, Stuart arrived at the house of William Smellie at a late hour. Smellie quickly discovered him to be drunk and put him to bed. In the middle of the night Stuart awoke and thought he was still in a brothel. The loud call of 'House! House!' roused the family. Smellie entered the room in his nightshirt; and Stuart, believing his friend to be in the same brothel, remarked: 'I never expected to find you in such a house. Get on your clothes, and return immediately to your wife and family; and be assured I shall never mention this affair to any one.'[100]

Encounters of the kind Stuart indulged in carried with them no uncertain risk. In a letter to John Murray in 1769 he hinted that he had contracted venereal disease and explained: 'My design in going to the country is on account of health rather than for pleasure or study. I have been complaining for some weeks; but I endeavour to live temperately.'[101] Stuart was well known for his intemperate habits. His boyhood friend Andrew Dalzel, later Professor of Greek at Edinburgh University, gave a short account of his daily activities. 'His usual way was to rise very early in the morning, to write till about two o'clock, and ... after dining on beefsteaks, to soak the remaining part of the day, drinking Burton beer, and, after supper, punch, till at last he finished a constitution, very strong.'[102] In Edinburgh and London Stuart sought out the best kept glass of Burton. Since the Navigation Act of 1698 this beer had been shipped through the Humber Estuary into Scotland.[103] Stuart expressed views on beer and alcohol generally in the context of a political debate over the high tax levied in Scotland on malt, which made the brewing of beer there prohibitively expensive. He criticised the way Scottish politicians entered into self-interested associations to produce whisky cheaply when it was clear

the stomachs of raw-boned and hungry Scotchmen are sufficient boilers and stills for all the grain that their country produces ...

The poor people of Scotland have no porter, no ale; the *cap-ale* which they had before, and a little after the union, being diluted by the taxes into a wash, in comparison of which, the common table-beer of England is Burton ale.(PH, II, 314–16)[104]

Consequently, Scots more often drank whisky, a drink 'ill qualified to quench the thirst of a palate spiced, salted, and peppered with a Glasgow herring, an oaten cake, and an onion'.(PH, II, 316)

Evenings in which Stuart and his publisher John Murray together drank six or eight bottles of wine were not uncommon. When Murray established himself as an agent for exporting beer to India, a ready supply of alcohol was always at hand. Even by liberal eighteenth-century standards, Stuart drank too much too often. Reports of his drinking rarely fail to be mentioned in published and unpublished accounts. In a letter to Murray, the Reverend Donald Grant reported: 'I saw Dr Stewart yesterday. I believe he was a little tipsy. I found him eating Oysters & drinking Drams.'[105] At Edinburgh Stuart was a member of at least one convivial drinking club, named the Chrochallan Fencibles. The group presented itself as 'Fensible men or Volunteers against dangers arising from invasion during the American War'.[106] Nevertheless, socialising was the first order of business. The Club met at Daniel Douglas' Tavern off Edinburgh's High Street in Anchor Close, just a few doors up from Smellie's printing shop. Among its members were Smellie, the advocate Henry Erskine, Lord Newton and, at a later date, the poet Burns, who 'undermined his constitution by excessive conviviality' with this group.[107]

At times the confines of Edinburgh could not satisfy Stuart's thirst. On one 'ramble of dissipation', he travelled on foot for many days between the Cross of Edinburgh and Musselburgh, stopping at every drinking establishment at which good Burton beer could be had. He entertained several friends who joined him in this expedition with his great wit and outlasted them all, probably in a quest for the best glass of Burton. The results of his researches are not recorded, although the route he took was a meandering one.[108]

Stuart's social pastime became an addictive and ultimately fatal activity. Moderation was not a feature of his personality. Drinking was a relaxing social antidote to intensive work habits, but it also became an escape from dissatisfaction with himself and his unfulfilled ambition. In spite of his drinking, or arguably because of it, he produced some innovative historical works and perspicuous literary and political commentary. Something of that heated energy, that mixture of passion and wit which animated his drunken conversations emerges in his writings and gives them a distinctively powerful character.

Just a few days after Stuart's death, John Murray reflected on his friend's intemperate habits and warned their literary associate William Thomson to 'be instructed by Stuart's example. Inebriety may even prove more fatal to you than to him; it may entail upon you poverty without death; and who would not rather die than become a beggar?'[109]

2

Living to Write and Writing to Live 1768–1773

Everybody is censured and abused. The satirist defies discovery, saying it will be impossible to find him out. One shall
hardly see such drawcansir-work
Joseph Warton to John Wilkes, 30 September 1797, *The
Correspondence of Wilkes* (London, 1805) IV, 335.

Like many young Scotsmen during the mid-eighteenth century,
Gilbert Stuart set off for London to find employment. It had
become clear that he would not find a suitable job in Edinburgh.
The *English Constitution* had brought him rather less recognition
than he might have hoped and no regular work. Nevertheless, he
must have felt a sense of relief that he had not resigned himself to
a stifling legal career. The future promised much and the prospect
of life in London for a twenty-five-year-old was exciting. With
letters of introduction, essential in an age of patronage, Stuart left
in January 1769 for the city where (as he wrote of John Arbuthnot)
'so many adventurers carry to market their virtues and their
vices'(EMR, II, 418).[1]

One important recommendation was written by Principal
Robertson, under the anxious eye of George Stuart, to David
Hume, then in London. Gilbert was well known to the Principal
and, as the letter suggests, well liked. Robertson described Stuart
as 'a modest, ingenious & high-spirited young man', trained as a
lawyer but with 'no great relish for that business. He wishes to fix
in London, & both his education & integrity fit him for any station
where something must be done.' The Principal further suggested
that Hume discuss Stuart's career prospects with Gilbert Elliot
who 'is his natural patron, & disposed to serve him', adding his
wish that Hume likewise offer assistance. 'There are few people',
he concluded, 'who have gone from this place, who will do so
much credit to those who patronize them'.[2] Robertson observed in
Stuart's character an eager desire to please those who held him in

their favour, and an equal contempt for those who did not. The genuine interest and good feeling which this letter exhibits contrast with the subsequent accounts of antagonism between the two. Neither Hume nor Elliot did much to further Stuart's career, though the mere association with these men could do him little harm.

From the outset Stuart found his ready pen in sufficient demand on Grub Street, the haunt of hack writers of all descriptions. Sometimes he would write a favourable article on a politician for one newspaper and a censorious one of the same man for another and receive his guinea from each.[3] In such anonymous pieces principles mattered less than the payment. London was an expensive place to live, especially in the gentlemanly manner necessary to make one's way in literary society. Boswell's entertaining 'Journal of my Jaunt' to London in 1762 provides a vivid picture of the setting in which Stuart found himself in 1769. In the coffee houses and taverns he met a variety of literary and political figures. He visited the British Museum (opened in 1759), attended the theatre, a public hanging, and experienced the less reputable side of London's nightlife which Boswell so keenly relished.

Stuart found lodgings in the house of a bookseller named Murdoch. Thomas Somerville, another young Scot first visiting London, shared these lodgings, and in his autobiography disparaged the selection of profligate and destitute writers with whom his companion regularly associated. Stuart, he noted, was 'assigned oracular authority' over these literary gatherings, where, to Somerville's indignation, 'contempt was expressed for the most esteemed authors living'.[4] Though disagreeable to some, Stuart possessed an engaging personality and a lively, if bawdy, sense of humour. His intelligence and wit entertained a growing circle of companions, especially if warmed by drink. At a late hour when the revelry concluded, Stuart retired to his lodgings, his mind flowing with energy, to write reviews and news articles. He usually prepared these quickly and sent them to his employer the following morning. Rarely was there a need for subsequent correction. By this occupation he earned an income which kept pace with his spendthrift nature. Somerville acknowledged that Stuart 'possessed transcendent intellectual talents ... with a capacity for patient laborious research. But what I most admired, and what was less known, was his facility and quickness in composing – the more extraordinary because his style has so much the appearance of art and elaboration.'[5]

During this first London visit Stuart established a long-lasting friendship with John Murray. Seven years Stuart's senior, Murray had left his native Edinburgh and joined the navy to fight in the Seven Years' War. He retired from this career in 1765 and a few years later purchased the business of the London bookseller William Sandby. Murray laid down the principles and gradually built up the lists of a publishing house which later published Byron, Jane Austen and Darwin and continues to this day. Included in the original transfer of Sandby's stock were unsold copies of Stuart's *English Constitution*. This may have led to their first meeting but the two probably knew each other in Edinburgh beforehand. This friendship proved to be the most important of Stuart's career. Murray readily acknowledged that 'we live in the greatest confidence and friendship'.[6] He had a share in the sale of all Stuart's historical works, and the two had many other mutual literary interests. The bookseller recognised Stuart's exceptional talent but was aware that it required prudent and often firm guidance. Their extensive correspondence covers the period from Stuart's return to Edinburgh in July 1769 to his death in August 1786. Unlike the deferential letters Stuart wrote to Hume and other social superiors, those to Murray reveal him as a passionate man who was easily flattered, self-critical, judgemental and full of ideas about literary projects.

Frankness and genuine affection and respect characterised their long friendship. In one instance Murray criticised Stuart for the vindictive tendency and general mismanagement of the *Edinburgh Magazine and Review*, and implored him: 'For Heavens sake know yourself better than squander your precious time to such an unprofitable purpose ... I beseech you seriously to lay to heart my remonstrances which my regard for you alone dictate[s].'[7] In a letter to a mutual friend, Murray elaborated upon his relationship with Stuart: 'I have occasionally opened myself to Dr Stuart with much more freedom than I ever did to you. And tho he felt my strictures, yet he recovered the nature from whence they proceeded and valued my attention to him.'[8]

Stuart was always eager to advise and assist Murray. During a six-month period when Murray was out of London, Stuart edited the publisher's magazine *The Repository: or Treasury of Politics and Literature for MDCCLXX*. To prepare the monthly issues Stuart selected political articles from the daily papers, including many of the letters of Junius and pieces relating to John Wilkes – two dominant issues of the year. The materials were collected to enable the reader 'to arrive at the truth of those Transactions and Events which have so much agitated the present times'. The editor also added occasional notes and references to distinguish 'the heat of Party-zeal ... from candid reasoning'.[9] For his efforts Stuart received nine guineas.[10] The publication itself continued for only one year.

Stuart frequently acted as a reader for Murray to determine if a work might be worth publishing, and helped him win the publication of new works by Scottish authors whom he knew, among them John Millar's *Observations concerning the Distinction of Ranks in Society* (1771), David Dalrymple's *Annals of Scotland* (1776–9), and Dr William Cullen's *First Lines of the Practice of Physic* (1776–84).[11]

The case of Millar shows the extent to which Stuart involved himself with Murray. Millar was a professor of law at Glasgow University. His lectures were so popular that many of Edinburgh's best known lawyers came through to attend them.[12] Stuart knew him well, admired his works and approved of his whiggish politics. Similar subjects and historiographic traditions engaged the two men. When the *Observations concerning Ranks* was nearing completion, the author entrusted Stuart 'to make what corrections you think proper, either in point of matter or the expression'.[13] David Hume and William Robertson also went over Millar's work before it appeared.[14] At Murray's request, Stuart persuaded the author to draw up an introduction and in effect present as a unified work what Millar had originally conceived to be five separate discourses. The bookseller judged this would make the book more successful, but Millar took some convincing by Stuart. Stuart's involvement did not end there. In a review of the work, he praised the author and explained the didactic value of conjectural studies:

> After learning by history and observation the effect of different circumstances on the manners and sentiments of men, we might infer, from these circumstances, how, on all occasions, they would think and act, and thence learn to conduct ourselves with propriety in every possible situation.[15]

Stuart considered this aim a 'distant prospect'; Millar was rather more optimistic. Except perhaps in the concluding comments on the hypocrisy of the rebellious Americans, there is little of the contentiousness which characterises Stuart's own conjectural compositions.[16] Where Stuart engaged in 'incidental discussions' and defended 'the novelty of [his] opinions' (VS, vi), Millar (according to his first biographer) 'discarded every idea not strictly connected with the subject of his inquiry'.[17] The format each adopted was fundamentally different. For Stuart footnotes and endnotes were speculative or controversial excursions, while Millar's notes are generally minimal references (although in later editions of his first work he did expand them). Where Stuart's prose is declamatory and stylised, Millar's language is 'neither the most striking, nor the most alluring, to the reader'.[18]

Millar shared Stuart's view that there was a republican form of representation in Saxon times.[19] However, he diverged from Stuart in refusing to adopt a nostalgic view of ancient liberty, and probably had Stuart's *English Constitution* or other whiggish works like it in mind when he commented in the *Observations concerning Ranks*:

> Many writers appear to take pleasure in remarking, that as the love of liberty is natural to man, it is to be found in the greatest perfection among barbarians, and is apt to be impaired according as a people make progress in civilization and in the arts of life ... There are many other objects of greater consequence than liberty, and which are preferred to it by all the world.[20]

In many important respects, the works of both men were responses to Hume's relativist view of history. Millar's *Historical View of English Government* (1787), like the *English Constitution* and the *View of Society*, took as a basis for its argument the thesis that man's changing conception of property had more influence than Hume imagined.[21] The point may not have been sufficient to bring Hume's *History of England* into disrepute, but the broad agreement of Millar and Stuart on this point and others did bring the two closer together. Millar was one of the few Scottish writers Stuart respected. 'Have you seen Professor Millar?' Stuart asked Murray.

> I cannot conceive what has taken him to London, if it is not to get the Principality of Glasgow [University] ... It cannot, surely, be a new publication. If it is, I shall rejoice. It is a torment to read perpetually idle books. A good one now & then is absolutely necessary.[22]

Stuart earned a considerable reputation in London literary circles as a perspicacious and at times innovative critic. As the brief excerpt from the review of Millar suggests, in his articles on contemporary literature he sought to mark out the qualities which separated the good books from the 'perpetually idle' ones. His reviews also reveal important aspects of his politics and personality. Some books reviewed are of interest because the subject matter relates to his own historical productions; others because of his comments on well known authors, such as William Robertson, Henry Mackenzie and Samuel Johnson.

The first periodical for which Stuart regularly wrote was the *London Magazine*. This monthly miscellany was edited by the Scotsman John MacMillan, who formed a close friendship with the new recruit.[23] James Boswell became one of the proprietors in the autumn of 1769 and was himself a regular contributor. One of the first articles Stuart wrote was a review of Robertson's *History of Charles V*, in which he praised the author and so confirmed a genuine interest in advancing the sale of this work. It was not Stuart's best effort. His prose is laboured and lacking in the 'art and elaboration' which Somerville noted. Curiously, he made no mention of Robertson's important introductory volume, the 'View of the Progress of Society in Europe', which had many similarities to the *English Constitution* and which he attacked nine years later in his own *View of Society*. Stuart did acknowledge the whole as a 'valuable acquisition to the world of letters', yet he offered little substantive criticism, and much of the review contains extended quotation so that, as Stuart rather unfortunately put it, 'our readers may relish the extracts from this very entertaining performance with greater gust'.[24]

Three years later, in the pages of the same periodical, Stuart wrote a 'Character of Dr. Robertson'. He marked the Principal's rise to fame and praised him as a man of uncommon ability, as a progressive leader in the Scottish Church and as a discerning historian. At the outset he declared Robertson's *History of Scotland* 'to be the best history in the English Language' and in closing described its author as 'one of the most perfect characters of the age'.[25] The extent of Stuart's hyperbole prompted Boswell to enliven the pages of the periodical with a challenge. At a dinner on 3 April 1772 he and Stuart met and almost certainly discussed the piece.[26] Two issues later Boswell offered some 'Strictures on Dr. Robertson's *Character*' in which he asked: 'Who takes upon him to pronounce Dr. Robertson's history of Scotland "to be the best history in the English language?" Alas! what fulsome panegyrick! Call it an Historical Essay, or an Historical Dissertation, and we will agree with you!'[27] By alluding to the title of Stuart's first work (*An Historical Dissertation concerning the English Constitution*), Boswell informed perceptive readers that this character of Robertson came not from an impartial London critic, but from a loyal supporter of the Principal and the institutions he headed. To some extent, Boswell had succeeded in undermining Stuart's intended compliment. Seven years later, Stuart wrote a new 'Character of a Certain Historian', far more defamatory than Boswell's, 'Strictures', reflecting the extent to which his relationship with Robertson had changed.

After a brief return to Edinburgh, Stuart moved into more permanent lodgings at 13 Southampton Buildings in Holburn, the centre of legal London in June 1770. His landlady was a Mrs Wait, who treated him with maternal affection and whom he charmed with amusing stories of his experiences in the capital. He was a short walk from John Murray's shop at 32 Fleet Street and in close proximity to his favourite tavern, the Peacock in Grays Inn Lane, an establishment renowned in London for its superior Burton ale. It had been serving since 1630, over 135 years before Stuart first drank there.[28]

During this extended stay in London Stuart established himself as one of the leading critics at the *Monthly Review*. Ralph Griffiths had set up this successful literary periodical in 1749, editing and contributing to it for fifty-four years.[29] Here Stuart's whiggish politics found an accommodating forum. Nevertheless he also contributed occasionally to the Tory-based *Critical Review*, conducted by Archibald Hamilton and, for a time, by Tobias Smollett.

Griffiths paid his writers relatively well at two guineas per sheet (16 printed pages) and demanded impartiality in return.[30] But if Stuart knew (and liked) the author, or John Murray was the publisher, a favourable review was usually produced. Percival Stockdale, a contemporary of Stuart, remarked in his *Memoirs* (1809) that 'the monthly reviewers had not the merit of ... moral principles in their decisions; but they had the merit of boldness; of some fire; and of a sprightly variety, that entertained you'.[31] While writing in the *Monthly*, Stuart matured as a critic. His success there encouraged him to return to Scotland in 1773 to establish the *Edinburgh Magazine and Review* where the 'boldness' and 'fire' which Stockdale observed were brought to his native land.

Stuart produced nearly 250 reviews, long and short, for the *Monthly*.[32] Very often he judged a work on the basis of whether the writer – be it an historian, a novelist or political pamphleteer – formulated his ideas from first-hand experience and from a knowledge of history, which, Stuart believed, could limit self-interest, and in the political sphere could minimise the differences between the ministry and opposition, while ignorance of it promoted faction. In his opinion the spirit of history, like the spirit of laws, was sadly rarely found in the latest publications. Such understanding required 'a force and extent of penetration, and a delicacy of precision, which are never possessed by ordinary men'.[33] Stuart was an advocate of works which studied mankind in all its variety.

Of the novels Stuart reviewed there were few which he could recommend but many which he characterised as 'in the highest degree disgusting', or 'the ravings of a deranged imagination'.[34] Reading these works could be a test of patience. His reviews show his heightened degree of sensibility to good fiction, with its capacity to involve the reader in the actions and sentiments of the characters. One novel, *Anecdotes of a Convent*, achieved this end and Stuart wrote: 'We feel everything it describes, and are alternately melted with tenderness, sunk in dejection, chearful [sic] through hope, and exalting with joy.'[35] More often Stuart was 'disgusted' with the books set before him and with the authors who regarded only 'the pecuniary recompense' they hoped to acquire.[36] In this frame of mind he commented:

> Literature, in the present age, seems to be reduced to a manufacture; and ... books multiply, without serving the purposes of information or taste. That passion for fame ... which made Montesquieu bestow twenty years on *the spirit of laws*, seems, in a great measure, to be lost. Hence it is that we have treatises on the state and constitution of Great Britain that have no merit to recommend them, systems of husbandry, by those who have seldom, if ever, seen a plough, and dissertations on points of philosophy, by those men who never looked into Locke, or into Hume.[37]

Most of the works on which Stuart passed judgement fell quickly into obscurity, but a few, such as Henry Mackenzie's anonymous *Man of Feeling* (1771) and Samuel Johnson's *Thoughts on the Late Transactions respecting Faulkland's Island* (1771), are of more interest. Even though Stuart knew Mackenzie from his days at the Edinburgh High School, it is not obvious that any influence was brought to bear by the author or his bookseller (Cadell) upon the reviewer. Stuart said that, although a first effort, it was 'not totally destitute of merit', but added, 'the knowledge of men it contains, appears to be rather gathered from books than experience'.[38] Stuart misjudged the reputation Mackenzie would obtain in his day when he remarked: 'We should not be disposed to think that he will ever attain to any great eminence in literature.'[39] In this review Stuart reaffirmed the idea that the sentiments of a writer should develop out of interaction with society rather than from imagination in isolation.

In a review of Johnson's Faulkland Islands pamphlet Stuart applied this principle in a political context. He opposed the author's Toryism, specifically the criticisms of Junius which occupy a large portion of the pamphlet. Stuart acknowledged that Johnson's 'literary merit is very considerable', but objected in other respects to the moral tone of his writings.

> The present publication is not entirely free from that disgusting petulance and affectation, which generally characterise the performances of its Author. Filled with that little vanity, which so frequently attends on contemplative and retired men, he delivers his oracles with an air of the utmost authority; and seems to consider himself as seated on the pinnacle of the temple of wisdom, from whence he looks down with a *sapient disdain* on the reptiles that crawl below him.[40]

Stuart's own 'disdain' for Johnson was shared by other Scottish literary men. This was true even before Johnson's occasionally deprecatory *Journey to the Western Islands of Scotland* appeared in 1773. Stuart adopted his attitude from Hugh Blair, whose 'strictures on *The Style of the Rambler* ... served as a high seasoning to his course' of lectures on Rhetoric and Belles Lettres at Edinburgh University (ER, I, 498).[41]

During his career as a reviewer in London Stuart earned additional income by editing a number of unfinished historical works. This was typical Grub Street hack work. In 1770 he compiled the fourth and final volume of Nathaniel Hooke's *Roman History, from the Building of Rome to the Ruin of the Commonwealth* (1771).[42] His rather censorious article in the *Monthly Review* suggests that he did little more than to see a work that was nearly completed through the press and that he had no financial interest in the sale. In the review Stuart praised classical writers, like Cicero, who acted in the events they recorded, and challenged modern historians for failing 'in the judgements they have given of those great men who have acted in difficult situations'.[43] This appeal to the *vita activa* was a commonplace civic discourse, adopted by Stuart. His censure specifically excluded William Robertson, 'whose genius ... has surmounted the disadvantages of his situation, and who, in the retirement of a college, has been able to discuss the transactions of men, with the experience and discernment of an accomplished statesman'.[44]

In other places Stuart defended Robertson against the aspersions of rival writers. In a review of William Smith's *History of
England* (1771), for example, he discounted Smith's remark that
Robertson's intention in the *History of Scotland* was to 'ingratiate
himself with the English; and, like a mercenary writer, to present
the public with an account of a few modern reigns, in which he
advances many well-dressed falsehoods'.[45] Stuart later attacked
Robertson on exactly these grounds, but in the early 1770s his
intention was to expose Smith's falsehoods and ingratiate himself
with the Principal.

In the spring of 1772 a London bookseller by the name of Nichol
engaged Stuart to edit and complete Richard Rolt's *History of the
Isle of Man*. Rolt, a prolific miscellaneous writer, had died a year
earlier. Stuart welcomed an historical project and was glad to have
the additional income. If he had had any real interest in the work
surely, as a regular contributor to the *Monthly*, he could have
arranged a notice, but none appeared. Comments in the *Critical
Review* referred to it as 'incapable of affording the least degree of
pleasure even to a Manksman'.[46] Stuart sent a copy to John Mackenzie, his former employer, telling him apologetically, 'I much
fear, that the work will not be worthy of your inspection' as Nichol
was 'in the greatest haste to have [it] published'.[47]

Stuart had, however, an important ulterior motive for writing
to Mackenzie to discount his role in an unsuccessful work. While
editing Rolt's compilation, he had formulated a plan for his own
comprehensive history of the Isle of Man. To this end he sought
the patronage of the 3rd Duke of Atholl, whose family had sovereign rights over the Island until 1765, when it was annexed to the
British Crown by an act of parliament known as the Revestment.
Mackenzie, the legal agent for the Duke, was the obvious mediator
for such a proposal.

Over the summer of 1772 Stuart gathered materials and began
to compose the history, to which he had given the title 'Memoirs of
the Isle of Man'. He wrote quickly, and in August sent Mackenzie
the first chapters. Four months later there followed a complete
draft on which Mackenzie made general comments and editorial
changes. Stuart was now writing narrative rather than conjectural
history, and consequently had a different audience in mind, as he
told Mackenzie.

> The Labour of minute details would perfectly fatigue the
> nobility of this age, & even the politer sort of Gentry. In order
> to have their notice, we must hold out something striking to

them ... That the treatise, notwithstanding, may be as perfect as possible, we shall have an Appendix for the men of business and Inquiry.[48]

Stuart divided the work into five chapters. The first four are essentially compilations from earlier published works on the island. The final chapter – described by Stuart as 'the great branch of our undertaking, the annexation of the Island to the Crown'[49] – is entirely original and by far the most interesting. In the first chapter Stuart runs through the island's history from before the invasion of the Romans to the period when it descended to the Dukes of Atholl. He placed particular emphasis on the Civil War period but acknowledged that the chapter 'will be the least interesting of the whole work'.[50] Chapter 2 contains a physical description of Man and a rather sketchy character of the Manx people; in Chapter 3 he describes the government and civil institutions of the island; and in the fourth he offers an account of its religious establishments. These chapters generally lack a philosophical approach to the material, and the picture of Manx society is two-dimensional, limited in its speculative or conjectural argument. Only in the final chapter could the reader fully enter into the sentiments of the Manx people and consider the larger social and political significance of the events.

As an historical narrative the work is inferior to his more mature productions. In an anonymous review written soon after he completed the 'Memoirs', Stuart pointed out the difficulty in giving 'dignity, interest and variety' to an historical composition:

> The happy selection of circumstance, the bright sally of vivacity, the deep and unexpected remark, the characteristic anecdote, the diction, now graceful and sublime, now delicate and forcible, have been exhibited by some writers; but they have been of the number of that select few, on whom heaven has bestowed its choicest gifts. (EMR, I, 98)[51]

Stuart included himself among the 'select few', but had failed to incorporate these qualities adequately in the Manx history. The work was doomed to fall into obscurity until the manuscript was located in August 1986 in the Manx Museum Library at Douglas.[52]

He began the work with characteristic enthusiasm. To Mackenzie he explained the historical and political interest of the subject: 'A feudatory, but independent kingdom, where the Lord [the Duke of Atholl] possessed all the flowers of prerogative & all the fruits of revenue, & where the ... Laws are sufficiently singular to excite curiosity, offers & forms a subject ... important in itself.'[53]

Politically, too, he acknowledged the pleasure it would be 'to record in terms of a proper censure, that low & encroaching policy, which ravished from your noble friend, in contradiction to equity & Laws, a jurisdiction & dignity, which no other subject could boast of'.[54] This policy was the work of George Grenville, who became Prime Minister in 1763. Grenville sought to regain the substantial revenue lost each year through smuggling from Man into Britain. The 'running trade', as it was known, had centred itself around the island at the close of the seventeenth-century after wars with France had put high tariffs on goods imported into Britain. Manx duties, paid to the Lord of Man, remained low; so goods were first brought to Man and then easily smuggled into Britain. It was not only Manxmen who gained; more often the profits went to British merchants who first benefited from tax relief on goods exported from Britain to Man, and then avoided import duties by smuggling these same goods back on to the mainland. Throughout the eighteenth century measures had been taken to stop the 'running trade', but these proved ineffectual. When the 3rd Duke succeeded to the sovereignty of Man in 1764, Grenville saw an opportunity to recover the estimated £350,000 annually lost in custom duties to the Crown, and wrote a letter asking the Duke to name a price for the property, customs revenues and regalities of Man. He received no reply. When he wrote again, the Duke was compelled to answer, though he claimed that, as he had only recently become the Lord of Man, it would be difficult to estimate the value. In a letter to Mackenzie he marked out his strategy: 'Our first plan is not to sell it at all if we can decently avoid it; the next to stave off the sale as long as we can, and if it must be parted with, to gett [sic] as much for it as we can.'[55] At this juncture the negotiation came to an abrupt close with the passage of legislation known as the Mischief Act, designed to prevent 'the mischiefs arising to the revenue and commerce of Great Britain and Ireland from the illicit and clandestine trade to and from the Isle of Man'.[56] The act gave the government power to intervene with a military force and gain control of the Duke's customs' revenues.

Stuart voiced a dismissive contempt for Grenville and the Mischief Act: 'It teemed with absurdities, & displayed a fullness of corruption, which never degraded, even in the most sanguinary times of Rome, the most degenerate of her statesmen, or the most ferocious of her tyrants.'[57] The Duke and Duchess were forced to set out the terms of an unwanted sale. The Duke's price of £300,000 for the land, customs duties, regalities and other items was an outrageous sum in the eyes of the government. But as Grenville was intent only on recouping lost customs' revenue, he decided to purchase the regalities and duties alone, paying out £70,000 and leaving the Duke the ownership of the land.[58] This arrangement, the basis of the Revestment Act, became law on 10 May 1765. It passed through Parliament in an unprecedented eighteen days from the first reading to the Royal assent.

With the Revestment came the loss of sovereignty of an autonomous state. Under its ancient and oddly mixed form of government the Island had maintained its independence from Great Britain until 1765. Although the island was ruled, and much of it owned, by a feudal lord, the Manx parliament, called the House of Keys, was profoundly republican. This ancient legislative body exemplified the type of Gothic representative government which Stuart had examined in the *English Constitution*. For centuries the House of Keys, together with the Tynwald Court, had provided a model system for the Manx people, balancing the autocratic sway of the Lord of Man. Yet neither body was consulted about the political revolution that took place with the Revestment.

In an age of British imperialism the idea of an independent principality so close to the mainland was an anomaly. Britain was building an empire that extended from America to India, yet through the eighteenth century it had failed, to its embarrassment and loss of revenue, to control trade from a small island off its western shore. The ultimate success of the British government in the Isle of Man contrasted with its failure to control a not dissimilar situation in the American colonies. For Stuart the constitutional issue was of central importance. If the rights of one individual were violated, those of all British citizens were in danger. The Revestment threatened the protection of property, the primary function of laws and government: 'When such an infringement takes place', Stuart wrote in the work, 'men return in some measure, to their first condition; the cement of society is loosened: they dissolve the compact they had entered into; & delegate dominion to more equitable governors.'[59]

Stuart hoped that the appearance of the work might rectify the situation, but Mackenzie and the Duke were more pragmatic about a history written to protest an event which had taken place seven years earlier. Mackenzie deferred to the Duke's 'clearer apprehension of things' as to 'how far you may think it worth while to Encourage the Scribbling friend of mine further to indulge his Genius (which I know in such matters to be a good one)'.[60] Mackenzie then added his support for the project.

I think I may answer for his Capacity. His Style is full as good and bold as Robertson's on Queen Mary and as Fluent as David Hume's Historical Essays which have pleased the world so much ... I do not know but a well pen'd History might have good Effects with some of the John Bulls & at any rate Justify the Surrender (however involuntary) made by your Grace and the Duchess under your hands to posterity. If this performance is Execute[d] with Chastity & spirit, I cannot see any harm can result from it. If it is not you only lose your 50 guineas and have the manuscript for uses improper to name.[61]

The Duke took up the suggestion. Should he ultimately approve, Stuart would have the 'whole benefit of the printed impression' as well as the fifty guineas.[62] Consequently, Stuart put all his energy into the composition.

It was welcome relief to turn from the drudgery of journalism to the dignity of narrative history. The fluency, to which Mackenzie referred was nowhere more apparent than in the opening paragraph of the work.

The origin & earlier state of principalities & kingdoms are concealed in darkness, & in time. Ignorance of the art of writing, & of the use of numbers make it necessary in rude ages, that the memory of transactions be entrusted to tradition; and, while the bustle & hurry of present occurrences are ready to destroy or impair the remembrance of the past; the love of wonder, & the pride of superior antiquity & greatness disfigure it. But though the exploits & the history of men, in their more ancient condition, were sufficiently known, they would contribute little to instruction or entertainment. Acting without premeditation or concert; and indulging in disorder & cruelties; the revolutions they undergo would offer nothing to excite attention or inquiry: We should be disgusted with their uniformity; we should be shocked with the atrocious circumstances, with which they would necessarily be accompanied.[63]

The similarity of this passage to the opening of the *History of England* would have been noticed by many contemporary readers.[64] Stuart meant the allusion as a compliment, and might have done worse than continue in this vein, but the essentially political focus of the 'Memoirs' (especially in Chapter 5) led him into a more polemical style. A letter to Mackenzie indicates the challenge he faced and his bravado in achieving an acceptable result.

If I do not raise ... a goodly Fabric, the fault will lie on my want of ability. I shall exert all that freedom which History can allow me in the freest country in the world; but while I impeach the understanding & integrity of the minister [Grenville] I shall be careful not to descend into meanness of abuse. The wounds to be inflicted must be mortal, while we behave with all that respectful gallantry, which may be expected from a generous enemy.[65]

When he read a draft of the 'Memoirs', Mackenzie questioned the handling of the attack on Grenville, but Stuart held firm in this regard, asserting that 'I have thought it necessary to express myself in the strong manner I have used because the class of men to whom we chiefly address the performance have contracted a kind of insensibility ... and because the Public has of late been accustomed to the utmost severity of satire.'[66] To encourage Stuart to develop an argument on patriotic grounds, Mackenzie posed a rhetorical question: 'Had that valuable Object belongd to Earl Temple in place of a Scots Peer of higher Rank Do you think that Mr. Grenville's financing zeal would not have contrived some other plan for the increase of the Revenue?'[67] Stuart adopted Mackenzie's suggestion, reserving this emotive challenge for the last paragraph of the work:

If the principality of Man had belonged to an English Peer, and Mr Grenville had made a similar attack upon it, all the rage of a gallant & indignant people had been awakened. They would have revenged the blow that had been given to their Laws, & to their constitution. The flames of civil discord would again have been kindled; and, the blood of another sovereign might have flowed to expiate their violated rights.[68]

These words brought the passionately and well-argued last chapter to a provocative conclusion. The patriotic, indeed seditious, tone of Stuart's prose is similar to that of the letters of Junius and of the speeches, pamphlets and articles connected with the Wilkes affair circulating at the time.

The reality of the situation proved far less dramatic than Stuart's prose, for the Duke in fact did little to redress the injustice of the Revestment. In March 1773 he received the manuscript, while Stuart impatiently waited for a decision about publication. The author's opinion of his work was extremely high. 'It will be a delightful thing', he explained to John Murray, 'one of those monuments, that God Almighty, once in a hundred years, allows a finite creature to create.'[69] Unfortunately, others did not think the history had reached such a perfect state. In the final instance the Duke refused to grant permission to publish probably because the work did not meet the required standard and perhaps because it would harm his political standing in an impending election. At any rate, the Duke's death in July 1774 brought an end to any hope of publication. Stuart, for his part, had received fifty guineas according to the bargain, but this sum, probably already spent, provided him with little consolation.

Another unrealised project from this period was a biography of Tobias Smollett. Stuart roused John Murray's interest in a work 'that will be useful to us both. A life of Dr Smollet [sic] written with taste & spirit and including a criticism on his writings & a key to his satire & allusions.'[70] Stuart calculated that such a work might earn him one hundred guineas and informed the publisher that 'to execute this undertaking is now in my power'. Commissary James Smollett of Bonhill, cousin of Tobias and the wealthy member of the family, had agreed to supply Stuart 'with original letters which contain almost all the transactions in which he was engaged'.[71] Stuart was likewise promised the assistance of the novelist's widow (Anne) and sister (Jane Telfer). In subsequent letters written in the spring of 1773, he asked Murray to gather literary anecdotes from those who had known Smollett and explained that the materials expected from the family 'will be connected with several original pieces, not published & some of them of considerable length'.[72]

Unfortunately, the papers were not immediately forthcoming. The project was temporarily set aside while Stuart began to edit the *Edinburgh Magazine and Review* in November 1773. The delay appeared to have ended in December 1775 when he reported to Murray that Commissary Smollett had died: 'I have just learned that he has left me a legacy to write a life of his relation Dr Smollet [sic]. I suppose, it is to be accompanied with original papers & letters.'[73] Still Stuart's efforts to procure the promised manuscripts were unavailing. To remedy the situation he enlisted the legal assistance of John Mackenzie. Optimistic that the affair would be brought to a successful conclusion, Stuart was nevertheless angry about the way he had been treated by Smollett's relatives. But the prospect of the financial gain and literary recognition the biography would bring gave him 'sufficient inducement to do the business, & to punish the Doctor's relations by exposing them, if they prove refractory'.[74] With increasing vituperation he added: 'If greed is their motive they will deserve all I can say. And after their long neglect, I will not be in a humour to spare them.'[75] George Stuart also wrote to Mackenzie on behalf of his son:

> Never was an author better qualified to write the history of his hero. Money is the spur to action with all writers & will be needed to obtain materials. The sooner it is procured, the sooner will the life appear & with greater spirit. Besides a journey on that account is intended to Glasgow.[76]

George's references to 'Tobie' and the legacy for Gilbert suggest a more than casual association with the Smolletts.[77] It is possible that there were ties of kinship through Stuart's mother, Jean Duncanson, who was from Dunbartonshire, although searches through parish records have not produced any concrete relationship. George Stuart wrote a Latin inscription for a monument to Smollett at Leven which Gilbert translated into English for the reverse side. 'This' wrote George, 'I did without fee or reward which makes it the more shameful to grudge such a pittance to a young man.'[78]

The inscription and translation were printed in 1777 in *Plays and Poems written by T. Smollett, M. D.* at the conclusion of the prefatory 'Memoirs of the Life and Writings of the Author'. The Smollett scholar P. G. Boucé has called these 'Memoirs' 'an important biographical landmark in Smollettian studies'.[79] It is possible that Stuart was their author and the editor of the volume, but the evidence is largely circumstantial: Thomas Evans, the publisher of the collection, was known to him and published Stuart's anonymous pamphlet, *Critical Observations*.

The 'Life' itself contains a chronological survey of Smollett's literary productions, beginning with *Roderick Random* (1748) and concluding with *Humphry Clinker* (1771). The frequent reference to the autobiographical features in these and other works set a precedent which other biographers followed. The 'Life' was by no means a panegyric. Smollett's editorship of the *Critical Review*, for example, was summarised in the following manner: 'To speak impartially, he was, perhaps, too acrimonious sometimes in the conduct of that work, and at the same time too sore, and displayed too much sensibility when any of the unfortunate authors whose works he had ... justly censured, attempted to retaliate.'[80] Smollett's political writings in support of Lord Bute were mentioned, as was his *History of England*. The writer supplemented the account with letters by Smollett to David Garrick and John Wilkes. A short critical piece entitled 'Observations on Dr. Smollett's Ode of Independence' appeared at the end of the volume. This posthumously published poem, with the accompanying 'Observations', was first printed in a small edition at Glasgow by the Foulis brothers in February 1773. The poem itself gained wider public circulation when it appeared in the *Edinburgh Magazine and Review* in November 1773 (EMR, I, 25–6). It was then published with the 'Observations' by Murray in 1774. It has been suggested that William Richardson, a close friend of Stuart's who was published by Murray, wrote the critique.[81] This may be the case, but it is worth noting that the writer's interest in Smollett's remarks on the liberty and independence of the Saxons corresponds with Stuart's own historical preoccupations. General remarks on lyric poetry as a genre are perhaps most striking: 'Without preparing the mind by a cool artificial introduction, rising gradually to the impetuosity of passion, they assail the imagination by an abrupt and sudden impulse; they vibrate through the soul, and fire us instantaneously with all the ardour and enthusiasm of the poet.'[82]

Clearly more concrete evidence is required to confirm Stuart's hand in the secondary material affixed to the *Plays and Poems*. *If* he was involved, it was probably in response to learning that he would not get the papers from the family to write an authorised biography. Around the time the work appeared John Murray explained the situation to John Moore, the eventual biographer of Smollett. 'Dr Stuart's Life of Smollet is dropped. The Relations of the latter discouraged the idea, and gave the former a premium, or rather compromised the Legacy which was left to Dr Stuart for the undertaking, in order to lay it aside.'[83] Moore's edition of Smollett's works with a 'Life' appeared in 1797. But neither did he obtain possession of the elusive Smollett papers. It would have been an inestimable addition to literary studies had more been known about the life of Smollett or had further writings and correspondence survived. As it stands, there are few original records of Smollett's activities. Early biographers like Moore, faced with this lack of primary information, made conjectures about the autobiographical nature of novels to recreate the writer's life. It would have been interesting, moreover, to see Stuart's talent for biography extended beyond the short character portraits found in the *Edinburgh Magazine and Review* and in his narrative histories or his talent for criticism of the novel extended beyond that found in his reviews. But Stuart's plan to write an extended 'history of his hero' was thwarted.

In 1776 Stuart wrote a 'Life' which indisputably appeared. His 'Short Account of the Life and Writings of Mr. Gray' was prefixed to Murray's edition of the *Poems of Mr. Gray* in 1776. The main source for the twenty-page account was William Mason's 'Memoir of Gray' published in 1775. Murray paid Stuart three guineas for the piece but soon after publication the publisher was surprised to learn that Mason 'is at this moment suing me in Chancery for piracy'.[84] Stuart's contribution was not the point of legal contention but fifty lines of poetry printed by Murray. Mason claimed these verses belonged to him exclusively, having been bequeathed by Gray and printed originally in the 1775 edition. Mason had himself borrowed portions of the 'Memoirs' from sketches of Gray's life written by James Boswell and William Temple which had appeared in the *London Magazine* of March 1772.[85] Murray lost the case in Chancery, despite justifying his actions in a printed pamphlet entitled *A Letter to W. Mason*. In subsequent editions of Gray's *Poems* he excluded the fifty lines in question but continued to reprint Stuart's short 'Life'. Other accounts of Gray supplanted this one but it did reappear in the elegant English edition from the Bodoni Press (Parma) in 1793.

Such commissions did not challenge Stuart's intellect, but they were necessary for survival on Grub Street. Translating popular foreign works was another area which provided him with income. Compared with historical composition, it was a vastly inferior literary activity: 'It is only those who cannot write who will translate', asserted Stuart; 'nor is it to be regretted, since the task of translation is certainly unworthy of a man of ability and genius' (EMR, IV, 660). Nevertheless it was an occupation he performed competently and regularly.

Murray engaged Stuart to translate a number of French works in whole or part. The first of these was Abbé Millot's *Elémens de l'Histoire d'Angleterre* (1769). The title page of the English edition, which appeared in 1771, attributes the translation to William Kenrick, a prolific miscellaneous writer and sometime editor of the *London Magazine*. Kenrick in fact only translated half of the work. Murray's account ledger records a payment to Stuart of over £27 for translating twenty-six sheets of the original edition, which was a quarter of the whole. The poet John Langhorne was enlisted to translate a further twenty-two sheets.[86] In the advertisement to the *Elements of the History of England; from the Invasion of the Romans to the Reign of George II* Kenrick, or perhaps Stuart, emphasised that this would not be a straightforward translation and acknowledged a source of literary (rather than political) inspiration.

> In giving an English dress to his work, the translator has endeavoured, rather to imitate than to translate him [Millot]. In several passages, where he betrays a partiality to his own country, or to the Romish faith, he ventured to suppress his sentiments, or to substitute, in their place, ideas more conformable to truth. As he has followed Mr. Hume, as his chief guide, the translator has sometimes, where it could be done with propriety, adorned his version with the expressions of that elegant historian.[87]

In an article in the *Monthly*, Stuart reviewed the translation of the *Elements* together with another of the same work by Frances Brooke. Taking sample passages from both works and placing them in columns, with the French original below, he left no doubt about which was the superior version: 'Ease and freedom, and the dignity of historical narration have been aimed at by the one. The ... other is faithful, but feeble.'[88] Of the work itself, Stuart said that Millot had 'executed his task with great accuracy and attention'.[89] In the next issue of the *Monthly* he reviewed Millot's *Elements of the History of France*. This translation, by Miss Roberts, prompted the chivalric remark: 'It is always with pain that we find ourselves under the necessity of censuring the literary efforts of a lady.'[90]

Stuart's interest in Millot did not end here. In March 1773 he planned a translation of the *Elémens d'Histoire Générale* (1772). He enlisted the assistance of Robert Liston, an old school friend who was free to do the translation before embarking on a diplomatic career. They were of the opinion that a fee of £90 or £100 for the four volumes 'would not be too extravagant'.[91] Stuart began to translate the work but Murray changed his plan: 'I do not intend to *drop Milot* [sic] but I mean to lay it aside for some time.'[92] The publisher thought it prudent to wait for the author to produce the 'modern history' sequel and then translate the complete work. Stuart did not return to this project.

In the meantime Murray had a more immediately profitable foreign work in hand: J. L. De Lolme's *Constitution de l'Angleterre*, first published in Geneva in 1771. The publisher wanted a 'masterly translation' and stimulated Stuart's interest with work and the promise of thirty guineas and a liberal supply of paper, quills and ink..[93] The author had begun his own English edition but Murray thought that Stuart's would be superior. De Lolme was in

London at the time and, according to Murray, 'meant to add notes'.[94]

Stuart worked quickly. Ever attentive to detail, he requested that the proof sheets be shown to him, by which means 'a thousand little improvements will be communicated to it'.[95] As he became engrossed in the subject, Stuart began to question the accuracy of the author's ideas and inquired, 'is this fellow De Lolme perfectly in his senses?'[96] The translation appeared in 1775 and was reprinted many times.[97] Stuart reviewed his own translation in the *Edinburgh Magazine and Review* where he was obliged to criticise the author's monarchical view of history. De Lolme regarded the period after the Norman conquest to be the real foundation of English liberty rather than the more democratic Saxon period, as Stuart asserted. He guessed that De Lolme adopted this view from Hume, who 'inadvertently gave a sanction to it' (EMR, IV, 595), a point made in *The English Constitution*.

Stuart continued to voice similar political principles in other publications. In 1774 he wrote an introduction, edited and added 'notes and authorities' to the second edition of Francis Sullivan's *Lectures on the Constitution and Laws of England* (1776). He undertook the task after the death of Sullivan, who had been the Professor of Common Law at the University of Dublin. This project involved a considerable amount of original effort. Stuart had a typically high opinion of his introductory 'Discourse concerning the Laws and Government of England', which he boasted to Murray 'is excellent, & of more worth than the whole book'.[98]

The Discourse is essentially an abridged history of the English monarchy from the invasion of the Romans to the Restoration. Stuart took as his theme the continuity of British political liberty and asserted the almost formulaic points of the Whig ideology – namely: the antiquity of the Commons; the importance of Edward, the Saxon lawgiver; the denial of a Norman conquest; the view that the Magna Charta only reaffirmed the original liberty of the people; and the corruptions of the Catholic Church. He also challenged the political views of David Hume no less than seven times. 'It is not with pleasure that I differ from this great authority; but, no man has a title to enquire who will not think for himself; and the most perfect productions of human wit have their errors and their blemishes.'[99] Stuart was among those critics who charged Hume with presuming 'to shed a generous tear for the fate of Charles I'.[100] In the Discourse he asserted that 'no authority and no precedent, no usage and no law can give a sanction to tyranny'.[101] Sullivan emphasised the Germanic origin of English law and his views were thus largely in sympathy with Stuart's.

Stuart had favourably reviewed the first edition of Sullivan's work for the *Monthly Review*. He praised Sullivan as a man 'enlightened by reflection, no less than by study',[102] and in the advertisement to the second edition paid 'a Tribute of Respect to the Writings of a virtuous Man and an ingenious Lawyer, whom an immature Death had ravished from his Friends and from Society'.[103]

In April 1775 Stuart completed the edition, but it did not appear until two years later. He complained to Johnson and Dilly, the publishers, about the delays and the slowness in making payment.[104] Conflict also arose over Stuart's plan (suggested by Murray) to dedicate the work to Lord North, the Prime Minister. The publishers questioned the propriety of such a dedication. However, North had already accepted the honour: 'I should appear the tamest idiot', Stuart explained to Murray, 'to withdraw a dedication to so great a man, which he had privately received with uncommon politeness.'[105] Stuart still hoped to obtain the patronage of the government, and North was the obvious target. He probably solicited North's favour through Henry Dundas, who had been appointed Lord Advocate of Scotland in 1775 and wielded considerable power in North's ministry. The dedication is similar in tone and substance to the earlier one to Lord Mansfield: 'You support the lustre of the Crown, while you guard the independence of the subject.'[106]

While working on the edition of Sullivan, Stuart began another project, a history of Edinburgh. In June 1774 he reported to Murray that both manuscripts (Sullivan and the history) 'are finished ... I wish Johnson & Dilly would finally settle payment of the first ... as to the last Creech is to pay me £100. But the fellow is perpetually in want of Cash.'[107] The *Caledonian Mercury*, under a new section headed 'Scottish Literary Intelligence', advertised 'A new History of Edinburgh compiled by Dr. Gilbert Stewart' among a list of other Scottish works.[108] Murray was typically cautious about the profitability of this kind of work and explained privately to Creech: 'The History of Edinburgh may do in Scotland but not much here. I shall like however to publish it for you if agreeable.'[109] For the Scottish market the history was a good commercial proposition. It had been over twenty years since William Maitland had written his compendious *History of Edinburgh, from its Foundation to the Present Time* (1753); and it would be another five before Murray published Hugo Arnot's *History of Edinburgh* (1779).

Stuart's work never appeared in print. However , it is probable that to some extent Arnot used the manuscript in preparing his own history. This was most likely with Stuart's approval as the two men were in close association. In a short letter Arnot told Murray: 'I have looked over the manuscript History & find it very defective.'[110] The content and the style of the more historical parts of Arnot's narrative suggest that he may have incorporated some part of the unpublished account, and Stuart's largely favourable review of Arnot's work in the *Monthly Review* might also imply a tacit agreement between the two men.[111]

The story of Stuart's role in chronicling Edinburgh's history probably did not end there. In 1787 Alexander Kincaid wrote and published the next important history of the city. Kincaid's father was William Creech's late partner and had been Lord Provost of Edinburgh from 1776 to 1777. Little is known of the younger Kincaid, apart from being credited with a small number of miscellaneous literary compilations. The first part of his *History of Edinburgh, from the Earliest Accounts to the Present Time* has a number of stylistic and thematic similarities to Stuart's other writings. The assertion of whiggish principles; the opposition of citizens to a tax for a standing army; a lengthy account of Mary Queen of Scots; a consideration of the development of the City's legal institutions; and the combination of a main narrative text supplemented by lengthy scholarly appendices suggest the possibility of Stuart's involvement.[112] Without more evidence, however, the story of Stuart's history of Edinburgh, whether destroyed, buried in some archive or dispersed in other publications, remains a mystery.

Although this work, with the Manx history and other projects, was not published as Stuart had hoped, the first years of his career as a writer were ones of productivity and diversity. As a reviewer he earned a reputation and a steady income. With the former he gained confidence, perhaps too much confidence; and with the latter he was able in a limited way to pursue the historical studies which he saw as his true vocation.

Calamity was never far away. Stuart's younger brother, Walter, had been in London for some time trying unsuccessfully to find regular employment in business. He was in poor health and Gilbert regularly supplied him with money out of his own modest earnings. Between February and October 1771 alone he gave him twenty-five guineas.[113] In November 1772 he told Murray:

My poor brother is just at the point of death ... Of his places, I can say nothing; a circumstance, that will probably surprise you. But I have long since learned not to be surprised at any thing ... I am more hurried than ever, & more than ever out of humour with every thing in this world – except you & a few friends whom I esteem heartily.[114]

In another letter he reflected more generally on death: 'We anxiously wish for life; and yet before our own mortality comes, we have to die fifty times with those we love.'[115] These shadows of gloom passed; in moments of optimism Stuart could turn from sorrow and disappointment to hope for the future. He commented on this in a review written some years later:

The passion of hope is not easily eradicated or depressed in individuals or kingdoms. No sooner is one subject of hope taken away, than another opens to the views of mankind: and it often happens, that the new direction which disappointed expectations give to our exertions, redounds greatly to our advantage.   (PH, II, 286)[116]

In London Stuart found both opportunity and friendship, especially in John Murray. The excitement of national politics captivated him and expanded his provincial Scottish experience. During his stay in the metropolis, public awareness of the potential for political reform had gradually risen with the success of Wilkes and other oppositional elements in society. Events took a turn in December 1773 when rebellious colonists dumped tea into Boston harbour. War was imminent, a war which formed a backdrop to Stuart's politics for the next decade.

When he returned to Scotland in April 1773, he brought with him the reformist attitude so pervasive in the capital. Although intending to stay just a few months, he remained over eight years. From the retirement home of his parents at Fisherrow, near Musselburgh, he wrote enthusiastically to Murray with 'a thousand things to say to you, & a thousand schemes to propose when we meet'.[117] The most important of these was his plan to establish a Scottish literary review.

3

The Edinburgh Magazine and Review
Redefining the Limits of Criticism 1773–1776

If I attack the vicious, I shall only set upon them in a body; and will not be provoked by the worst usage I can receive from others, to make an example of any particular Criminal. In short, I have so much of a *Drawcansir* in me, that I shall pass over a single Foe to charge whole Armies.

Joseph Addison, *Spectator*, Number 16 (19 March 1711)

Edinburgh's literary scene was a narrow one compared with London. Most Scottish authors, successful or otherwise, held posts in the church, university or the courts.[1] Hume was among the few writers in Scotland who, lacking substantial private means, attained eminence as a man of letters. Stuart had similar aspirations, but he had found it difficult thus far to establish himself as an historical writer. Necessity led him to the career of a critic in London, a profession for which he had a natural flair. He was confident that a Scottish review could achieve a national reputation and earn him a good profit. With these hopes, Stuart established the *Edinburgh Magazine and Review* in November 1773, at the time he celebrated his thirtieth birthday.

In this venture he enlisted two able associates: William Smellie and William Creech. Though a printer by trade, Smellie was no stranger to literature, and Creech was a successful Edinburgh bookseller. The skills of the three men brought together considerable literary talent and business acumen. Stuart and Smellie were the main writers and therefore each took two of the six shares in the periodical. A further share went to Creech and the last to John Murray.[2] Murray provided an essential connection with London and the provinces where new books were obtained for review and where a wider readership was cultivated. He also distributed the *Edinburgh Magazine and Review* to the Continent and to the American colonies.[3] In addition to printing the work at his shop in Anchor Close, Smellie took an active role with Stuart in preparing the 'History' section, for which they wrote accounts of domestic happenings in various countries, but particularly in England and Scotland. He also wrote a number of reviews. Other contributors were Thomas Blacklock (the blind poet), James Beattie, the Reverend Alexander Gillies, William Richardson, William Baron and the Reverend Alexander Carlyle. Kerr, in the *Life of Smellie*, lists these contributors and some of the articles they wrote.[4] The information is based on a copy (not extant) partially annotated by Smellie, but this is not always accurate. The review of Gibbon's *Decline and Fall of the Roman Empire* (EMR, V, 144–54), for example, is attributed to Stuart but was in fact written by Carlyle.[5] There were good reasons why men who occupied prominent positions in society, such as Carlyle, would want to be discreet about their involvement. His example begs the question, who else wrote for the *Edinburgh Magazine and Review*? In a letter to Murray, Stuart reported that 'Hume (Dav.[d]) gives an essay, for No. 3',[6] but this piece has not been indentified.

The *Edinburgh Magazine and Review* became a forum for the expression of religious, political, moral and literary opinion. Stuart produced work in many respects representative of his society and of his positive association with establishment figures. In others it was a departure to a new and controversial style of journalism. Through its pages his spirited character and contentious opinions emerge. This brand of criticism met with opposition from those writers who were unaccustomed to it; polite Scottish readers were also offended to see public figures challenged. As a consequence, the periodical ceased to be published after a run of less than three years. Nevertheless, Stuart's approach left its mark. In a modified form it reappeared more successfully thirty years later in Francis Jeffrey's *Edinburgh Review*.

In Stuart's best reviews a dynamic commentary emerges from the dispassionate surface of polite eighteenth-century criticism. He is at once an insightful observer and an arrogant antagonist. By employing the vocabulary of controversy as a rhetorical tool he engaged the attention of the reader and charged him with emotion. The review thus became a literary piece in its own right as well as a vehicle for judging literature. What had been once an exercise in cursory judgement and a series of lengthy quotations became a display of imaginative journalism. Stuart attempted to transform the formulaic eighteenth-century review from what Derek Roper calls 'an objective chronicle of cultural progress'[7] into an editorial piece which expressed opinions on subjects or individuals, sometimes only marginally related to the work at hand. This approach suited Stuart's nature, as it could stimulate his interest or channel his impatience with the work. But the public was not fully ready for this type of criticism, nor could Stuart refine his style sufficiently to accommodate his readers' sensibilities.

Throughout his life Stuart reviewed books. He was prolific and innovative, but more often than not literary criticism was a means of making money. 'If I had been born to independence', he remarked of this profession, 'I should sooner have been nailed like an imposter to a tree, than have submitted to it.'[8] It was more than financial necessity that led many authors to take up the critical pen: Hume, Smollett, Godwin, Wollstonecraft, Coleridge, Walter Scott are just a few whose contributions in this area are noteworthy.[9] Stuart's lament obscures the extent to which his criticism and his historical writing were interdependent intellectual activities. Publications were multiplying at such a rate that no one could hope to read in full all the contributions to a given field of knowledge. Criticism of a certain type could bridge this gap and belie the paradox that as more was known knowledge became more difficult to absorb. As an intellectual activity, criticism could be a model for judicious reading. As an analytical and imaginative way of approaching a book it could also be a guide for good writing. Practice as a critic made Stuart a better historian. He certainly lacked the critical refinement of Jeffrey, Sydney Smith and the other contributors to the successful *Edinburgh Review*. Often his attempts at lively and controversial journalism deteriorated into slanderous attack. With hindsight it might be said, however, that despite his somewhat misdirected efforts he redefined Scottish criticism for his successors.[10]

Initially, I will describe what place the *Edinburgh Magazine and Review* occupies in the tradition of eighteenth and early nineteenth-century Scottish periodical literature. Then I shall address the work itself to discuss some of the more important religious, political, moral and literary issues which Stuart and other contributors addressed in articles and reviews. I do not pretend that this chapter provides a comprehensive account of the work, as the focus is on Stuart. During the course of his editorship he wrote two interesting pamphlets to which he devoted a certain amount of attention in the periodical. These works will be examined and in the final part of this chapter I will consider the failure of the periodical.

The *Edinburgh Magazine and Review* stands between the short-lived *Edinburgh Review* of 1755–6, established by Alexander Wedderburn, Adam Smith and others, and Jeffrey's well known journal of 1802. Interest in the contributors of the former and the success of the latter have overshadowed Stuart's periodical. It is not the similarity of title alone that makes it important in the history of the Scottish periodical. It appeared when new publications were filling the booksellers' shops at an unprecedented rate and new forms of religious, political and philosophical debate were heard in the tavern, the lecture hall and the kirk. The power of the printed word was increasing. As a consequence, the periodical became a forum for opinions about culture and politics – Scottish, British and international.

In the preface to the first *Edinburgh Review* Wedderburn described the cultural setting from which the idea of a Scottish literary review developed. Since the Union, Scottish writing and publishing had advanced to a level rivalling other European capitals, so it was decided that important philosophical and scientific works produced in Scotland should be discussed in a public forum. Wedderburn contended that 'shewing men the gradual advances of science, would be a means of inciting them to a more eager pursuit of learning, to distinguish themselves, and to do honour to their country'.[11] His hopes for a Scottish journal were only partly realised. First, there was an insufficient number of new Scottish publications; second, the deistical bias of the reviewers, evinced in their criticisms of publications by the more orthodox clergy, met with open opposition.[12] After two numbers the *Edinburgh Review* was discontinued. In the mid-1750s the Moderates' control over Scottish institutions was still in its early stages. In the 1760s, when Lord Bute's interest at the Court of George III made itself felt, the Moderates and their friends gained a firmer hold on Edinburgh establishments.

By the time Stuart established the *Edinburgh Magazine and Review*, these men had moved to the controlling centre of church and civic affairs. However there was still vociferous opposition from the Popular party and the political network of Lawrence Dundas which loosely supported that faction of the church. To some extent the periodical reflected the ideas and supported the aims of the Moderates and their circle of supporters, but, under Stuart's independent editorship the work was no mere mouthpiece. Any individual, any book, was a potential object for an attack from his belligerent and satirical pen. But he proved too indiscriminate and too fractious. As a consequence, public disapprobation was such that after thirty-five monthly issues the periodical ceased publication.

Nearly fifty years after the first *Edinburgh Review*, Francis Jeffrey confidently outlined a new editorial policy:

> Of the books that are daily presented to the world, a very large proportion is evidently destined to obscurity, by the insignificance of their subjects, or the defects of their execution ... The Conductors of the Edinburgh Review ... decline any attempt at exhibiting a complete view of modern literature; and to confine their notice, in a great degree to works that either have attained, or deserve, a certain proportion of celebrity.[13]

The provincialism of Wedderburn and Stuart was judiciously set aside in favour of a cosmopolitan approach. It is true that the earlier periodicals had reviewed works by English and European authors, but their accounts of ephemeral Scottish sermons and pamphlets had given the works a narrow aspect. In 'A Letter to the *Edinburgh Review*' of 1756 Adam Smith suggested that the editors consider only those works that 'have yet a chance of being remembered for thirty or forty years to come'.[14] But this prudent advice was not adopted. John Murray similarly told Gilbert Stuart 'to be more general' as 'there are complaints that you pay too many comp[limen]ts to Scotch authors'.[15] Jeffrey's review, by contrast, added to the literary reputation of Scotland not by emphasising the merits or demerits of native productions but by dictating literary taste and judgement from Scotland. Moreover, the quarterly rather than monthly interval for publication gave the editors of the nineteenth-century review 'a greater variety for selection' and enabled them to be 'occasionally guided in their choice by the tendencies of public opinion'.[16] As a consequence this quarterly became the most widely circulated journal of its type in Britain.

A common theme of social and political liberty runs through the three Scottish reviews. In the first, writers whose religious views were formed within the framework of a post-Newtonian science of man challenged the orthodoxy of the Scottish church. In the second, Stuart and his associates asserted freedom of expression, however indiscriminately, against religious enthusiasts, corrupt politicians and certain literary men they believed to be misguided. In the third, radicalism and the Reform movement provided new political direction. While the two earlier reviews attacked the fanaticism of Calvinistic clergymen, the later one attacked the 'absurdities' of the Methodists.[17]

For the 1756 *Edinburgh Review* the most important political event was the commencement of the Seven Years' War; for Gilbert Stuart it was the American Revolution and for Jeffrey the French Revolution. Through the accounts of these events, the writers expressed a common desire for liberty – the liberty of the people to be an integral part of government and the liberty of the press to shape and reflect public opinion.

An analogy of the 1756 and 1802 reviews concerning the development of a Whig tradition in post-Union Scottish society allows us to place Stuart's periodical. Wedderburn formulated his conception of a review from the vantage point of a child looking forward to that tradition and Jeffrey as an adult looking back nostalgically.[18] The tone of Stuart's work then reflects the period of adolescence, or to borrow from Keats' phrase in the preface to *Endymion*, 'the space of life ... in which the soul is in a ferment ... [and] ambition thick-sighted'. A near contemporary critic stated similarly that Stuart was 'full of the arrogant confidence of youthful genius'.[19] On the one hand he sought, as he wrote in the Preface of the periodical, to 'spread Knowledge, and diffuse Taste' to an intelligent public; on the other he was often rebellious against the leaders of religious and civic establishments and contemptuous of eminent literary figures.

Alexander Gillies spoke more positively of a Scottish periodical when he asserted:

> Such a Magazine is a right thing in our country. The Scotch have sense enough to instruct, and wit enough to divert one another ... Thus the flimsy, frivolous things that come from London, to steal our money and vitiate our taste, will remain in the land of their nativity.[20]

Stuart's pride in Scottish achievement and his audacity in criticising whatever or whoever he found objectionable formed central elements of his journalistic approach. Through the *Edinburgh Magazine and Review* he endeavoured to entertain men and women and improve society by establishing sound principles on which literature could be evaluated and public figures judged. Unfortunately, he did not succeed as he had hoped. The periodical promised much but it never became a profitable venture. None felt the disappointment more than Stuart. From this endeavour re-emerged two prominent yet conflicting forces which shaped his critical and historical writings. One was the increasingly disputatious tone he adopted, which helped to draw attention to what he had to say and won him a modest degree of public approbation. The other, at times causing him at times to sacrifice the cogent expression of his ideas, was the excessive expression of contempt.

In his introductory 'Address to the Public' Stuart alluded to the instructive lessons which might be learned from the first *Edinburgh Review* when he wrote: 'The imperfections of former attempts ... evince the difficulty of such publications; they point out the dangers to be avoided; and they ought to excite to greater vigour of execution.' (EMR, I, 3.) He marked out 'variety' as the 'great object' and explained the division of the work into two parts: first there was the 'Magazine' section presenting 'historical anecdotes and details, state papers, singular characters and inscriptions ... facts and relations descriptive of mankind in the different stages of civilisation and refinement ... original pieces of poetry, and discoveries and views in all the different branches of philosophy and science'; second there was the 'Review' section containing accounts of 'the more capital literary performances which appear in England, and of every new production which is published in Scotland' (EMR, I, 4). The combination of a 'Magazine' containing a range of essays, poetry, and local and international news together with reviews of the latest publications makes the *Edinburgh Magazine and Review* a fascinating, almost encyclopedic microcosm of Scottish society at the time. The divisions of the periodical do not obscure a general editorial unity. Themes and opinions on various matters carry over from one section to another. Stuart could not possibly write everything, or even the majority of the material, but as editor he kept a watchful eye over all that was included. Thus the work reflects his taste and opinions more than those of any other contributor.

Stuart perceived the appeal of a monthly periodical that incorporated the entertaining features of the popular *Scots Magazine* and *Gentleman's Magazine* with original literary reviews like those found in the *Monthly Review* and *Critical Review*. It was not his intention to compete with the successful *Weekly Magazine, or Edinburgh Amusement*, begun in July 1768 by his cousin Walter Ruddiman and mainly compiled from other sources. Instead he anticipated that this new work would make its mark by the originality of its articles and reviews.

For a number of years some of the most talented Scottish literary critics (Smollett and Hamilton in the *Critical Review*, MacMillan and Boswell in the *London Magazine*) had contributed to, and in some cases owned and managed, successful London publications. Now it was time for Scotland to boast its own critical forum. Stuart's enthusiasm and expectations were characteristically high. Murray warmly received Stuart's news that 'the Literati of Scotland ... are all eager to advance the undertaking'.[21] But the publisher was more cautious about the rumour that 'the timid proprietors of the Scots Mag have come to the resolution of dropping their work at the end of the year'[22] and advised that a sufficient budget be allotted for advance advertising. On 30 October 1773 notice appeared in the *Caledonian Mercury* for 'Number 1 of a new monthly work; entitled the Edinburgh Magazine and Review ... embellished with a handsome frontispiece ... and priced at six pence'.[23]

Each number (or issue) contained fifty-six pages of text.[24] These were issued stitched in blue wrappers. On the front wrapper Smellie printed the contents for that month and on the back advertisements for books sold by Creech and Murray.[25] Initially, Smellie printed 500 copies but this figure soon rose to 2,500 (1,500 for Scotland and 1,000 for London). Some were sent quickly to London by waggon, others less expensively by sea. Towards the end of its run in the summer of 1776, no more than 1,000 copies were printed, but many of these remained unsold.[26]

In the 'Magazine' section there are extended essays on Scottish emigration (EMR, II, 512–15, 561–73 and 741–3) and on architecture 'as a subject of taste' (EMR, II, 286–90 and 402–6). There are pieces of original fiction, such as Stuart's 'Anecdotes of Laura and Petraque' (II, 414–17 and 469–71); and William Nimmo's 'Antiquities of Stirlingshire' (EMR, I, 230–38, 348–52; II, 409–14, 459–64, 575–80, 617–26, 729–39; III, 3–10, 57–62, 130–37), which appeared as a separate publication in 1777.

Stuart pursued his interest in biography by preparing a series of short character sketches of famous Scots, including: Mary Queen of Scots, William Carstairs, Duncan Forbes of Culloden, George Buchanan, Dr Alexander Monro, Archibald Pitcairne, John Arbuthnot, Admiral Crichton, John Knox and George Drummond.[27] His work 'Anecdotes of Scottish Literature' (EMR, I, 5–13 and 113–17) reflects a similar interest in composing a catalogue of national biographies. These, together with articles such as the 'Scots Patriot' (EMR, I, 173–8) and others of a more historical kind, show a tendency to promote patriotic sentiment.

Alexander Gillies' lengthy essay entitled 'A Modest Defence of Blasphemy' (EMR, I, 185–90, 246–52, 295–302, 353–8; II, 505–10) and the 'Patriot', purportedly written by Dr Johnson, show the editors' readiness to discuss controversial religious and political issues.

Not all the articles were written especially for the periodical; the editors regularly included extracts from contemporary literature. On a monthly basis it became more and more difficult to fill the necessary pages with interesting original material. From the start articles of all kinds were actively solicited from the public, and aspiring writers were requested to leave their compositions in a box outside Smellie's print-house. In the 'Notes to Correspondents' the editors passed a cursory judgement upon the submissions. Some were to appear in subsequent issues; others were described as 'obscure and frivolous' (EMR, II, 560) and consigned to the flames. Stuart had hoped that correspondents would send in better material for inclusion, but this source could not be depended upon. He reported to Murray that 'in the course of eleven months ... not a single paper has been sent which could be inserted'. Though an exaggeration, it was true that, in sorting through these papers, 'the trouble is greater than any advantage that can acrue from it'.[28]

The poetry section (usually two to four pages) was one department where there was a good response from correspondents, even if the verse often was of a rather inferior kind. An unpublished poem or two from Robert Fergusson, whose first volume of poetry was published in 1773, might have been expected, but this was not forthcoming. Stuart engaged Murray's assistance to obtain poetry from the most popular writers of the day, among them Swift, Pope, Gray, Hawkesworth and Smollett. Some of these pieces were still unpublished, or at least such claims were made (EMR, II, 529). Latin verse was not uncommon, even in the curious form of translations of popular English works, such as Beattie's *Hermit* (EMR, II, 700). In all, about 150 poems were printed in the pages of the periodical.

The 'History' section appeared at the end of each issue and occupied from two to six pages. The heading was something of a misnomer, as politics and other current affairs were the main focus. Over the course of the periodical's existence the divisions of this section along geographical lines varied. At first, readers were given news of events in countries such as Russia, Turkey, Poland and France, along with more detailed notices of happenings in England and Scotland. After six months, affairs in England (including 'America') and Scotland came to dominate the section. From August 1774 the editors devoted a separate column to

American affairs during the critical period leading up to independence and war. Scottish clergymen and other public figures, both pro- and anti-American, were given an opportunity to voice their views. Smellie himself entered the dispute in a heated exchange of letters with the Reverend Charles Nisbet, who was radically pro-American.[29]

Topics of Scottish interest, such as Highland emigration and financial disasters, were reported impartially on the whole, but the same could not be said of local Edinburgh political and religious affairs, which occupied an increasing amount of space in the 'History' section. Readers were left in little doubt about the views of Stuart and Smellie in these matters. Nevertheless, the reports they gave of elections, General Assembly debates, causes in the Scottish Court, Edinburgh building projects, the poor, and other social topics make this news department an invaluable source for local information. At the end of each 'History' section the editors included lists of marriages, births and deaths. They also printed the dates of the circuit courts and lists of government and church preferments.

Stuart regarded the 'Review' section as the most important part of the periodical, indeed his real aim as a journalist was to edit his own critical journal. In the wake of the initial success of the *Edinburgh Magazine and Review* he told Murray of his plan: 'We now begin to think seriously of a *Review*. I have had time to look around me; & I have persons, who are able to do it, with an eclat that no work of the same kind! ever attained in England. Think of *this*.'[30] Stuart, Smellie and others wrote over 150 critical articles for the periodical. The length of the reviews varied considerably, from a few lines for an ephemeral novel such as *Ideal Trifles* (EMR, III, 44) to extended articles continued over many months for important philosophical works.

Books as well known as Johnson's *Journey to the Western Isles of Scotland* (EMR, III, 155–62), the first volume of Gibbon's *Decline and Fall of the Roman Empire* (EMR, V, 144–54) and (if less known) Joseph Priestley's *Institutes of Natural and Revealed Religion* (EMR, II, 701–21) stand out among the English works reviewed. Another work by Priestley which received considerable attention (from Smellie) was *An Examination of Dr Reid's Inquiry into the Human Mind, on the Principles of Common Sense: Dr Beattie's Essay on the Nature and Immutability of Truth; and Dr Oswald's Appeal to Common Sense, in behalf of Religion* (EMR, II, 771–81; III, 33–7, 96–102, 146–55, 199–209 and 260–275).[31] The issue was of considerable importance, but it was odd that the review was almost as long as the work itself. The criticisms of Priestley in both reviews demonstrate Smellie's understanding of the philosophical questions at hand and his bias towards the Scottish (or Aberdonian) writers who were involved in the dispute.

The emphasis on Scottish publications reflected the number of important works written at the time by native authors. The two which were given the fullest treatment were Lord Kames' *Sketches of the History of Man* (EMR, I, 310–20, 376–86; II, 430–7, 494–9 and 555–7) and the second and third volumes of Lord Monboddo's *Of the Origin and Progress of Language* (EMR, I, 320–8, 367–72; II, 423–30; V, 88–97, 155–64, 208–216 and 249–67). No English review gave these books such attention. In a letter to Murray, Stuart indicated his editorial policy with respect to such important books: 'The 2nd volume of Monboddo is published & will appear in our next with Kaims [sic]. The former is a childish performance; the latter rather better. We are to treat them with a good deal of freedom, especially the former.'[32] These reviews bear more resemblance to Jeffrey's thorough articles in the *Edinburgh Review* than to a typical review of the period. Stuart allotted considerable space to these works because he realised their importance, even if he had unfavourable, even severe, remarks to make upon them.

Books published by Creech and Murray received considerable attention. Although the reviewer would certainly be encouraged to favour such works, the articles were not generally puffs. Even a work such as De Lolme's *Constitution of England*, received Stuart's unqualified disapprobation: 'It is a pain to us, that we cannot recommend this performance to the public. To those who are well informed, it contains nothing to gratify curiosity; and into inexperienced readers it might infuse pernicious and deceitful tenets.' (EMR, IV, 602.) Three works by David Dalrymple fared better.[33] Of these, the *Annals of Scotland* was praised for the 'liberal spirit which runs through the whole of this work, both with respect to religion and politics' (EMR, IV, 768). However, Stuart challenged the author's too frequent reliance on English sources: 'They ... are not always impartial ... ; and surely, when English records or chronicles fail, Scottish history or tradition should be held good, except where it exceeds probability.' (EMR, IV, 768.)

As indicated, many of the articles and reviews reflect important philosophical and religious issues then under debate in Scottish society. The dissemination of sceptical ideas, particularly in the writings of David Hume, was a topic not only for the clergy but for the whole community, and it was a trend which required public refutation in a Christian society. An anonymous commentator in the *Weekly Magazine* voiced his concern about the spread of unorthodox ideas and succinctly summed up eighteenth-century British philosophy with the rather cynical remark: 'Berkeley banished matter out of the world: H[um]e has sent the soul after it; and nothing remains now but ideas. Some succeeding genius may banish these also, and leave the world a perfect vacuum.'[34]

The leading Moderate clergy such as Robertson, Blair, Ferguson and Carlyle could be friends with Hume but they could not condone irreligion. They read Stuart's periodical with interest and could not but be pleased by the attacks on their rivals. However Stuart did not share all of their religious concerns. Although he opposed the more orthodox views of the Popular party, he hailed James Beattie's *Essay on the Immutability of Truth* (1770), as an antidote to Hume's religious scepticism, and offered the pragmatic observation that 'if the *Treatise on [sic] Human Nature* had never appeared, we should not have seen the *Essay on the Immutability of Truth*' (EMR, II, 522).[35] He saw moral and religious inquiry as a dynamic cultural process. Collective social happiness was more important, in his view, than the opinion of a single individual, however truthful. In a description which may have been modelled upon Hume, Stuart wrote:

> The infidel, from respect, either real or pretended, to the laws, and the interests of morality, does not commonly permit himself to disturb the public peace. His indolence or indifference about all religion, induces him rather to satisfy himself with a sneer or a laugh, at the folly and credulity of his fellow creatures.[36]   (EMR, IV, 440)

He reserved harsher treatment for the fanatic, 'the most dangerous member of society' whose 'violent and uncharitable spirit … render him peculiarly pestilent and fatal' (EMR, IV, 440). The attack on religious enthusiasm began in the first article, 'Anecdotes of Scottish Literature'. Here Stuart followed Hume's Tudor volumes in censuring the fanaticism of the early Scottish reformers. Elsewhere he challenged the Reverend Daniel MacQueen, the author of an attack on Hume, who

> meant possibly to do a service to religion, by extolling the characters of the reformers beyond what history or nature will permit; and it is by such well meant, but futile endeavours, that our most holy religion receives its worst wounds; the great source of infidelity being the contemptible bigotry

of too many of the defenders of christianity.[37]

(EMR, III, 259n)

The editors singled out Robert Henry, then leader of the Popular party, on similar grounds. William Smellie criticised Henry's sermon, *Revelation, of the most Effectual means of Civilising and Reforming Mankind*, in the first number; Stuart continued the attack with a scathing review of Henry's *History of Great Britain* in the second. Opponents of the *Edinburgh Magazine and Review* challenged the implication of a connection between the enthusiasm of the first reformers and that of the Popular clergy of the day. One critic remarked that 'the Reviewers are as angry at the living spreaders and maintainers of the reformed religion, as they are at the ashes and memory of the reformers themselves'.[38] In reply to this charge and to attacks 'from different quarters' Stuart reported to Murray: 'I am about to be persecuted by the whole Clergy; and I am about to persecute them in my turn. They are hot and zealous; I am cool & dispassionate like a determined Sceptic.'[39]

The links between religion and politics in eighteenth-century Scottish society opened to Stuart and Smellie another area for attack. Henry's brother-in-law, Gilbert Laurie, was then the Lord Provost of Edinburgh. Charges of nepotism and corruption were therefore levelled at Laurie and his political boss, Sir Laurence Dundas.[40] He was the Member of Parliament for Edinburgh, influential with the ministry in London and one of the wealthiest men in Scotland. The *Review* exposed the faction of Dundas, Laurie and Henry and presented this triumvirate as a genuine threat to the public interest.

In the spring of 1775 Stuart wrote an account of the proceedings of the General Assembly, where he clearly expressed support for the Moderates and offered a description of the two religious parties and their leaders. Written with sincerity at the time, his comments on William Robertson would carry a retrospective irony.

> The Rev. Dr. understands how to lose with a good grace, as well as to win. As the head of a great party in the church, he knows he must sometimes follow, as well as lead; and he is too wise to think of obtaining the affected praise of an hundred enemies, at the expence of losing a single friend.

(EMR, III, 365)

By contrast, Stuart attacked the opponents of the Moderates for affecting 'to be thought the most zealous guardians of religion and pure morals' (EMR, III, 364). In the *View of Society*, which he was writing at the time, he penned his thoughts on the role of the clergy in a more evocative manner:

> Were it possible to destroy the comments, the explanations, the catechisms, and the systems of divines, a very considerable blow would be given to infidelity. One can respect the honest doubts of philosophy. But, is it possible to with-hold indignation or scorn, when ability stoops to be uncharitable and disingenuous, when bigotry presses her folly, and spits her venom?   (VS, 305)

Stuart came to regard religion as an element of an essentially secular structure, 'the great end of which is to make mankind happy, by making them good and wise' (EMR, III, 40).[41] Reformed Christianity was a benevolent force which should bring men together under what he called 'the powerful principle of worthy conduct'. He rejected the concept of 'faith without works' which he considered a 'source of discord and animosity' (EMR, III, 41). Civic virtue, the antithesis of religious enthusiasm, was the force which best benefited the individual in society. Later, in the *History of Mary Queen of Scots*, Stuart clarified in a most trenchant manner the growing extent of his anti-clericism. He compared the spiritual benefits which religion offered the individual with the dangers which religious institutions posed to society.

> The guides of every church ... contend respectively for the tenets entrusted to them ... They give check to religion in its happiest principle of universal benevolence ... and perhaps it would be fortunate for human affairs, if the expence, the formalities, and the abuses of religious establishments were for ever at an end; if society were deprived alike of the sovereign pontiff with his tiara, the stalled bishop, and the mortified presbyter; if no confessions and creeds were held out as standards of purity and doctrine; if faith and futurity were left unfettered like philosophy and science; if nations were not harnessed in opinions like horses to a carriage; and if every man's heart were the only temple where he was to worship his God.   (MQS, II, 77)

For Stuart a civil jurisdiction was preferable to clerical despotism. He condemned the means by which some groups of clergymen, such as the Popular party, incited the populace; he also questioned the more subtle ways others, such as the Moderates, managed civic affairs. It is significant, too, that these comments conclude his portrait of John Knox, the most ardent and implacable of all the Scottish reformers. Stuart first expressed a condemnatory opinion of Knox in the July 1774 issue of the *Review*. He argued that Knox's tenets 'had a tendency to subvert both moral and political order' (EMR, II, 521). To such criticisms and others more severe, Stuart added qualifying remarks which show how he thought best to combat scepticism and win public support for the Moderates.

> It must be obvious ... to every person of observation and candour, that the imperfections of Knox reflect not disgrace on Christianity, any more than those of many of the preachers of our own age; and that a censure of his conduct may be given with no less justice, than of those factions which now disturb the church of Scotland; and which, under denominations of *moderate* and *wild*, foster the most bitter animosities. Men of sense and virtue can respect religion without adorning its teachers. (EMR, II, 522)

This was not wholly a one-sided defence of the Moderates. When Stuart challenged the view that Knox almost singlehandedly brought about the Reformation in Scotland, he directed the reader to Robertson's overly laudatory portrait of Knox in the *History of Scotland* as the source of this misapprehension (EMR, II, 521). In comments directed at his female readers, Stuart criticised the reformer's low opinion of women; and to a quotation from Knox's *Blast against Women*, he added ironically: 'Such is the liberal spirit of this celebrated tract' (EMR, II, 521). Finally, he subjoined to this provocative picture of Knox a call on the public to send in 'remarks in opposition'. In this way 'its errors ... will lead to advantage' (EMR, II, 522).

The challenge to scepticism and fanaticism continued, though less obviously, in the response to a review of the second volume of Robert Henry's *History of Great Britain*. David Hume wrote a favourable account of the work for the *Review* which Stuart later rejected. Stuart, in turn, prepared his own critique in its place (EMR, I, 199–207 and 264–70). A discussion of the suppressed article by Ernest Mossner concluded that Stuart subjected Henry's *History* 'to a deliberate campaign of persecution designed for the ruin of the author, such as can scarcely be paralleled in the annals of literature'.[42] Mossner's main source was a chapter on Stuart in Isaac D'Israeli's *Calamities of Authors*. D'Israeli called his account 'Literary Hatred: Exhibiting a Conspiracy against an Author'. The piece itself is based on letters Stuart wrote to John Murray.[43] It gives an amusingly sensationalised picture of Stuart which begins with an elaborate characterisation of a self-destructive 'literary assassin':

In the peaceful walks of literature we are startled at discovering genius with the mind, and, if we conceive the instrument
it guides to be a stiletto, with the hand of an assassin –
irascible, vindictive, armed with the indiscriminate satire,
never pardoning the merit of rival genius, but fastening on
it throughout life, till, in the moral retribution of human
nature, these very passions, by their ungratified cravings,
have tended to annihilate the being who fostered them.[44]

Stuart's attack on Henry was severe, but information to which
neither D'Israeli nor Mossner had access clarifies the affair to a
greater extent and offers a better explanation of his behaviour.

Stuart's association with Henry dated from a period over two
years prior to the establishment of the *Edinburgh Magazine and
Review* when he favourably reviewed the first volume of the *History of Great Britain*.[45] Hume was (Mossner tells us) 'determined to
do something tangible for his new clerical protégé',[46] and may
therefore have asked Stuart to write this commendatory piece. If
so, when Henry's second volume was published early in 1774, it
would have been natural for Hume to turn to Stuart again, this
time to publish what he had written himself. But had the philosopher been aware that Henry was probably the writer who had
referred to 'the sophistry and pernicious metaphysical subtleties
of Mr Hume's essays',[47] he might have reconsidered giving his
assistance. At any rate, Stuart would have none of Hume's patronage, as he told Murray: 'He wanted ... to review Henry, but that
task is so precious, that I will undertake it myself. Moses were he
to ask it as a favour should not have it.'[48]

William Smellie offered an explanation of the affair (as it stood
up to this point) more sympathetic to Stuart than that found in
Mossner or D'Israeli. In his opinion Hume's review 'appeared to
be so high-strained, that the Reviewers ... agreed that Mr Hume's
account was meant as a burlesque upon the author'.[49] Was Smellie
merely offering a defence for his friend's behaviour? Or were the
editors sincere in their interpretation of Hume's sentiments? A
passage towards the end of the review may clarify whether
Hume's regard for Henry's work was genuine or whether he was
simply writing with characteristic irony.

> The reader will scarcely find in our language, except in the
> work of the *celebrated* Dr Robertson, any performance that
> unites together so perfectly the great points of entertainment
> and instruction! It is happy for the inhabitants of this metro-
> polis ... that the same persons, who can make such a figure in

profane learning [Henry and Robertson], are entrusted with the guidance of the people in their spiritual concerns, which are of such superior, and indeed of unspeakable importance! These illustrious examples, if any thing, must make the infidel abashed of his vain cavils, and put a stop to that torrent of vice, profaneness, and immorality, by which the age is so unhappily distinguished.[50]

Stuart was in no doubt about Hume's motives and exaggerated Hume's comments to the extent that no one could mistake his criticism of Henry.[51] When this altered copy arrived, Hume was surprised at the changes and wrote to Stuart requesting that he admonish the 'Printer with some Severity for the Freedoms he uses; I suppose to divert himself. He has substituted the Name of Dr Mac Queen, whom certainly I did not think of, instead of Dr Robertson, to whose Merit I meant to do some Justice.'[52] Stuart took pleasure in the humorous conceit that Hume (even in an anonymous review) should compliment his old antagonist MacQueen. Hume's anger was probably caused by Stuart challenging him in this underhand way, turning an ambiguous censorious review into an outright attack. It was an instance of Stuart the satirist engaging in battle with Hume the ironist.

After this exchange Stuart finally decided to prepare his own account of Henry's *History*. His unfavourable review affected adversely the initial sale in Scotland, but Henry was not discouraged and journeyed to London to muster support. His plan to have Hume's review printed in the *Monthly* failed when Stuart and Murray employed their own superior influence with the editor. Stuart himself told Murray of his wish to come to London and review Henry's work.

A fire there, & in the Critical would perfectly annihilate him ... To the former I suppose David Hume has transmitted the criticism he intended for us. It is precious and would divert you. I keep a proof of it in my cabinet for ye amusement of friends. The great philosopher begins to doat [sic].[53]

Murray assured Stuart that 'Hume's *critique* is rejected from the monthly' and that a deprecating one would appear in its place. Hamilton, the editor of the *Critical Review*, had 'settled Henrys damnation. In the *Monthly* he cannot expect a better fate.'[54]

Ultimately Stuart's attempts to deprecate the *History* and its author had little effect. Henry's work on a 'new plan' appealed to the public, went into many editions and brought the author ample financial reward. According to Henry's biographer, Stuart censured the work 'with an unexampled acrimony and perseverance'.[55] In the review itself he challenged Henry (as he had Hume) for failing to adopt the whiggish argument that British political representation and its associated liberties dated from the Saxon rather than Norman period. Further, he claimed that Henry dismissed 'whatever was worthy to excite curiosity [and] amassed all the refuse and lumber of the time he would record' (EMR, I, 270). He labelled the author a mere annalist and compiler who failed to remember 'an observation made by father Paul, and ... repeated by Mr Hume, that every performance should be as complete as possible within itself, and should never refer, for any thing material, to other works' (EMR, I, 270). Stuart must have relished the irony of complimenting Hume, even though it would have been appreciated only by those few who knew of the suppressed review.

Stuart's attack upon Henry was vitriolic, possibly because the prospect of the success of another historian recalled his own interrupted literary career. A year after the commencement of the affair, his resentment ran high. 'Poor Henry', he reported to Murray, 'is at the point of death, & his friends declare that I have killed him. I received the information as a compliment, & begged they would not do me so much honour.'[56] Such malicious comments show Stuart to be an over-enthusiastic antagonist. He was risking the reputation of his periodical with little thought for the possible consequences. At the height of the affair, Murray wrote to Edinburgh to discover the truth about its effects: 'I am glad to hear', he told Smellie, 'that your Mag[azine] thrives. But your account does not correspond with the *man of feeling* [Henry Mackenzie] who says you have had an amazing decline since the Review of Henry.'[57]

John Murray was a calm, more prudent man. Why he encouraged Stuart in such behaviour is more difficult to explain. When the third volume of Henry's work appeared in 1777, the author visited Murray to discover the origin of Stuart's antagonism and to reconcile himself to the publisher. Murray understood that Henry was mainly concerned about the reception of his work and consequently did 'not find that I am much his friend'.[58] The publisher even asked Stuart to prepare a scathing piece on Henry's third volume for the *Critical Review*.[59] To Henry, however, he wrote a conciliatory letter in which he assured him that Stuart 'does not think of publishing the review in question' and explained that he had 'long thought [Stuart] carried his resentment too far'.[60] The severe review led to a public exchange of letters in the *Critical*[61] and the composition of a satirical epitaph by Stuart:

Here continue to rot,
The writings of Dr. R[obert] H[enry]
Who, with an indefatigable constancy
And inimitable uniformity of manner,
Persisted
In spite of Age, ignorance & stupidity,
In the arduous task
Of composing a Complete History of Great Britain ... [62]

Even ten years later Stuart continued his belligerent campaign against Henry. When the fifth volume of the *History* appeared in 1785 he targeted the author and other 'flatterers of prerogative' who employed their literary talents to 'write away the liberties of their country'. Just as with Henry, it was 'from this servile motive, that pensions were bestowed on Mr. Hume, Dr. Johnson, and Dr. Robertson' (PH, I, 213).[63]

In the course of the affair Stuart reflected more generally on the state of literature in Scotland and expressed the view that 'there are very few men of taste or erudition on this side of the Tweed. Yet every idiot one meets lays claim to both. For one Robertson or Hume we have ten thousand Henrys and McQueens.'[64] In Stuart's opinion, Scotland's 'hotbed of genius' had generated a large amount of inferior literary produce. It was here among the 'select few' that he sought to mark out ground in which his own historical productions would flourish.

The compliment to Hume in this reflection did not prevent Stuart from attacking him openly in the *Edinburgh Magazine and Review*. The publication of John Whitaker's *History of Manchester* (Book 1 in 1771 and Book 2 in 1775) also gave Stuart opportunities to advance the divergent political views and historical approach he had set out in the *English Constitution* and in the introduction to Sullivan's *Lectures*. Whitaker was an English vicar with literary talent and ambition whom Stuart had met in London through John Murray. His book was not merely the history of a city; it was written to encompass a general view of British history. The first book dealt with the British and Roman period and the second with Saxon times. Whitaker planned to produce two further volumes, bringing his account forward to modern times, but they were never completed. In 1773 John Murray published a second edition (of Book 1) to which Whitaker made many additions. The most important of these was a lengthy appendix which contained critical remarks on the histories of Mr Carte and Mr Hume. Stuart did not hide his interest in this part of the book in his review. He set Whitaker above two types of historian with whom he found fault: those who 'corrupt and disfigure the writings of their predecessors'; and those who 'please the ear and the fancy, but inform not the understanding' (EMR, II, 490). By the first example he alluded to Hume and by the second to Henry. His conclusion was emphatic: 'We are fully disposed to allow to Mr Hume all his merits: The same justice we owe to Mr Whitaker; and we hesitate not to pronounce; that, as far as his criticism goes, the wounds he inflicts are deep and mortal' (EMR, II, 490).

Whitaker's censure of Hume and Stuart's favourable review had created a Scottish market for the work. Murray therefore encouraged the author to continue the attack in the Saxon sequel.

> I make no doubt of your throwing light upon the saxon Period much superior to Carte and Hume. Your Review of these authors will certainly promote the sale of your Book ... Hume is alive & in the zenith of his Reputation. Spare him not therefore but wield your weapon like a Gentleman. By this time you will have seen our Friend Stuart's Review of your first Volume, which I am told has nettled David so much that he has taken up the Pen against you. What he will produce I know not.[65]

The rumour that Hume was preparing a reply was unfounded, and Stuart was encouraged to 'nettle' him further when Whitaker's Saxon volume appeared in the spring of 1775. In the second review Stuart observed that it was 'somewhat remarkable, that, while the philosophy of Mr Hume has been assailed by such a number of combatants, his history, though in many respects, exceptionable, should have been the foundation of so little animadversion' (EMR, III, 259). He singled out Whitaker and Robert MacQueen as the only two writers 'formally to censure him as an historian' and preceded to contrast 'the quickness and penetration' of Whitaker with the 'wild pertinacity' of MacQueen (EMR, III, 259). Whitaker could be a useful ally in the campaign to undermine Hume's historical views; at the same time Stuart could achieve another end in the censure of MacQueen and his party. Stuart's enthusiasm was heated to a high degree. As always, whether engaged in an act of praise or of censure, he carried his point well beyond a reasonable level. His comments to Murray are characteristic.

[Whitaker's] correction of Mr Hume is inflicted with great

spirit, & in general most strikingly just. In a word, I am perfectly in admiration of the whole work; and, I do not know, but I may be tempted to offend the nationality of our countrymen by saying of it what it deserves. I am only afraid, that I should irritate *you* beyond measure. I know your admiration of Hume & Robertson; and, if it should venture in opposition to them to assign the palm of history to Mr Whitaker, you would never forgive me.[66] Stuart fought battles on many fields in the *Edinburgh Magazine and Review*, in the course of which he believed he had attained a victory over Henry and the Popular party. Therefore it was time to challenge the political figures who stood behind them. 'Now that the Clergy are silent', he reported to Murray, 'the Town Council have had the presumption to oppose us.'[67] Behind Henry and Laurie stood others with real power and considerable wealth. The influence of Laurence Dundas with the government, for example, enabled him to obtain the legislation and funds necessary for Edinburgh's improvement.[68] His career reflected a shift in British politics which enabled financially independent men to enter more easily into the largely aristocratic national political forum. This development was opposed by politicians (the Earl of Bute, Duke of Buccleuch and Henry Dundas among them) who represented the landed interest and were supported by the Moderate party. The appointment of Henry Dundas as the Lord Advocate for Scotland in 1775 signalled the waning of Laurence Dundas' influence. It was an event which Stuart and his editorial team looked forward to. In October 1774 the *Review* issued a long account of the corruption surrounding the election of Laurence Dundas as a member of parliament for Edinburgh. They challenged the City Council and their newly elected Provost James Stoddart for yielding to Dundas' influence, as Gilbert Laurie had done before (EMR, II, 726). Laurie's record became a fruitful object of attack. Aspects of his administration, including the preferment of Robert Henry to a lucrative church post, were noted as especially corrupt and almost resulted in a prosecution (EMR, I, 334), but his mismanagement of the funds of George Heriot's Hospital was a matter of special interest.

In April 1774 Stuart wrote an anonymous pamphlet on the subject. He boasted that his *Address to the Citizens of Edinburgh, Relative to the Management of Heriot's Hospital*, by a Free Burgess, 'included a direct proof of perjury in the Provost in repeated instances'.[69] By introducing the piece with a passage from *Exodus*, he established a declamatory and moralising tone that made the pamphlet read more like the exhortatory sermon of a Popular party minister than a political attack. The satire was a way of silencing the opposition with its own 'artillery'.

Stuart complained that governors of Heriot's Hospital were mismanaging the large fortune which George Heriot gave to the town in 1623 to support a charity school. The relevant social context for understanding the pamphlet is the building of Edinburgh's New Town.[70] Vast funds were necessary to finance the project, and the city was often in difficulty. National economic uncertainty increased the problems, and avarice among officials was not uncommon. A large portion of the land on which this plan of urban development was being realised belonged to Heriot's. In the 'History' section of the second number of the *Review* the editors reported on an important legal case which had been decided in favour of Walter Ferguson against the city magistrates (EMR, I, 110–11). Ferguson held land in feu from Heriot's, and as security against the duties he intended to build a square according to the plans of the architect James Craig. This was to become St James' Square, at the east end of Princes Street.[71] The editors contended that the magistrates opposed the plan mainly because the property was 'not subject to imposts and duties' (EMR, I, 111) as the proposed square was outside the royalty. Heriot's Hospital, they argued, should not bear the burden of the city's poor financial state, when its capital had already been reduced by poor management.

In his pamphlet Stuart followed the lead which Ferguson's victory established and pursued civic leaders for other dubious activities in connection with urban development. Though land owned by Heriot's was 'held in perpetuity', as Stuart explained, the magistrates 'have found a method of eluding this, by the most scandalous equivocation that any set of men were ever guilty of. In short, they have made it a practice to feu out parcels of ground to their favourites, often at shameful under-rates.'[72] In other instances they sold the school's lands outright.

A condition in George Heriot's will set out that gross mismanagement would mean reappropriation of his legacy for the maintenance of poor students at St Andrew's University. Stuart presented a copy of the *Address* to its chancellor, the Earl of Kinnoull,[73] then reviewed the pamphlet in a highly favourable manner (EMR, I, 212–15) and so reinforced the attack against the magistrates and Popular party ministers who were mismanaging the resources of Heriot's.

The topic was sufficiently popular that Stuart published a second edition of the pamphlet with the new title *Considerations on the Management of George Heriot's Hospital*. Under the republican pseudonym Lucius Junius Brutus he added a three-page dedication to Gilbert Laurie, 'the Most Impudent Man Alive' in which he told the former Provost:

> The disaffection of the inhabitants is notorious; their complaints and reproaches resound from every quarter; and, whatever *self-love* may dictate to you, a remedy must be sought for them, though at the expence of your *honour*; or, of what, perhaps, you value more highly, your *interest*.[74]

Stuart revelled in the sale of three hundred copies on the morning of publication and boasted to Murray: 'It is perhaps the strongest paper that ever was written in this country. A prosecution was expected but did not happen.'[75] He reviewed his own work again in the *Edinburgh Magazine and Review*, where he explained that 'the liberty of expression, in which the author ... indulges himself, may, to many, appear reprehensible. But, perhaps, it is impossible to consider the ruinous state to which Mr Heriot's most magnificent donation has been reduced, without feeling a lively sentiment of indignation' (EMR, II, 781).

Stuart enjoyed seeing his attacks in print and overhearing conversations in which the question of their authorship was debated. He played the role of a party propagandist with enthusiasm. In the heat of the moment, he believed his contribution would have some impact, though in reality its effect was transitory. The Heriot's affair as a whole may have been little more than what Hugo Arnot termed in the *History of Edinburgh* 'a popular topick for scandalizing the magistrates of Edinburgh, when any political job makes it expedient to spread such calumnies'.[76] But it showed Stuart's ardent support for the Moderates against the faction of Laurence Dundas.

Behind the rhetoric of justice and liberty Stuart was basically pessimistic about the ability of elected officials to act in the public interest. To some extent this may be an accurate assessment of mid-eighteenth-century politics, but it also showed a selective application of moral and political principles. Though he attacked the self-interest which pervaded society, he was himself as much subject to it as others. Reviewing his own works was but one example. In an article entitled 'Thoughts and Maxims', Stuart, or a like-minded contributor, wrote:

> In times of corruption the engaging in public affairs is a

traffic. The representative buys his seat, and sells his voice. Against the prosperity of his country he stakes his particular interest; and, what to him are the miseries of his fellow citizens, or of mankind, when he procures, by promoting them, the costly materials of luxury, and the affectations of a sickly fancy?   (EMR, II, 696)

Another reason for Stuart to attack Laurence Dundas and the Town Council arose over an attempt to remove Adam Ferguson from the chair of moral philosophy at the University.[77] When Ferguson accepted a temporary post as tutor to the Earl of Chesterfield, the Town Council initially approved of the plan to appoint John Bruce, the Moderates' choice, to give lectures in his absence. Then, at a critical moment, the Council declared the post vacant and made clear their intention to appoint James Beattie to the chair (EMR, III, 279–80). The debate between the enlightened tolerance of the Moderates and the orthodoxy of the Popular party, and the growing scepticism in Scottish society, were central issues in the affair. Stuart argued that Ferguson's dismissal 'would tarnish the reputation of the university, by removing one of its greatest ornaments' (EMR, III, 279). He then took the offensive and explained to his readers that 'though it is not to be supposed, that mechanical and uneducated men are proper judges of the qualifications or the conduct of professors, it is yet to be expected, that they would, at least, endeavour to behave with common decency'. Laurence Dundas, though not named, was implicated as the man who 'planned this pestilential measure' (EMR, III, 279–80). Ultimately, Ferguson retained the chair and Bruce was allowed to act as his substitute. The episode itself reaffirmed the influence of the University and its Moderate professors in civic affairs.

Stuart again supported the Moderates when he favourably reviewed Ferguson's pamphlet on the question of American independence. In the *Remarks on a Pamphlet Lately Published by Dr. Price*, Ferguson criticised Richard Price's defence of the rebellious Americans. Placing the issue in a Scottish context, Stuart challenged members of the Popular party who, like Price, 'have of late been acting as the friends of America, and disseminating sedition and wildness with an open effrontery' (EMR, V, 325). Since August 1774 the editors had presented a regular section on American news. They had also reprinted selections from pamphlets opposing and supporting the Americans, including Dr Johnson's *Taxation No Tyranny* (EMR, III, 225–7) and Joseph Priestley's *New Considerations on the Disputes between Great Britain and America*

(EMR, III, 116–21).[78] The editors advocated a policy in support of the government which was similar to the Moderates' own and generally consistent with Scottish public opinion.[79] But at the same time they provided a forum for the opposite views of Scottish clergymen in America, such as John Witherspoon, and John Erskine at home. As war drew closer, toleration became more difficult and challenges more frequent to those members of the Popular party who 'actually prostitute their pulpits by railing against the government, and invoking the Almighty to crown with success the American arms' (EMR, V, 271).[80]

When war became a reality, Stuart's politics, like that of many others, became more conservative. This may conflict to some extent with the republican assertions of his earlier years, but localised factors, such as the threat of invasion and the swing in public opinion, overcame the necessity of maintaining absolutely consistent political beliefs.

In other instances Stuart was less inclined to go along with prevailing trends. With the appearance of his review of John Hawkesworth's *Voyages in the Southern Hemisphere* (1773) in the first number, the morality of both the *Edinburgh Magazine and Review* and its editor became a focal point for public censure (EMR, I, 28–36). Stuart's criticisms were scathing; but he also damned the book in a more subtle way, choosing to quote passages which gave an inaccurate impression of the nature of the work. An account of a sexual act between a six-foot-tall man and an eleven-year-old girl, together with descriptions of other curious sexual behaviour in a tribe of American Indians observed by Hawkesworth, may have confirmed Stuart's view that the manners of one nation cannot be judged by the standards of another, yet he knew that such accounts would do little to recommend the book to an essentially polite and religious society.

An anonymous critic for the *Caledonian Mercury* stated that such selections tend 'to destroy all distinction betwixt virtue and vice, modesty and beastly turpitude'.[81] Ostensibly Stuart praised the author, but his true motives became apparent when he told Murray with a hint of remorse: 'Hawkesworth's death makes me sorry we have reviewed him.'[82] Was it the wonder of cultural differences that prompted him to include these explicit passages? Was it the wish to shock an unassuming public and incite the ire of the clergy? Or did the content reflect something of his own sexual preoccupations? In any case it was a dangerous way to advance the reputation of the periodical. In the *View of Society*

Stuart explained the attitude with which he regarded these issues:
> In times of refinement and delicacy, virtue takes the alarm,
> even at the recital of such facts; but the philosopher, struck
> with their universality over all societies, however distant
> and distinct, is disposed to inquire, Where it is that nature
> has placed her barriers; and what, on this head, in the codes
> of nations, is to be explained by natural law, and what by a
> policy civil and religious? The topic is full of curiosity.
>
> (VS, 198)

Pedagogical debate also stirred Stuart to take an active role in
shaping public opinion. In the first number he reviewed his own
pamphlet, *Animadversions on Mr. Adam's Latin and English Grammar*. He wrote this polemical attack upon the Rector of the High
School of Edinburgh under the pseudonym John Richard Busby,
the seventeenth-century grammarian and headmaster at Westminster whose name had 'become proverbial as a type of the
severest of severe pedagogues'.[83] In private Stuart typically described the work as 'sixty full pages of the strongest satire &
reasoning you ever saw. I am amazed at it. The Rector will be more
so.'[84] Alexander Adam's *Principles of Latin and English Grammar*
was published in May 1772, and for fifteen years was the subject of
vociferous disagreement in Edinburgh. Adam intended to replace
Thomas Ruddiman's popular grammars, the *Rudiments of the Latin
Tongue* (1714) and the *Grammaticae Latinae Institutiones* (1725–31)
with his own.

Family loyalty was one important motive behind Stuart's challenge. It was not only Ruddiman, his mentor and relation, who
stood to suffer in posthumous reputation, but George Stuart, who
would lose financially from Adam's success. Adam argued that it
was unnecessary for students to enroll in George Stuart's Latin
class at the University if they studied with him for an additional
sixth year at the High School. As the professor's income was
dependent upon enrolment (and already at the low end of the pay
scale) it was in the interest of the Stuarts, as Gilbert put it, that 'the
Grammar be damned'.[85] Their attack was especially vehement
because Adam, when he came to Edinburgh as a poor scholar, was
taught Latin free of charge by George Stuart, who afterwards
recommended him for a post at George Watson's Hospital. He
was also taught Greek by Professor William Hunter on the same
terms, and his attempt to introduce a beginners' Greek class at the
High School was perceived in an equally detrimental light.

As the Scots took their classical teaching very seriously, a committee was formed to consider the issue by the governing body of Edinburgh University, the Senatus Academicus. In November 1772 the members 'unanimously expressed a favourable opinion' of Adam's work, but they 'declined giving a final report until they had an opportunity of conversing with the Masters of the high School'.[86] Even though George Stuart was not on this committee, his influence and Hunter's was brought to bear. At the next meeting notice was given of the encroachments Adam had made 'of Manifest detriment to the Professor'.[87] Adam, explained Gilbert, 'wanted as far as he could to hurt the very people who had advanced him. He joined ingratitude with stupidity. What hurts me more than any thing, he conceived the design of throwing out of the schools, the latin Rudiments of my most worthy & esteemed friend Thomas Ruddiman.'[88]

In the preface to the pamphlet Stuart asserted that it was in the 'interests of education and science' that he wrote the attack.[89] But while he employed the rhetoric of public interest to justify his condemnation, the expectation of gratitude that would acrue to him was not hidden:

> The task I undertake is, I confess, an unpleasant one; but it may be attended with signal advantages. The prejudice that may happen to a single individual, is lost in an enlarged view of utility. I shall be entitled, I perceive, to the thanks of many an anxious parent; and this must console me for stooping to engage a contemptible enemy. One hates to achieve a victory that is to bring no laurels.[90]

To further Adam's damnation Stuart enlisted the support of John MacMillan, his former employer at the *London Magazine*, to write a 'burlesque song' against the Rector. Stuart told Murray he himself would have written 'a ballad to be sung through the streets of old Reeky, against this most contemptible author ... if the study of the middle ages had not utterly ruined my rhyming talents'.[91] Apparently it had not, because he wrote and published a Latin poetical satire which described in the language of a Roman funeral 'the remains of an inauspicious book, never again to be resurrected'.[92]

Stuart's pamphlet is most relevant in the context of a general debate in Scotland over the value of perpetuating that distinctive Scottish humanist tradition which had started at the time of George Buchanan and had been promoted more recently by Thomas Ruddiman.[93] Latin, which was the embodiment of everything intellectual for Ruddiman and a central feature of the Stuart household, was losing its importance in Scottish society. Stuart aligned himself with those who sought to preserve this classical legacy.

His antipathy towards Adam continued for many years, though ultimately the Rector turned public opinion in his own favour. What was probably Stuart's final remark on Adam appeared in a review of the latter's *Summary of Geography and History* in 1785. This sums up his scathing opinion of the author: 'If we are to look for his equals, we must ... survey the ox, the elephant, and the hippopotamus.'[94] Stuart then referred to the honorary doctor of laws degree which Adam received from Edinburgh University and drew William Robertson (a more formidable rival) into his condemnatory metaphor. He described the degree as 'a distinction which we might suppose the animals we have mentioned might procure, for a bribe from ... the *learned* principal of the college of Edinburgh'.[95] Stuart's remarks were more severe because Adam's award called into question the status of his own honorary law degree. Furthermore, it demonstrated to him the extent to which he had become alienated from the Edinburgh establishment.

The vitriol of Stuart's writing and the decline in sales of the *Edinburgh Magazine and Review* were related. Rather than employing controversy judiciously, Stuart used it as a means of compensating for the routine of mundane editorial tasks. He entered into disputes with enthusiasm, but if his opponents did not respond, he lost interest. In a letter to Murray he lamented the state of the periodical.

> It is an infinite disappointment to me, that the Mag does not grow in London ... I thought the soil had been richer. But it is my constant fate to be disappointed in every thing I attempt. I do not think I ever had a wish that was gratified, and never dreaded an event that did not come. With this felicity of fate, I wonder how the devil I could turn projector. I am now sorry that I left London; and the moment that I have money enough to carry me back to it, I shall set off.[96]

Had he thought more carefully and remembered the fate of the first *Edinburgh Review* he would have realised that a preoccupation with local affairs – with the Robert Henrys and Alexander Adams of his world – would make unneeded enemies. Such affairs, moreover, were of little interest to readers outside Edinburgh. Yet Stuart was disposed to think that his own concerns would be shared more widely. Edinburgh, for its part, was still a provincial city in many ways and he was too caught up in the detail of its religious, political and literary goings on to see their irrevelance elsewhere.

Stuart's moments of self-criticism, if intense, were of short duration. His anger turned from himself to others, and he burst into a tirade against the literati in the 'hotbed of genius':

I mortally detest & abhor this place; and every body in it. Never was there a city, where there was so much pretension to knowledge, & so little of it. The solemn fopping & the gross stupidity of the Scottish literati are perfectly insupportable ... Nothing will do in this country, that has any common sense in it. Only cant, hypocrisy, & superstition will flourish here. A curse on the country, & all the men, women & children in it![97]

Such outbursts were brief and quickly gave way to optimistic reports of new articles and of other literary projects in which he was engaged. If disaffected with certain individuals among the literati, he still wished to enter the fold. But he began to see that the periodical was not advancing him as quickly in that direction as he had hoped.

There was another factor contributing to Stuart's unsettled state of mind. He explained rather mysteriously to Murray in a subsequent letter that his 'peevishness & dissatisfaction' were caused by an event 'which broke my peace & ease altogether for some weeks'.[98] This 'event' may have been an unrequited love affair. Evidence for this conjecture is circumstantial, but at this time Stuart wrote a curious and entirely uncharacteristic piece for the 'Magazine' section entitled the 'Anecdotes of Laura and Petrarque' (EMR, II, 414–17 and 469–71). This was a sentimental story of the Italian poet's tragic quest for the love of a woman who was engaged to another. Stuart had read and reviewed many romantic novels, but it was another thing to write one, however short, and base it upon his own situation. The protagonist, Petrarque, grew despondent when he was unable to 'rid himself of an unhappy passion: 'His reason and his love waged a war, of which he was the victim. Sadness and woe invaded those years of his life which nature seems to set apart for joy. He determined to forsake the world ... He hastened to bury himself with his books' (EMR, II, 416). Petrarque did not totally despair however. A new plan formed itself in his mind: 'He must rise in her estimation, and be distinguished by a renown that enobled none of his contemporaries. A project, extravagant and wild, suggested itself to his ambition' (EMR, II, 417).

In the second part, which appeared the following month, Stuart showed how his hero attempted to win poetic laurels and 'soften the pride of Laura' (EMR, II, 469). Petrarque succeeded in the first (as his sonnets demonstrate), but was thwarted in the last. 'The agitations of his mind affected his body ... A fatal, yet agreeable melancholy wasted his force; and he seemed to look forward with pleasure to his dissolution' (EMR, II, 470). Even his wish to die before his beloved was unrequited, for Laura fell victim to the plague.

Whether Stuart's speculative mistress met a similar end or simply would not respond to his romantic advances is impossible to know. Were she alive, the imagined scene of her demise would have been a sharp rebuke from a man who bore the burden of an unhappy affair. This fictional conceit was an indulgence on Stuart's part, whether or not it was the consequence of personal suffering.

The poor management, provincialism, quarrelsomeness and bias of the periodical were increasingly evident, rendering it unappealing to the public in the long term. After less than one year of publication Murray could no longer refrain from expressing to Stuart his concern about the periodical's fate. 'Indolence and carelessness seem to have seized the whole ... Does the gratification of your spleen and resentment ... against a few obscure individuals recompence you for the odium you sustain in conducting the work?'[99] Murray's harsh words were well meant and to some extent Stuart heeded his remonstrances. At such a distance, however, his influence could not be relied upon. The bookseller was also concerned about the demand for a stamp duty on the work: the profit margin was narrow, and this expense had probably not been calculated into the sale price.[100]

The periodical continued to be produced for twenty more months but sales declined after its initial popularity. With the start of the third volume (December 1774) the 'Magazine' section was printed in double columns. This allowed for more articles but most of these were now culled from other periodicals and from new publications. Stuart explained sardonically, and mistakenly, to Murray that 'adapting it to vulgar or clerical comprehension will increase the demand for it'.[101] In a note to readers at the end of the second volume he said more optimistically: 'This improvement is the suggestion of several correspondents, to whom the work has been much indebted; and it is hoped will, in general, be acceptable.' (EMR, II, 786.)

A specific reason for the increase in public disapprobation of the *Edinburgh Magazine Review* was Stuart's severe criticism of Lord Monboddo in a review of the third volume of the *Origin and Progress of Language*. It was unacceptable to denounce publicly a leading figure in Scottish society. Smellie's efforts to tone down the article were resisted by the author. The consequences were dire. 'My reason and my only reason, for giving up the Review', wrote one subscriber, 'is the shocking scurrility and abuse in the late articles of it concerning Lord Monboddo's book ... . Every gentleman with whom I have talked ... is of the same way of thinking.'[102] Murray told Smellie that he was 'sorry for the defeat you have met with. Had you praised Lord Monboddo instead of damning him, it would not have happened.'[103]

Stuart was not one to submit to the dictates of polite society; he saw Monboddo as an opinionated eccentric who took advantage of his public position to gain a literary reputation. Many shared this view, though today his works, particularly the *Origin and Progress of Language* have received scholarly attention for their interesting linguistic, evolutionary, and anthropological themes. Stuart expressed his opinion of Monboddo most clearly in the lengthy review itself:

> The unsuccessful attempts of this author to acquire the estimation of the public, seem to have affected both his temper and reasoning ...
>
> The idea of his own importance, which never forsakes this writer, has also induced him to indulge a strain of unmannerly abuse against those, whom he terms 'the fashionable authors of this age'.   (EMR, V, 88–90)
>
> It seemed to him that the ancient and the modern literature were at variance; and that he could not testify his admiration of the former,without detracting from the latter.
>
>   (EMR, V, 266)

One biographer of Monboddo wrote that Stuart 'attacked his book ... with all the fierce malignity of a Portuguese inquisitor enjoying the sufferings of a detected Jew; or of an American savage putting his captive to death, amidst every refinement of torture'.[104]

Stuart was not alone in his condemnation of the work. David Hume told Adam Smith that 'it contains all the Absurdity and malignity which I expected', though he added, it 'is writ with more Ingenuity and in a better Stile than I look'd for'.[105] In a subsequent volume, Monboddo himself expressed contempt for the treatment he had received from 'some nameless scribblers' who 'abuse me in Magazines and Reviews' and explained that he wrote 'chiefly for the scholars in England and for the few that the prevalence of the French learning has left yet remaining in other parts of Europe'.[106]

Stuart held a dismissive opinion of the judge even before the review appeared. He considered Monboddo's evolutionary theories preposterous. In June 1773, while planning the *Edinburgh Magazine and Review*, he had asked Murray to procure 'as an ornament for our first number ... an engraving of the Print of Lord Monboddo in his quadruped form ... We are to take it upon the footing of a figure of an Animal, not yet described; and are to give a grave yet satirical account of it in the manner of Buffon.'[107] Murray thought it prudent not to encourage Stuart in mocking Monboddo for his assertion that men once had tails. An important legal figure was involved, and a libel action might be brought.

The reviews of Monboddo did in fact result in a legal action against Smellie who, as printer, was ultimately responsible for the contents of the periodical. In June 1776 Murray told Creech: 'I am sorry you have lost the blasphemy cause, which L[or]d Monboddo[']s damnation no doubt occasioned; but you know the proverb "Those that play at bowls &c".'[108] Murray discouraged the owners from appealing against the decision because of the expense involved and the improbability of a reversal. His hope that the defeat would 'serve to make the authors of the Edinb. Mag more cautious in their strictures of living authors' was not realised.[109]

Another factor which prompted Stuart's caustic treatment of Lord Monboddo was the judge's singular and unpopular opinion voiced in an important literary property case.[110] The decision, a landmark in the history of publishing, set a fourteen-year limit to the copyright of a work and broke the monopoly of the established London trade. The Court of Session judges reached their decision in November 1774, shortly before Stuart's first review appeared. Monboddo, alone of all the fifteen judges, decided in favour of the English bookseller Becket against the Scottish printer Alexander Donaldson, who had been selling cheap reprints of works originally printed in England.[111] The judge asserted that an author's work belonged to him as a perpetual right and was not limited to a given number of years as stipulated by an act of Queen Anne's reign. Had Becket succeeded in re-establishing perpetual copyright, the Scottish reprint would have become illegal. All but the old guard of the London trade (who published Monboddo's works) would suffer, including Smellie, Creech and Murray. For this reason Murray, who traded in London and stood to benefit most from the decision, encouraged his friends in the Scottish trade to join him in opposing a bill of appeal which had been presented.[112]

In April 1776 Murray told Smellie to stop sending the periodical to London as there was no demand for it there.[113] This news and the consequences of the Monboddo 'blasphemy' affair hastened the end of the *Edinburgh Magazine and Review*. In the August 1776 issue Stuart announced 'that the publication ... must be interrupted for some months'. He went on to state that 'it will afterwards appear in an improved form' (EMR, V, 392). But that event never took place. It was a poignant coincidence that the last item of news in the work should report the death of David Hume, 'author of the history of Great Britain, and other ingenious works' (EMR, V, 392).

After the demise of the *Edinburgh Magazine and Review*, Stuart returned to a study of the Middle Ages on which he had been engaged sporadically for a number of years. He lived and worked at the home of his parents at Fisherrow, where, somewhat removed from friends and temptations at Edinburgh, he could better concentrate on the project at hand. It was now necessary to economise as he had no regular income. His distance from the University Library was compensated for by the liberality of David Dalrymple, who opened his extensive collection of books at nearby Newhailes to him. 'I am quite ashamed', wrote Stuart deferentially, 'of having recourse so often to your library, and wish the trifle I am busy about may, in some sort, apologise for it.'[114] This 'trifle' was the *View of Society*. It was published in 1778 and was followed a few months afterwards by the *Public Law of Scotland*.

4

Conjectures on Society 1776–1779

Then might Distraction rend her graceful Hair,
See sightless Forms, and scream, and gape, and stare.
Drawcansir Death had rag'd without controul:
Here the drawn Dagger, there the poison'd Bowl.

George Colman, *The Jealous Wife* (London, 1761),
Prologue (by Evan Lloyd)

After a year of concentrated effort, Stuart completed the *View of Society* in the summer of 1777. He referred to this project at the conclusion of the work itself as the 'aspiring fruit of my studies and ambition' (VS, 408).[1] Murray read the manuscript and offered £150 for the first edition; it was a fair sum for a work in the conjectural manner and more than the hundred guineas the publisher had given John Millar for the *Observations concerning Ranks* in 1771. Still, it was nothing like the £4000 Robertson received for the *History of Charles V* from Strahan and Cadell. Murray was a cautious businessman even with a close associate like Stuart. Careful to keep personal and financial matters separate, he assured him 'whether I have the book or not ... will make no alteration in my friendship for you'.[2]

Stuart had told the publisher a few years before that 'the vanity of getting much for the child of one's understanding is very strong'.[3] It was therefore no surprise, though it must have disappointed Murray, that he took up what he considered to be a better offer from the Edinburgh bookseller John Bell. Bell agreed to give him £100 up front with the promise of £300 more upon the entire sale of the first edition of 1,000 copies.[4] Murray warned Stuart to 'leave nothing indefinite', for Bell, 'from the particular turn of his mind is difficult to deal with'.[5] The arrangement did prove an unfortunate one, as Murray predicted; and it was seven years before a legal decree forced the Edinburgh bookseller to give over to Stuart just £25 more than the initial payment, his 'share of the money arising from the sale'.[6]

The *View of Society* is essentially a study of European civilisation during the Middle Ages. It consists of two books: in the first Stuart described the state of equality and liberty to which he and other Whig historians believed Europe returned after the fall of Rome. As in the *English Constitution*, the concept of property, and its development from an object of communal to private interest, provided the basic framework for his discussion. Where Stuart had nostalgically evoked the ancient liberty of the Saxon barbarian and set it against Norman oppression, now he took a wider view, glorifying the European feudal system in its original mutually beneficial condition and contrasting it with subsequent corruption. As in his first work, Stuart applied this whiggish principle to the whole throughout the narrative.

He introduced his subject with a Tacitean picture 'Of the Germans before they left their Woods' (Chapter 1). Then he turned to consider 'The political Establishments of the Barbarians after they had made Conquests' (Chapter 2). Central to these subjects is an account of the condition of women in pre-commercial society. Sections in these two chapters of Book I on 'An Idea of the German Woman', 'Of Marriage and Modesty', 'Of the Property of Women' and 'The Pre-eminence of Women' are designed to show the high status accorded to the sex before property came to be vested in the individual. Women, Stuart wrote, 'felt, as well as the noble and the warriour, the cares of the community. They watched over its interest, considered its connection with other states, and thought of improving its policy, and extending its dominion' (VS, 16). The knights were their counterpart and possessed similar virtues. In sections headed 'Arms, Galantry, and Devotion', 'The Origin of Knighthood and the Judicial Combat', and 'The Institutions of Chivalry', Stuart described the role that knights played in society:

> Intent on the fame of their lovers, watchful of the glory of their nation, their affections were roused; and they knew not that unquiet indolence, which, softening the mind, awakens the imagination and the senses. Concerned with great affairs, they were agitated with great passions. They prospered whatever was most noble in our nature, generosity, public virtue, humanity, prowess ... Their softness mingled with courage, their sensibility with pride. With the characteristics of their own sex, they blended those of the other.
>
> (VS, 61–2)

In Book II Stuart described the rise and, more importantly, the fall of the legal and military institutions of feudal society. He began this part with an account of the 'Spirit of Fiefs' (Chapters 1 and 2).[7] Topics discussed include 'The Feudal Incidents', 'The Invention of Knight-service' and 'The Æra of Hereditary Fiefs'. Next Stuart turned to the 'Military Power of a Feudal Kingdom' (Chapters 3 and 4) to show how the rise of commerce and the refinement of manners brought about the decline of the feudal militia. 'The Fine for Neglect of Service' and 'The Fall of Chivalry as a Military Establishment' are two of many related topics that come under discussion. He then surveyed the 'Military Arrangements which prevailed in the Declension of Fiefs and Chivalry' (Chapter 5). Mercenaries, standing armies, and taxation are a sample of a number of subjects discussed in order to show the reader the extent to which modern-day social institutions can be traced to the period of Norman dominance in Europe.

> The disorders of the feudal militia produced mercenaries, and the use of mercenaries gave birth to taxations. Taxations were begun to be levied, in all the states of Europe, at the will of the prince. This occasioned contentions between sovereigns and their subjects. The victory of the kingly authority over the liberty of the people, continued in many princes the power of taxation; and this power, and the command of mercenaries, are the completion of despotism.   (VS, 127)

This picture of Norman oppression would have served to heighten anti-French sentiment, as war with France (declared in 1778) brought with it the danger of another 'Conquest'. 'From the time that William Duke of Normandy had mounted the throne of England', wrote Stuart, 'the two kingdoms entertained a jealousy of one another' (VS, 131). The events of the Seven Years' War and the American Revolution, though not specifically mentioned, were nevertheless in the minds of his readers. With regard to this national threat, Stuart devoted a significant portion of the narrative to the history of the feudal military system, a theme which recalled Scotland's own attempts to re-establish a militia, most recently by means of Lord Mountstuart's parliamentary bill of 1776.[8]

Stuart looked upon the passing of the age described in Book I with regret and upon the progress of corruption in Book II with qualified pessimism. The two books form a history of chivalry in Europe in which the knight emerges as the central figure. In the final chapter of the second book he gave a more general review of the events which changed the face of society from one of 'romantic grandeur and virtue' (VS, 141) to one of 'venality and corruption'

(VS, 142). His survey of the changes in roles of the sexes, the place of religion and the state of manners recalls, by way of contrast, the beginning of the work, and a lament brings the *View of Society* to a somewhat abrupt conclusion. This book is more than twice as long as the first, but its supplementary notes are proportionately shorter, making the total length of each book nearly the same.

The most distinctive feature of the *View of Society* is the unusual proportion of main text to notes. Over two-thirds of the work consists of what Stuart calls 'Authorities, Controversy, and Remarks'. There, the edifice of information and opinion about the Middle Ages is built upon an impressive scholarly foundation. Stuart, the architect, guided his reader over a detailed model of European history. He placed the lengthy note section after the main narrative and divided it into corresponding books, chapters and sections. The reader (if he is patient enough) moves continually between these parts and benefits from the complimentary role of each. The notes are as much an impressive display of scholarship as an example of Stuart's discursive and contentious nature.

> My proofs ... appear by themselves; and, in consequence of this arrangement, I might engage in incidental discussions; I might catch many rays of light that faintly glimmer in obscure times; and, I might defend the novelty of my opinions, when I ventured to oppose established tenets, and authors of reputation. (VS, vi)

These 'proofs' are an integral part of the *View of Society* and the most interesting. However they do not represent all the additional material. At the very end of the work Stuart included six appendices. These contain primary documents relevant to his inquiries and curious in their own right, at least to the eighteenth-century antiquary.[9] In a posthumous 1792 edition an anonymous editor (possibly George Stuart) translated all the foreign quotations and thereby made many of the notes more accessible.

Enough has been said above about the different types of references Stuart included in his conjectural writings. In this work those distinctive features are exaggerated to the point where there are notes on the notes. He tapped newly published sources, such as Halhed's translations of the *Code of Gentoo Laws* (1776) and the travel accounts of Adair, Lafitau and Charlevoix. He also attacked recent works of contemporaries, such as Blackstone's *Commentaries on the Laws of England* (1764–9), Kames' *Sketches of the History of Man* (1774) and Robertson's *History of America* (1777). Hume's *History of England* came under fire as it had in the *English Constitu-*

tion: 'From the most able historian of our own and foreign nations, who might naturally be expected to be intelligent guides ... I could derive no advantage' (VS, vii).

On the subject of the place accorded to women in medieval society, he challenged Millar, Kames and Robertson. These men, he believed, were wrong in concluding that in pre-commercial society women were 'in an abject state of servility, from which they advance not till the ages of property' (VS, 12). He claimed to oppose their opinions 'from no captiousness of temper, but because, if they are just, mine must be ill founded and improper' (VS, 188).[10] Women, he wrote, 'went to the public councils or assemblies of their nations ... and were called upon to deliver their sentiments. And, what is worthy of particular notice, this consequence in active scenes they transmitted to their posterity' (VS, 16). Occasionally Stuart conceded that Millar's 'observation is not to be controverted' (VS, 189), but more often his argument was 'direct against the opinions of my Lord Kaims and Mr. Millar' (VS, 193).

When the public first read the sections in the *View of Society* examining the condition of women, they would probably have recalled an important Scottish legal case from 1771. The decision in the Court of Session upon the Sutherland peerage affirmed that the daughter of the lately deceased Earl was entitled to that peerage, the oldest in Scotland, in preference to two male relations. Many well known Scottish legal figures came to the aid of the young Countess, including David Dalrymple and John Mackenzie. Stuart respected these men and his arguments in favour of women served as a subtle compliment to them for their efforts in this case.

More than three years before the *View of Society* appeared, Stuart had confided to John Murray his hopes for a work 'on which I mean to rest my reputation, if I shall get any'.[11] The original title he gave it was 'An Introduction to the History of Europe; or A New version of the treatise of Tacitus, concerning the situation of Germany, its Inhabitants and their manners; with explanatory notes & illustrations'. His plan was to supply what he felt had been lacking in his own legal education:

> The whole work will be like a school book for preparing the student of English law and history for entering with the greatest advantage on these studies by opening up to him whatever is most curious in the customs of the middle ages, & in the constitutions & policy of the Gothic kingdoms.[12]

This work and the *English Constitution* were to form the first two of a series of textbooks on which he would base his lectures when he advanced to one of Edinburgh University's law chairs. The *View of Society*, according to a plan Stuart outlined in the preface, was only one volume of a larger study, where Stuart discussed the laws, manners and government of European society in the Middle Ages. Afterwards he would continue to publish works on 'civil jurisdiction, nobility, constitutional law, and cultivated manners' (VS, vi). It was his goal 'to explain the complicated form of civil society, and the wisdom and accident which mingle in human affairs' (VS, v). Following the conjectural approach of the day, he asserted that 'it is in the records of history, in the scenes of real life, not in the conceits and the abstractions of fancy and philosophy, that human nature is to be studied' (VS, v).

Stuart had often acknowledged that he was not the first to study feudal society from a conjectural point of view. Montesquieu, John Dalrymple, Lord Kames, Adam Smith, Adam Ferguson and others had preceeded him. But when William Robertson published the introductory 'View of Europe', knowledge about the Middle Ages was thrown open to a wider audience. For Robertson feudalism was not just a subject for the antiquary or law student; it could engage the interest of educated men and women alike. Stuart felt this approach undervalued the breadth of understanding necessary to master such a complicated subject. Jurisprudence was a masculine study for the specialist, not an amusement for the polite company of a drawing room. He explained to Murray that his work 'will show a reading somewhat uncommon, & will treat of all the topics on which Dr Robertson has *touched* in his illustrations [i.e. notes] to his first volume. I say *touched*; for he has not examined them with attention, and has little knowledge of Jurisprudence.'[13]

Robertson had planned his introductory volume to the *History of Charles V*, entitled 'A View of the Progress of Society in Europe, from the Subversion of the Roman Empire, to the Beginning of the Sixteenth Century', as a wide-ranging introduction to the reign of Charles V, and had deliberately excluded the more detailed aspects of legal and military inquiry in favour of a general approach. He divided the work into three sections. The first contained an outline of the progress of society 'with respect to interior Government, Laws, and Manners'. This section related most closely to the subject matter of the *View of Society*. In the second short section, Robertson considered the military institutions of the Middle Ages;

and in the third, the political systems in Europe during this time. These last two sections were written in a more narrative manner and served to introduce the events of Charles' reign. In general, Robertson wrote in the popular tradition of Voltaire rather than in the scholarly manner of Montesquieu.[14] He explained that 'to sketch out the great lines which distinguish and characterize each government, is all that the nature of my present work will admit of, and all that is necessary to illustrate the events which it records'.[15] Stuart clearly felt that more was required.

Robertson also acknowledged that an inquiry into the political constitution of European states was difficult and conclusions therefore could only be tentative; and concerning one point of deliberation, he added, 'this conjecture I propose with that diffidence, which I have felt in all my reasonings concerning the laws and institutions of foreign nations'.[16] Stuart adopted a bolder approach with such remarks as 'I will venture another conjecture' (VS, 217). At other moments, however, confidence mixed with temerity and deference: 'When I consider what many great men have written before me concerning human affairs, I know not, whether it ought to flatter my pride, or to fill me with shame, that I, too, have yielded to my reflections and my sentiments.' (VS, 408.) Where Robertson emphasised the gradual improvement of society, Stuart saw only the corruption of once ideal institutions as a consequence of man's inability to alter or even know his destiny. Within Robertson's panoramic landscape, European society advanced from the barbarism of the Middle Ages to the civility of his own time. Behind Robertson's historical notion of man's continual improvement was the religious disposition of a clergyman. Stuart did not believe that man so actively shaped his world. When he referred to 'the wisdom and accident which mingle in human affairs' (VS, v), the latter force was seen as dominant.

A comparison of Robertson's and Stuart's accounts of the Crusades indicates the extent of their differences. Robertson did not deny that the Crusades were a source of destruction, but he emphasised that they brought 'the first gleams of light which tended to dispel barbarity and ignorance'.[17] Stuart was less equivocal:

> The age, in which so many armies, inflamed with zeal, were to fight for the recovery and possession of the holy sepulchre, was remarkable for the most criminal depravity. The pilgrims and crusaders exported the vices of Europe, and imported those of Asia. Saint Louis, during his pious and

memorable expedition, could not prevent the most open
licentiousness and disorder. (VS, 146)
Where Robertson sketched broad outlines, Stuart coloured and
added detail to the complicated picture of feudal society. The
evolution of custom fascinated Stuart: he believed that what was
curious became explicable if traced to its origin. An example of
this is his commentary on the social significance of human hair. In
ancient times, he explained, 'it was a mark of refined attention in a
person to present a lock of his hair to a friend on saluting him ... To
give a slave the permission of allowing his hair to grow, was to
offer him his freedom' (VS, 404–5). A discourse of this type also
permitted him to indulge in observations that might offend common morality, such as his comment that 'it was not the hair of their
heads only, that the women were curious to deck out' (VS, 404).
Remarks in Latin follow – a form of modesty also employed by
Gibbon in the *Decline and Fall* when discussing similarly delicate
subjects. Stuart traced the progress of the customs relating to hair
which were transmitted in modified forms through European
culture to Stuart's own time. He then offered a more general
observation:

> There seems something wild and romantic in such usages;
> yet they produced the locket and the hair-ring of modern times;
> and we smile not, nor are surprised, that these should teach us
> to employ our moments of softness in melancholy recollec-
> tions of absent beauty, or departed friendship. What is dis-
> tant and remote, affects us with its ridicule. What is present
> and in practice, escapes our censure. In the one instance, we
> act with the impartiality of philosophers; in the other, we are
> carried away by our passions and our habitudes. (VS, 405)

This kind of passage is characteristic of Stuart's best writing. By
thus engaging the reader he leads him to reason about history and
makes him see the connection between an ancient custom and the
locket of hair he carries in his pocket.

Stuart repeatedly celebrated the condition of ancient chivalry in
its heyday and mourned its gradual corruption, a subject which
was not perhaps of entirely pedantic or ideological interest. James
Boswell expressed a similar opinion in a conversation with Dr
Johnson and Sir Alexander MacDonald. Boswell 'argued warmly
for the old feudal system' while MacDonald 'opposed it, and
talked of seeing all men free and independent'. Boswell 'maintained that ... the vassals or followers, were not unhappy; for there
was a reciprocal satisfaction between the lord and them: he being

kind in authority over them; they being respectful and faithful to him'.[18] The prospective Laird of Auchinleck undoubtedly envisaged such an arrangement on his own estate. Stuart was less positive than Boswell or Robertson concerning what progress had achieved and would achieve, and at times he yielded too much to the rhetoric about the corruption of commercial society. This difference in tone distinguishes Robertson from Stuart, and it equates broadly with their divergent temperaments and stations in life. Stuart's provocative dissent contributed to his alienation from the Scottish establishment; Robertson's deliberate equivocation helped to make him one of its most important and enduring leaders.

In a conversation with Thomas Somerville, some years after Stuart's death, Robertson

> spoke with just indignation of that notorious writer's treatment of himself. He said, 'Every man who has written history knows that the most difficult part of his work has been the arrangement, but Gilbert Stuart saved himself that trouble, and followed my arrangement exactly. His dissertations on the middle ages were ... stolen from me.'[19]

Dugald Stewart, in his *Life of Robertson*, acknowledged that Stuart was 'the most acute and able of all his adversaries', but like Somerville argued that he 'was guided by Dr Robertson's example in almost all his literary undertakings; and, that his curiosity has seldom led him into any path, where the genius and industry of his predecessor had not previously cleared the way'.[20] Stuart did compromise originality and scholarly integrity by attempting too insistently to undermine Robertson's general view of history, although critics have to some extent misinterpreted or, more likely, disregarded his polemical and scholarly intentions.[21]

No one would deny that Robertson's 'View of Europe', is a masterful narrative, but some have questioned the extent to which he himself borrowed from other sources. The author himself freely acknowledged a debt to Voltaire. However, Alexander Carlyle noted that Robertson was 'so much addicted to the translation of other peoples thoughts, that he sometimes appeared tedious to his best friends'.[22] It has also been suggested that an important source for the work was the series of lectures on jurisprudence which Adam Smith gave publicly in Edinburgh in the early 1750s. The early nineteenth-century antiquary George Chalmers recorded that Smith believed 'Dr Robertson had borrowed the first vol. of his history of Cha[rles] 5 from them; as every student could testify'. Smith is also reported to have said rather unfavourably of Robertson:

> His judgement enabled him to form a good outline, but he wanted industry to fill up the plan; that Robertson inverted morals, by blaming what he should have praised, and praised, what he should have blamed: that he liked Robertson better when at a distance than he did upon nearer inspection.'[23]

Stuart undoubtedly concurred.

The publication of the *View of Society* marks the point at which 'an irreparable Breach' took place between Stuart and William Robertson.[24] This conflict was largely the result of Stuart's failure in 1777 to obtain the professorship of Public Law at Edinburgh University, which he attributed partly to the Principal's influence. Stuart's disappointment led him to change his original plan of offering an elaboration of Robertson's introductory 'View'. Instead he added overt criticisms of Robertson's methods and conclusions and referred to the man he had once admired in an unmistakably poor light:

> I make not this remark to detract from the diligence of an author whose laboriousness is acknowledged, and whose total abstinence from all ideas and inventions of his own, permitted him to carry an undivided attention to other men's thoughts and speculations; but that, resting on these peculiarities, I may draw from them this general and humiliating, yet, I hope, not unuseful conclusion, that the study and knowledge of the dark ages are still in their infancy. Are we for ever to revel in the sweets of ancient lore? Are we never to dig up the riches of the middle times?   (VS, 377–8)

Had Stuart included such remarks beforehand, he could not realistically have hoped for success. It was one thing to challenge implicitly the scholarship of important literary figures such as Hume and others, as he had done before. It was quite another to engage in what even by eighteenth-century standards was character assassination.

What led him to such an irrevocable position? In a society so entrenched in patronage, Stuart expected a reward for the services he rendered in the interest of Robertson and the Moderates as a critic in London and as the editor of the *Edinburgh Magazine and Review*. A university chair appealed to him most and was a real prospect just prior to the publication of the *View of Society*. The chair of Public Law became vacant when James Balfour, a success-

ful Edinburgh advocate who did not lecture, made clear his wish
to sell the lucrative post.[25] Stuart's intention was to turn this
sinecure into a proper lecture course and thus earn an additional
income from class fees while repaying the considerable purchase
price. Traditionally, the post had been held by members of the
Faculty of Advocates and appointments were made with their
approval for which reason alone Stuart would have found it
difficult to succeed. But failure was far from his mind. In May 1777
John Murray wrote to Stuart with congratulations 'on the Reversion you have obtained of the Professorship'.[26]

> I wish with all my heart your negotiation for the resignation
> of the present professor may prove successful. But I will own
> to you in confidence that I have no opinion of R[obertson].
> And would disuade you from communicating to him your
> plan before the reversion in your favour is *unalterably fixed*.
> For if you do it before, his machiavellian politics may be set
> at work to *out* you. His professions in your favour I can easily
> believe. He is afraid of you as the Indians are of the Devil,
> and therefore he is crafty enough to parade and to flatter; but
> if he could demolish you altogether I am not certain he
> would not prefer it.[27]

These comments refer to Robertson as a shrewd manipulator and
to the complex influence of patronage in both academic and commercial matters. Murray was disappointed by his own recent
failure to win the publication of the Principal's new work on the
Americas. Stuart had acted as an intermediary on his behalf and
wished as much for the success of his friend as a publisher as he
did for his own prospects as a professor.[28] Robertson's view of
Edinburgh academic society, however, did not include Gilbert
Stuart.

Alexander Carlyle remarked of the Moderate leader, who he
knew extremely well: 'The softness of his temper and his habits at
the head of a party, led him to promise what he was not able to
perform which weakness raised up to him some very inveterate
enemies.'[29] After the law chair Gilbert Stuart placed himself at
their head.

Printed notices written at various times after the event provide
conflicting reasons for Stuart's failure. He provided the basic
information for an account favourable to himself which appeared
in the *European Magazine* for February 1782, following a review by
William Thomson of a new edition of the *View of Society*.

About the time of the publication of the first edition of this performance he had turned his thoughts to an academical life; and he asked for the professorship of public law in the University of Edinburgh. But, though this place was promised to him by the Minister [Henry Dundas], he was defeated in the nomination by the arts of Dr. Robertson, which appeared the more surprizing, as that gentleman was known to have many obligations to him ... It entirely broke the intimacy of two persons, who were understood to be on the most friendly footing with one another. In this quarrel, the blame has been imputed altogether to Dr. Robertson.[30]

Some years later Henry Brougham offered an account of the affair more favourable to his kinsman Robertson. He explained how Stuart

fancied that he owed his rejection to the influence of the Principal. Nothing could be more fitting than that such should be the case; for the life of Stuart was known to be that of habitual dissipation, in intervals only of which he had paroxysms of study. To exclude such a person ... would have been a duty incumbent upon the head of any university in Christendom ... but no admission was ever made by the Principal's friends that he had interfered ... But the disappointed candidate had no doubt upon the subject, and he set no bounds to his thirst for revenge.[31]

Perhaps Robertson was genuinely concerned that Stuart's reputation for dissipation would set a poor example for the young men at the University. Perhaps he did not approve of the controversial tone of Stuart's writings, so different from his own balanced and dignified manner. Perhaps, too, the patronage of the eventual successor, Robertson's kinsman Allan Maconochie, took precedence over the advancement of a qualified but temperamental candidate.[32] Maconochie was an advocate, and as such met the first qualification for filling the law chair. After his appointment he gave a regular course of lectures which went some way towards establishing Edinburgh University's reputation for legal education.[33]

This failure was a great blow to Stuart, who wished nothing more than to return to the University, his home for over twenty years, and to pursue the further historical study he had always envisaged. The event mortified him and brought to mind many other unrealised expectations. Had he established himself among the literati of Edinburgh, the future would have been very different. He might have become the Edinburgh counterpart to John

Millar and possibly have brought his University similar laurels; he would also have gained financial security. As it was, money remained an endless source of difficulty. The wound he sustained over the law chair was reopened at the end of 1779 when another academic post looked to be within his grasp. Murray even wrote to congratulate him on his 'promotion to the professorship of Modern History', adding his hope that it was 'fixed and determined'.[34] Murray probably meant the chair of Universal Civil History, which from 1765 to 1780 had been occupied by John Pringle. Alexander Fraser Tytler, however, won the appointment and re-established a lecture course.[35]

Stuart openly challenged Robertson and the Edinburgh establishment when it became clear that he could not be part of it. He might have realised from the similar failures of his friends John Brown and William Smellie to gain professorships that men of their temperaments would not be admitted into the elitist cleric-dominated fold of the University. Unable to become part of the polite academic society, these three men entered into a loosely connected opposition against its members and supporters. At a distance of over two hundred years their contributions to the wider culture of the period, so overshadowed by their more successful rivals, are only just beginning to be explored.[36]

Stuart soon seized an opportunity to undermine the authority of Robertson as well as that of Henry Dundas (the Lord Advocate) and the Duke of Buccleuch, the political figures who stood behind the Moderates. He supported the rival party of Laurence Dundas in a scurrilous pamphlet exchange over a political dispute in Edinburgh. Stuart now championed the side he had opposed while editor of the *Edinburgh Magazine and Review*. Acting as a propagandist for Laurence Dundas he wrote an anonymous pamphlet entitled *Faction Displayed or, a Genuine Relation of the Representation of the Trades, and the Late Political Contentions in the City of Edinburgh*. Stuart's style, with its mixture of scholarship and controversy, suited direct political attack. Whether the object was Henry Dundas or Laurence Dundas did not entirely matter.

The political issue on which the power struggle between the two parties centred was a movement to reform the 'Set' of Edinburgh, or the leet (list) system by which City magistrates (made up of men from the Guild of Merchants and the Incorporation of Trades) were elected.[37] The Lord Advocate attempted to reform the City Council's electoral process in order to win more influence. By reducing the power of the merchants and giving more to the trades he sought to wrest control of city government and the parliamentary seat that went with it from Laurence Dundas. To this end he enlisted the agency of the former Provost James Stoddart. As it stood, the incumbent council (then controlled by Laurence Dundas) could prevent the election of its opponents because councillors in effect re-elected themselves.

It was ironic that the conservative landed interest of Henry Dundas and Buccleuch favoured democratic reform. But the times were such that both sides sought control by whatever means seemed most expeditious, while political ideology was set aside. Similar attempts to reform this system in 1729 and 1763 had been unsuccessful. Like these and other civic constitutional crises such as the Drysdale 'Bustle' of 1762–3 or the encounters over Heriot's lands, the importance of the event lies not so much in the principles espoused by each party but in the consequences for the City and for those involved.[38]

Stuart wrote *Faction Displayed* along the stylistic lines of a Ciceronian legal speech.[39] He began the twenty-five page pamphlet by tracing the history of Edinburgh's political constitution from 1508, when 'the trades first thought of being represented' (FD, 3) to the current affair when the trades sought 'emancipation … from the council' (FD, 12). His point was to show that the power of this body was already considerable, and any further concessions would set a precedent for further encroachments on the merchant representatives, who by right of 'positive law, antiquity of practice, natural justice, political expediency, and national advantage … are properly the representatives of the community' (FD, 14–15). From this carefully argued if less than impartial outline, Stuart warned the public of the consequences of the proposed reform and turned to more direct political attack.

> Amidst the general profligacy which would ensue, they [the trades] would grow the mere objects of contempt, and their contagiousness give infection to the nation.
>
> Into this state would the arts of Mr St[oddart], with the patronage of the D[uke] of B[uccleuch], and the counsels of a Crown Lawyer [Dundas], force the metropolis of Scotland!
>
> … They would alter the statute-law of the kingdom; they would destroy a *sett* which ought only to die with the community; they would introduce the most desolating corruption, undermine whatever is most valuable in manners; and, by one blow, strike at the root of all trade, emulation, and industry. (FD, 19)

Though this issue was essentially political, Stuart reinforced his position by arguing that 'the interests of religion would suffer in this conflict' (FD, 20). Introducing this subject gave him the opportunity to draw William Robertson into the fray. The connection of Henry Dundas 'with the head of the moderate party of the church; and the ascendancy maintained over him by the Reverend and crafty politician, would concur to the advancement of Clergymen the most unfit' (FD, 20). From Robertson, Stuart turned his scorn upon Buccleuch and called upon the Scottish nobility 'not to permit, without disgrace and insignificance, a young Peer to attain a super-eminent and exclusive jurisdiction' (FD, 23). Dundas, 'his conductor and associate' (FD, 23) then received more severe personal assault.

> Pushed beyond his natural consequence, the ministry will not endanger their credit ... by advancing his to a greater height. Giddy already, he cannot bear any higher elevations ... An interest in the House of Commons, founded on superior ability, is indeed a sure engine of greatness. But a provincial accent, a manner rather presumputous [sic] than insinuating, agitations, where passion is ridicule, and a frothy incoherence of matter, can neither impose on, nor command.   (FD, 24)

The plan for reform moved from pamphlet exchange to legal dispute in the Court of Session. There, the failure of Buccleuch and Henry Dundas enabled Laurence Dundas to retain control of Edinburgh's political machine. It was only a matter of time, however, before Henry Dundas would assert his authority in Edinburgh and in Scotland generally.[40] This was Stuart's first attack on the Lord Advocate, but it was anything but his last or his most severe.

John Murray read a copy of *Faction Displayed* 'with great pleasure' and approved of 'the historical account of the origin and progress of the Leets' and of the 'just & conclusive' reasoning in favour of the party espoused. 'The stroaks against the A[dvocate] & [Buccleuch] his Cats paw [are] laughable as well as severe.'[41]

It was satisfying for Stuart to be on the winning side, but less than amusing to see himself and his failure to secure the law chair mentioned in a scurrilous opposition pamphlet entitled *A Plan for Discharging the Incumbrances of the City of Edinburgh*. The author, writing under the Scriblerian pseudonym of Walter Waaggstaffe [sic], proposed ludicrous ways (many of them scatological) by which Laurence Dundas could raise local revenues without levying a new tax. The last of these proposed employment for Stuart and Hugo Arnot, another propagandist for Laurence Dundas:[42]

Considering that Dr G[ilber]t S[tuar]t has been disappointed of the reversion of a professorship, let him be appointed conjunctly with Mr H[ug]o A[rno]t ... to teach the new method of exposing the Scriptures, and the doctrine of the soul's immortality. As the gentlemen I now refer to, have an utter aversion to the inside of a church, let an arch be thrown over the Cowgate, under which they may discourse.[43]

The author set the admission fee for this mock extra-mural lecture at half a crown; one fifth was for Stuart and Arnot, the rest for City revenues. In the section headed 'A True Account of what passed at the Ordination of Doctor G[ilber]t S[tuar]t and Mr H[ug]o A[rno]t at the Oyster-cellar in the Cowgate' (a well known brothel), the writer derided them for their religious scepticism, immorality and flippant allegiance to Laurence Dundas. The 'ordination' began when Satan (in place of the intoxicated City Chaplain) 'told them, That as they had kissed the breech piece of Sir L[aurence] D[undas], as a mark of their duty and attachment, that they must do the same to him'.[44] This severe portrayal of Stuart and Arnot as reproachful sycophantic figures, tenuous in their allegiance and impervious to religious morality or civic virtue, parodied masonic ceremonies. The Dantesque imagery, would suggest that in supporting Dundas they had descended into the Inferno.

Stuart's role in Edinburgh politics did little to enhance his reputation as a serious historical writer. But he remained confident that the *View of Society* would establish him more securely. A review of the work by the orientalist John Richardson featured as the lead article in the *Critical Review*, where the work was praised as 'a valuable acquisition' with 'an expressive elegance of style; an uncommon vigour of mind; with a spirit of research and investigation, which judiciously refuses implicit confidence in ... *great authorities*'.[45] The influence of Stuart and Murray was such that commendable notices appeared in some (but not all) of the periodicals. Murray attributed a less than favourable article in the *Monthly Review* by John Gillies to the influence which Robertson and his booksellers brought to bear upon the editor. 'Gillies certainly meant you well in the Monthly, but some alarm was received by both R[ose] and G[riffiths] concerning your work by the art of R[obertso]n and I am uncertain if G[illes] did not write in fetters or if his article did not undergo alteration in some part after it was given in.'[46]

In Stuart's lifetime the *View of Society* met with moderate success, and somewhat more afterwards. It appeared in seven English editions over a twenty-five year period after its publication, was often cited by contemporary writers, and found its way on to many university history course reading lists well into the nineteenth century.[47] The work also received attention on the Continent. A German translation by Friedrich von Blankenburg appeared in 1779, soon after the original. In 1789, just before the eruption of the French Revolution, Antoine Boulard produced a translation at Paris. Boulard prefaced the *Tableau des Progrès de la Société* with remarks urging a series of political reforms designed to remove many detrimental features of feudalism. Stuart's idealised descriptions of the ancient republican spirit appealed to the translator and the revolutionary leadership; his account of Norman oppression, paradoxically, could be useful propaganda. Although Stuart did not live to witness the Revolution, he would have approved, at least initially, of its ideals. Here liberty, brought from the woods of Germany, reasserted itself in the streets of Paris.

At publication the *View of Society* sold slowly. The remarks directed against Robertson made the Edinburgh booksellers wary of handling it; indeed Murray believed that John Bell had 'totally surpressed' the sale in Scotland.[48] In 1782 he eventually succeeded in buying hundreds of unsold copies of the original quarto edition from Bell. He affixed a new title page to these and they sold moderately well.[49] A review by William Thomson appeared at this time in the *European Magazine*. He praised the work and marked out Stuart's section 'containing authorities, controversy, and remarks, as ... the most valuable part of the performance'.

> It is from the collision of opposed bodies that the truth of light is struck out. It is from the fermentation of different opinions that the philosophic spirit is extracted. The liberty of the press is of no avail, if the liberty of the mind is to be circumscribed. Whenever names are worshipped, and authority set up as supreme, enquiry is at an end, and science hath received the finishing blow.[50]

The *View of Society* is characterised by its refusal to adopt what one nineteenth-century law professor called 'the middle course'.[51] Stuart's challenging style in its genuine and rhetorical modes stands in contrast to most of the productions of his contemporaries – to William Robertson's deliberate equivocation, to John Millar's avoidance of controversy or equivocation and to Hume's relativism. To a certain extent his attitude was evident in the *English Constitution*, but it became much more pronounced in the *View of Society*. It was in Stuart's nature to point out the errors of others, but controversy was also a response to his increasing sense that the traditional avenues of success were being closed to him. The failure over the law chair stands out among the disappointments he met with as well as marking the point at which he set himself against Robertson.

A posthumous Edinburgh edition of the work was seen through the press by George Stuart in 1792, and a letter intended to boost support for the author was included among new prefatory material. The letter challenged the justice of the praise lavished upon Dr Robertson and his works and cast Stuart into an amusing biblical role.

> His criticisms on Dr. Robertson pleased me much. Well does the Reverend Doctor deserve it all ... The magnitude and gigantic size of some characters in lifetime, are like the Goliah of the Philistines. They intimidate whole hosts of pigmies; but a David, or a Gibby Stuart, will now and then arise and level them to the common size ... Mr Stuart has shewn how carelessly and superficially the good Doctor has read Tacitus, and what chimerical conclusions may be drawn ... I wish, for the sake of truth, and of true historical criticism, that more Gilbert Stuarts may be found.[52]

In reality Stuart was more of an Ishmael than a David. He foresaw, as he told David Dalrymple, 'that I would offend very much the admirers of Mr Hume, & that Dr Robertson and his friends would be surprised at my method of mentioning them. And yet', he continued, 'I still think that they are treated not only fairly, but with greater respect than they merit.'[53] This attitude could only lead to isolation. Stuart justified his position by comparing the confrontational method he adopted with the polite approach of his contemporaries: 'In a country, where the spirit of inquiry is expiring, the plainness of controversy will ever pass for satire. And men, who are adored by the vulgar must be approached with adulation.'[54] Intellectual elitism buffered him from an anticipated rush of criticism. Armed with both controversy and satire he turned to write the *Observations concerning the Public Law, and the Constitutional History of Scotland: with Occasional Remarks concerning English Antiquity*, where he would conjecture and offend even more.

In the last few months of 1778 Stuart quickly completed the new book while living at Fisherrow. John Murray offered him just £25 for the manuscript, but William Creech, his former partner in the *Edinburgh Magazine and Review*, was willing to pay more. As part of an agreement to purchase a number of copies from Creech, Murray's name was included in the imprint as the publisher in London, where Stuart knew his friend would attend to the sale. On 20 January the *Caledonian Mercury* advertised that the *Public Law of Scotland* could be purchased at Creech's shop for five shillings in boards, or six 'neatly bound'.[65]

In the Scottish papers advertising the book the leading news was the opposition then mounting against proposed Catholic relief legislation. Articles and letters against the repeal of penal laws imposed on Catholics and announcements concerning the activities of Protestant associations, formed in communities across Scotland to ensure that the legislation was defeated, filled the press throughout the second half of 1778. During the last days of January 1779 this simmering anti-Catholic sentiment erupted in rioting; mobs roamed the streets of Edinburgh vandalising and setting fire to the property of Catholics and their sympathisers. William Robertson, a leader of the campaign promoting religious toleration, was among those threatened. He and his family were forced to seek refuge in Edinburgh Castle. It was no coincidence that the Principal was the central target for criticism in *Public Law of Scotland* and Gilbert Stuart an opponent of such social reform. Although the text itself contains few references to Popery or Protestantism, the strident tone of Stuart's assertions in favour of the authority of public opinion and the extended attack on Robertson as an historian connect the book with the volatile topic of religious intolerance.

Other issues relating to political and social reform in Scotland also throw light on Stuart's extra-scholarly purposes in writing a book about public law and constitutional history. One is the proposal of Lord Mountstuart (to whom the work is dedicated) to re-establish a Scots militia; another is Stuart's call to reform those features of Scots law which allowed the exercise of an arbitrary authority by Court of Session judges. The three topics – religious, military and judicial reform – are the themes around which the discussion of Stuart's book is organised.

The challenge to authority was apparent from the start. On the title page Stuart included an epigram from Horace's *Odes*: 'I walk over fire placed underneath treacherous ash'.[56] The typically lengthy endnotes, headed 'Proofs, Illustrations, and Controversy', included an even more provocative quotation from Livy, which translates as 'Each man should like or dislike men and should approve or disapprove of things according to his own judgement; and he should not depend on the expression or nod of another, nor should he be influenced by the mind of another (PLS, 147).[57] To an even greater degree than in the *View of Society* the notes dominate the work. A number are almost separate discourses, only marginally related to the main text to which they refer. In its conjectural approach and range of legal and martial subject matter the work is similar to the *English Constitution* and the *View of Society*. Once again, Stuart offered a two-stage model of feudal society, with emphasis on the first period of freedom and mutual benefit between lord and vassal. An examination of social change using the example of Scottish history is a distinguishing feature of the book. In the introductory chapter Stuart justified the study of Scots law by asserting its individuality, antiquity and original liberty. He reiterated the view central to his conjectural method: that the institutions which characterised feudal society in Scotland 'were not the effect of a plan, or the creation of a projector. They unfolded themselves under the influence of human passions and human conduct, in a certain condition of society' (PLS, 4). Supplementing this chapter is a single, albeit lengthy note in which he argued against the opinion of Lord Kames that Scottish laws and customs were borrowed from England (PLS, 149–55).

In the second chapter he focused on military institutions as they progressed from the era of the knight to the time of the standing army. The rise and progress of the Scots militia was as much a source of historical fascination to Stuart as it was of pride. His note on 'The Introduction of Fire-arms into Scotland' concludes with a typically philosophical remark:

> It was not possible, in those times, to predict their future efficacy, or to forsee that battles were to be less bloody, and more terrible; and that contending states, advancing nearer to equality by the means of this military artifice, a stability unknown before was to be given to kingdoms, and a period put to those destructive and desolating revolutions, which mark the conquests of the antient world.   (PLS, 168)

Other curious notes include an explanation of why stags' antlers and birds' beaks are displayed as trophies (PLS, 245–6) and a discourse on the origin of blackmail (PLS, 251).

Chapter 3 is headed 'The Revenue of the Sovereign, and the Expences of Government'. Stuart began with a concise chronological account of the Scottish monarchy, but his main purpose was to show that 'in every period of the history of Scotland ... the revenues for the royal state were fully sufficient for its wants and its grandeur' (PLS, 54). Patriotism distinguishes the main text while opposition to authors 'who have been solicitious to describe the monarchs of Scotland as abject' (PLS, 55) characterises the notes. Chapter 4, on 'Jurisdiction and Courts', and Chapter 5, on legislation and representation, recall corresponding sections in the *English Constitution* ('Of the judicial arrangements in Germany and England' and 'Of the great council, or parliament in Germany and England'). Again Stuart criticised the 'writers for prerogative' like Hume (PLS, 311–15), who failed to see that such institutions in Scotland, as in England, 'were founded in freedom, and had freedom for their object' (PLS, 122) and that 'selfishness and commercial ideas could not accord with the generous principles of the Gothic and the Celtic manners' (PLS, 123). In the fifth chapter Stuart directed his attention to the history of municipalities (or towns and boroughs). His examination of early legal charters led him to conclude that in ancient times towns possessed liberty and thus were represented in the national assembly.

> The first condition of the towns and the people ... must have been a scene of freedom or of happiness. And, in this condition, corporations and boroughs were actually known, and of importance. The second æra of their history was deformed with miseries. And it was from this wretchedness, to the felicities of their former independence, that the charters of community were to contribute to restore them. (PLS, 319–20)

Again, he contradicted Robertson (PLS, 320), but also challenged Hume and Robert Brady for their views on this subject and charged the three with being 'advocates for the crown' (PLS, 327).[58] The Magna Charta of King John, to which these historians ascribed the birth of municipal liberty, according to Stuart, 'actually alludes to the *freer* and the *happier* condition which the people had enjoyed in the Saxon times' (PLS, 312).[59] It was clear to contemporary readers that Stuart's assertions of the political independence of towns could relate to the activities of local Protestant associations.

On the whole, Stuart was more optimistic in this work than in his other conjectural writings. He was also less nostalgic about the lost freedom and equality of ancient times and now looked more to the future. While he noted those features of Scottish society which were corrupt, he held out the prospect of reform and improvement. One example is his challenge to the 'infinite profusion of *Scottish Lairds*, who have so long been a subject of ridicule; and who, retaining pride of feudal times, in the midst of meanness, repress at this moment the spirit of improvement, in every county in Scotland' (PLS, 260–1). This was a bold criticism, for Stuart knew that these same men formed a considerable part of the book-buying public.

The final chapter of the *Public Law of Scotland* focuses on events from the union of the Crowns in 1603 to the political union of Scotland and England in 1707. The absence of controversial notes in this part allows the optimism of former chapters to emerge in a greater degree. Stuart acknowledged that there had been much criticism and bloodshed over the events of more recent Scottish history, but in the larger view of the Union, he asserted, 'the best interests of freedom, and justice, and trade, were consulted, established, and maintained' (PLS, 143).

One dominant threat in the mind of many Scots as they read the *Public Law of Scotland*, was the prospect of Catholic relief legislation. The widespread antipathy towards Catholics, not only in Scotland but also in England, had many sources. The revolution of government in 1688–90 had removed a Catholic monarch from the British throne and established a Protestant succession. Since these events and the rebellions of 1715 and 1745, Catholicism and Jacobitism were closely associated. Although over time this came to be less of a political threat, as a popular conception it held force, particularly in Scotland. More recently, the Seven Years' War had accentuated the political rivalry between Catholic and Protestant countries. In May 1778 a parliamentary bill to remove many of the religious and legal restrictions on Catholics in England became law with little opposition. The necessity of raising troops from the Catholic population to fight the Americans and their allies required the passage of relief bills for Ireland, Canada and Scotland as well. Anti-Catholic laws, although often not enforced, punished priests for saying mass, prohibited heirs from inheriting property and disallowed entrance into public office or military service. Henry Dundas was the political force behind the Scottish bill, which was to be voted on in May 1779. In previous months, however, it had met with such adamant extra-parliamentary opposition, culminating in the Edinburgh riots, that it ultimately failed. Dundas realised that he would jeopardise his political influence 'if the religious passions of the nation were roused against him'.[60] Reactions against religious toleration were not unprecedented: in 1753, for example, there had been a great public outcry against the naturalisation of British Jews. In enlightened Edinburgh in 1779 the voice of the common man overwhelmed that of the tolerant intelligentsia. The struggle tested William Robertson's leadership of the Scottish church and the result was an important factor in his retirement from this sphere of action. It was a sign of the decline of the 'Moderate Revolution' in the Scottish church.[61] Catholics had to wait until 1829 for legislation guaranteeing their rights.

For Stuart, Robertson's defeat was gratifying. His comments in the *Public Law of Scotland* had helped to undermine the civic authority of the Moderate leader. It was illiberal to oppose Catholic relief, but the voice of public opinion (and Stuart's continued anger at the Principal) outweighed the politically expedient argument of an elitist circle of men in favour of religious freedom. Stuart viewed the progress of the Association movement, not as intolerant fanaticism, but as a sign of 'the people' claiming the right to have a larger role in government. In the *Public Law of Scotland* he pointed to historical precedents to justify the ultimate authority of public opinion in politico-religious matters. Events during the reign of Charles II, 100 years before, provided a formative example:

> While the spirit and forms of the antient government were invaded, and while the civil rights of the people were objects of mockery, the freedom of religious principle was also attacked. The most retired and private sentiments of men were to suffer violation. Every art was employed to divide the protestant interest, and to give countenance and encouragement to popery. A tyranny, extensive as well as cruel was about to strike deeply its roots into the soil, to lift up its head, and to threaten defiance.   (PLS, 137)

Such remarks highlighted the common ground between just political reform and the need for the Association movement to secure liberty. Stuart also alluded to the activities of Protestant associations in discussions of municipal liberty. In their early period each association organised support within their local provincial synod, but, to further their opinions, began to petition the governing bodies of their respective boroughs and towns. The strategy of gaining government sanction unified and politically ratified the anti-Popish cause. Here was an example of public opinion at a metropolitan level making itself heard. It is probable that Stuart was a member of the Protestant association, and as a propagandist, he justified their actions by historical precedent. The riots, a consequence of public opinion making itself heard, did little to advance the principle of municipal or individual liberty. Stuart nevertheless defended popular authority as the foundation of government. Writing in 1785 in the *Political Herald*, in an article headed 'Scots Reform', he recalled the anti-Catholic riots when he remarked that 'the pretence of popular disturbance has ever been employed to cut up the very principles of popular power. It is a curious maxim which despotism has invented', he added 'and upon which that species of government is supported, that the voice and actions of the people are ever hostile to their own happiness, and to their own important and fundamental rights.'[62]

The example of Protestant activism, culminating in the Scottish riots, repeated itself shortly afterwards in London where the public sought to repeal the existing Catholic relief act. The Scottish opposition to proposed legislation was successful while the English attempt to repeal existing law was a catastrophic failure. The leader of the English 'No Popery' movement was the Scotsman Lord George Gordon, after whom the infamous Gordon Riots were named.[63] Although Stuart grouped together Catholic relief opposition and the general movement for parliamentary reform, it was inevitable that the violence spawned by the former would disrupt the larger aims of the latter and produce hostility between the two.[64]

Anti-Catholic activity in Britain shows the gap between the theoretical ideas about the nature of society which writers like Hume, Smith, Ferguson, Millar and Stuart himself were articulating, and the reality that while their works were being read, the populace of Britain's great cities was totally out of control. But a systematically delineated historical discourse like the *Public Law of Scotland* could explain the relevance of volatile and emotional current events.

William Robertson's controversial role in support of Catholic toleration presented Stuart with an opportunity to attack when his adversary was in a vulnerable position. Throughout the book Stuart challenged Robertson. He neither forgot nor forgave the law chair episode, and the alterations he made to the *View of Society* exacerbated rather than exhausted his anger. In the course of writing he explained to John Murray the 'motives' behind the work. The publisher, however, knew that by indulging too much in controversy, Stuart had compromised the scholarly integrity of his writings and, more to the point, had hurt their sales. He also had observed the calculating manner in which Robertson distanced himself from public argument and recommended a similar tactic.

> I thank you for your candour in disclosing to me the *motives* of the publication and I have no objection to its answering your purpose; as I am by no means an adorer of the great man against whom your attack is levelled. I even think he merits your discipline ... Disguise the object of your attack; let the author be mentioned handsomely, and permit nothing rancourous to be said against the man.[65]

Stuart did not follow this useful advice. Creech also was concerned about this matter and wrote during the printing of the work to remonstrate over the animadversions on Robertson. The meaning of Stuart's reply is open to interpretation: if taken ironically it reveals the extent of his antipathy; or if taken seriously the extent of his vindictive delusion:

> The idea you mention, that my work is altogether against Robertson is a fiction of idle people. I sincerely declare to you that I will never submit to do so much honour to that gentleman as to write a book against him. I do him, indeed, the respect to oppose some of his opinions; but this business does not even employ my text. I only treat of him in some Notes.[66]

This did little to calm the anxieties of the bookseller, who seriously considered Stuart's proposal that John Bell replace him as publisher. Creech's name did appear on the title page, though he regretted his involvement and did little to promote the sale. He was remiss in sending copies to Murray, who wrote angrily some months later that 'it is my opinion you did not mean it to succeed'.[67] Creech's wish to preserve his reputation with Robertson, the Edinburgh literati and the powerful London booksellers who sold their works and supplied him with many others, mattered much more than the success of the *Public Law of Scotland*. Murray perceived that a campaign against Stuart's work was being mounted by the London trade and he told Stuart that their sales of Robertson's works 'will be affected exactly in proportion to the credit which is paid to your book by the public'. He added that not only were some of Stuart's associates being 'sucked into the vortex' of his adversaries, but also that, 'those persons who wish to damn you as an author have it next at heart to ruin me as a publisher'.[68]

Against this challenge, Stuart and Murray enlisted their own considerable literary connections. A favourable account appeared in the *Critical Review*, where the reviewer remarked that Stuart 'enjoys a great advantage over historical writers and antiquaries, who are not conversant in the laws of the country'. The *Monthly* voiced more guarded approval.[69]

The work did not sell well. Murray even sent back unwanted copies to Creech and could no longer protect Stuart from reports that 'every person I converse with censures [it]'.[70] Alexander Carlyle prepared some 'Notes on Gil. Stuarts Book', possibly with a view to publishing a defence of Robertson. He concluded with the following summary: 'I am tired of this peevish Writer, who has not a grain of candor from beginning to end of his book, nor hardly a word of truth ... Stuarts whole stile is turgid, affected, conceited & full of shallow Brilliantcy.'[71]

Stuart was not daunted by the strength of his adversaries. To heighten public antipathy against Robertson around the time of the riots and further vent his spleen, he wrote an anonymous broadside. The attack was entitled the 'Character of a certain Popular Historian, now Ministerial Agent, for Reconciling our Complaisant Clergy to the Church of Rome. From the Writings of a Celebrated Philosopher now Deceased'.[72] Stuart led the public to believe that the piece was written by David Hume, whose highly controversial *Dialogues concerning Natural Religion* had recently appeared. It was a poignant though less than plausible way to undermine the Principal. The antiquary George Chalmers later described the broadside as 'a character of the Principal very disadvantageous but I am afraid not far from truth'.[73]

In the text itself Stuart cast Robertson in the role of a self-seeking, Judas-like betrayer. He introduced the broadside with the couplet: 'Our Modern Iscariots, with Hypocrite Face,/Support Popish Measures for Pension or Place.' Stuart was intent on showing the extent to which Robertson's religious liberalism was politically motivated:

> The Earl of B[u]te, who has loaded him with all the Offices he now enjoys, he postpones to the Duke of B[u]cc[leuc]h; and when the latter has conferred his favours, he will bow to another Idol. To his resentment, he fixes no bounds; yet he has not Magnanimity enough to be an open enemy. He wounds secretly, and in the dark.

As an individual, a clergyman and a civic leader Robertson was severely defamed, and in a manner which presented an ironic contrast to the praise bestowed upon him in Stuart's favourable

'Character' seven years before. As a popular historian, Stuart criticised his former mentor for 'adapting his compositions to Women and Children'.

In the *Public Law of Scotland*, the attack was more sustained, if less severe than in the 'Character'. The main text, as he told Creech, was free of controversy, or almost. But the notes, which make up nearly two-thirds of the whole, contain a great deal of invective. In eleven of the twenty-nine notes Stuart specifically criticised the introductory narrative in Book I of Robertson's *History of Scotland*. These criticisms of Robertson are the most distinctive feature of the book, and they emphasise the corrective role which Stuart, as an antiquarian, assumed for himself.

Stuart challenged what he regarded as inaccurate generalities in Robertson's survey of early Scottish history, choosing not to see that the purpose of an extended hypothesis about the progress of feudal society was to recall the ambience of an age vastly different from the modern commercial world. Robertson wrote the *History of Scotland* for a wide and generally educated public with a view to promoting Anglo-Scottish relations.[74] In Stuart's mind this gave an inaccurate picture of feudal society in Scotland. He also saw Robertson's portrayal of Scotland's institutions as inferior to their English counterparts as an attempt to ingratiate himself at Court. Stuart did not accept a 'manifest destiny' for Scotland. He wrote the *Public Law of Scotland* for pedantic, republican Scotsmen in order to heighten patriotism and undermine his rival and the establishment he led.

> I felt the affections and the ardour of a good citizen. If my general principles are right, their application will be allowed to be extensive ... If I have fallen into errors, I shall be proud to forsake them. For, my view is to investigate the truth, and to illustrate a portion of knowledge, the most difficult. I affect not popularity and declamation. What I have written is to the few, and not to the many.   (PLS, x)

Stuart objected to the appearance of deep scholarship in Robertson's work where in fact he had largely synthesised the conclusions of others.[75] Stuart himself acknowledged that he was 'far from being insensible to the peculiarities of his [Robertson's] merit' (PLS, 367). Nevertheless he censured Robertson for judging earlier times by contemporary standards, for copying from other historians and for presenting an inaccurate description of feudal society. In the role of patriotic Scot, he criticised Robertson's 'propensity to embellish other men's notions, without considering enough on what authority they are founded' (PLS, 366). This was 'a constant and a teeming source of mistake to this showy and elegant historian ... [who] holds out many a frail opinion to glitter and to perish' (PLS, 366). With an air of indifference he added: 'To collect these cannot be interesting to me. But, though I could not submit to make a chronicle of his errors, I have been induced to wipe away, and to dispel, in part, the stains and the gloom they would fix upon our story' (PLS, 366). *The Public Law of Scotland* concludes (in the final note) with a censure thinly veiled by the rhetoric of sympathy. Here Stuart is at the height of his satirical style.

> It must be a pain, I know, to many of his readers, that the most widely amusing of all our writers, is not, at the same time, the best informed, and the most able. They must regret, that a work which forms so general, so easy, and so pleasing a pastime, is not also fraught with instruction, and loaded with wisdom. And, that the author, who is deservedly so eminent in all the arts of courtly and popular composition, is not likewise remarkable for those superior qualities, which alone can secure and establish admiration, the power of thought, and the originality of sentiment.   (PLS, 367)

Robertson was so offended by these attacks that he determined to take legal action against Stuart. However advisors dissuaded him from this course because in the matter of such literary disputes at the time, 'judges as well as juries were inclined to give great latitude in encouraging a spirit of criticism'.[76] Robertson's decision not to pursue Stuart was prudent. A public opportunity to confute the opinions of the leading historian of the day would have pleased Stuart and gained the Principal little advantage. 'If those who censure me would speak out to the world', Stuart complained to David Dalrymple, 'their conduct would be generous; because I should then have an opportunity to defend myself.'[77] Despite this lament, Stuart continued his challenge.

Athough Robertson maintained a cautious distance from such encounters, his eldest son did not. So angered was he by the aspersions cast upon his father, that he found himself involved in a quarrel with Stuart that led to a duel. In the *View of Society* Stuart described the duel as something 'dishonourable to refuse, and illegal to accept' (VS, 339) and added that 'in the observations of Dr Robertson on the same subject, the confusion is evident and palpable' (VS, 335). Henry Brougham reported of the affair that 'neither party was hurt, an accomodation having taken place on the field'. He concluded his account with the remark 'Stuart's second ... was obliged, knowing his friend's intemperate habits, to oppose the proposal which he made with his usual want of conduct ... That second, an able and an honourable man, always admitted Stuart's unjustifiable conduct towards the historian.'[78]

In the following years Stuart mounted even more determined attacks on the Principal over other aspects of Scottish history. Although he met with more success in this respect with his own *History of Mary Queen of Scots* than with the *Public Law of Scotland*, he could not hope to surmount entirely the political and literary monopoly which Robertson had built, even when events like the Catholic relief affair put the leader at a disadvantage. The interest in their encounter is not so much to determine who was right about points of feudal history, such as the relative wealth or poverty of the Scottish kings, but to clarify the cultural climate in which Stuart wrote.

Not all of Stuart's 'motives' in writing the *Public Law of Scotland* were as belligerent as his challenge to Robertson. His review of the state of land in Scotland shows the inquiring and educational nature of his scholarship. Stuart asserted at the outset that the way land gradually became hereditary was distinctly Scottish: 'Wherever feudality was to flourish, it was to grow from the root. The tree could not be carried to a foreign soil. Its native earth could alone preserve it in existence, and give the aliment that was to make it rise into height' (PLS, 10). The soil metaphor appears frequently in the work: first in the preface, where the records of jurisprudence 'are hid in the ground, and must be sought for with ingenuity and toil' (PLS, viii); and in the closing passages of the main narrative where the feudal law becomes a

> venerable oak which had expanded its branches so widely ... was to deposit in its grave the skeleton of that prodigious system, which had risen to so great a height, which had endured for so many ages, and which had known so much glory and mischance, so much stability and confusion.[79]
>
> (PLS, 146)

This language emphasises a principle central to eighteenth-century thought: that the land and the rights and duties associated with such property are the basis of law and society. Military service was the bond between the feudal lord and his vassal which secured property rights. Stuart accordingly reviewed the history of the Scottish militia from early times to the Restoration. He began with the assertion that 'to be free, was to have a title to go to the war and to seek renown' (PLS, 17) and argued that the right of Scotland to re-establish its militia was 'a claim which cannot be controverted' (PLS, 38). The appeal to the authority of 'the people' also provided an historical justification for the bellicose anti-Catholic rioters.

By advocating a national defence on practical and historical grounds, Stuart placed himself in a line of patriotic Scotsmen which included Andrew Fletcher of Saltoun, Gilbert Elliot, Alexander Carlyle and others. There were many reasons why the Scots demanded a militia and many instances after the Union when they tried to establish one.[80] Stuart was certainly familiar with the militia bill of 1760–62 proposed by Gilbert Elliot at the time of the Seven Years' War. Though unsuccessful, it had the active support of the Moderate party and served to animate Scottish national spirit. More recently he had supported Lord Mountstuart's militia initiative, which was proposed in November 1775 in the context of debates on the American conflict. Backing in Scotland for the bill was strong. Stuart inserted a notice in the *Edinburgh Magazine and Review* in which he referred to Scots patriots like Mountstuart 'whose names will ever be revered by their country'. He believed the establishment of a militia was important both constitutionally, to 'render the union more compleat' and pragmatically, to allow the Scots to defend themselves against 'revolted America' and its European allies (EMR, IV, 671).

Mountstuart's bill was also an effort to reassert his family's political interest, somewhat eclipsed by the rise of Henry Dundas and the Duke of Buccleuch. After the bill's defeat in April, James Boswell recorded a conversation in which a friend of his 'talked of the Duke of Buccleuch's imagining that he should be Prime Minister for Scotland, and that Harry Dundas was to act along with him … Lord Mountstuart heard this with contempt, and said of Dundas, "I hate the fellow."'[81] The dedication of the *Public Law of Scotland* to Mountstuart over two years after the defeat of his bill shows that Stuart's loyalties (or hopes of preferment) were anything but transient. Mountstuart was after all the pre-eminent opposition leader in Scotland.

His defeat did not dampen down the issue for long, for early in 1778 the piratical activities of John Paul Jones on Scotland's western coast prompted another revival of the Scots militia issue. Alexander Carlyle was active in mustering support for this initiative. Like Stuart in the *Public Law of Scotland*, Carlyle saw the issue in the context of a Union-based equality with England. In the minds of many Scots, defence against foreign invasion or against Catholics (even at home) amounted to much the same thing. In Stuart's mind it was politically consistent to be pro-militia and anti Catholic relief. In both cases public opinion dictated the course of action.

The threat of a Jacobite rebellion had once been a source of English objection to a Scots militia. However by the 1770s Jacobitism was, as Stuart put it, 'retiring to seek obscurity and repose in its grave' (PLS, 39), and was thus no longer a valid political fear. Like many Scots of his generation, Stuart was an advocate of the Union with a nostalgic non-political regard for the House of Stuart. In the tradition of a good Hanoverian Whig, he defended 'the most important transaction in the history of Scotland' (PLS, 140) as an event from which Scotland had much to gain. To prove this, he appealed to the Article of Union, which allowed the level of Scottish representation in the British Parliament to be proportionally greater than the land tax which the Scottish people paid and from which a militia was raised. Dr Johnson, in a typically anti-Scottish moment, told Boswell that the Scottish scheme 'was to retain so much a part of your little land-tax, by way of making us pay and clothe your militia'. Boswell replied: 'You should not talk of *we* and *you*, Sir: There is now a Union.'[82] Dr Johnson was also critical of the Scots, and of Scottish writers in particular, for their excessive praise of one another. But a reviewer, referring to this trait, noted that 'an opposite propensity seems to belong to a distinguished historian – See Dr. Stuart's observations on Dr. Robertson's *History of Scotland*' (ER, 5, 419n).[83]

Stuart's advocacy of the Union went beyond the representational and monetary advantages, with the assertion that Scotland 'may confide more securely in the democracy of England' (PLS, 142). He had made this point ten years before in the *English Constitution*, and now he emphasised that this fact did not lessen the importance of Scottish history. The subject had not been studied as thoroughly in Scotland as it had been in England: 'No Selden, no Spelman has arisen, to cast a light upon the gloom which conceals our laws, government, and customs; and our historians have copied one another with a convenient and disgraceful servility' (PLS, 3). Stuart saw himself as the Scottish counterpart to these English jurists of the seventeenth century. He believed that jurisprudential studies were necessary to understand how the Union was achieved; to this end he traced the progress of

Scottish liberty from 'the woods of Germany' through to the mid-eighteenth century. Though Scotland lost its parliament in 1707, it retained its own legal system so the historical study of Scots law was still profoundly important. Only by understanding how it evolved could Scotland prosper and resist further absorption into the English system.

For all his praise of the Scottish legal system from an historical point of view, Stuart was still aware that the advent of a modern commercial society made reform necessary. He believed that the largely principle-oriented Scottish civilian system would benefit from the introduction of reforms such as the removal of the Court of Session's *Nobile Officium*. This arbitrary power, which he traced to the ancient royal office of the Chief Justicier, invested the judges 'with a power that is above law and above equity' (PLS, 272). It entitled them to make and repeal laws and thus infringed upon legislative authority. Stuart described it as an example of 'the unprincipled rudeness of a barbarous age' (PLS, 268) and as 'Turkish jurisdiction in a country of liberty'(PLS, 275).

He anticipated the disapproval such comments would incur among the Lords of Session, and in defence drew attention to the precedent set by George Buchanan who had been reproached for voicing 'his sentiments with too much liberty' (PLS, 276). Stuart then asked rhetorically, as if to a jury of readers:

> Is there a quality in an author so honourable, so useful, as that of expressing what he thinks? Is it proper that science and learning should be put in prison, and dishonoured by confinement and fetters? Miserable is that nation where literature is under any form but that of a republic. (PLS, 276n)

Stuart argued that the *Nobile Officium* contravened the liberties guaranteed since 1707 by the English constitution. This appeal to Whig principles to promote Scottish legal reform was in advance of his day. Henry Cockburn in his *Life of Lord Jeffrey* (1852) confirmed that the 'sole object' of the Whigs during their reform campaign of the 1780s 'was to bring Scotland within the action of the constitution. For this purpose it was plain that certain definite and glaring peculiarities must be removed, and the people be trained to the orderly exercise of public rights.'[84]

James Boswell, himself the son of a Court of Session judge, shared Stuart's views about the need for judicial reform. In connection with such improvements he wrote two anonymous pamphlets. The first, *A Letter to Lord Braxfield* (1780) sought to correct abuses of the Court's prerogative; the second, *A Letter to the People of Scotland* (1785), sought to prevent a reform proposed by Henry Dundas to reduce the number of judges from fifteen to ten. Both pamphlets have a connection with Gilbert Stuart and the *Public Law of Scotland*.

Shortly after the publication of the first, Boswell was curious to know the speculations of various legal people about the authorship of the pamphlet. When asked directly, he denied having written it and proceeded to remove suspicion from himself by asking if Gilbert Stuart was the author. The reply to Boswell (from a Mr Norris): 'Give him (G. Stuart) the Materials, he could write it.'[85] A few days later Boswell attempted a similar deception while walking along Edinburgh's New Bridge in the company of William Robertson. In the Journal for 15 May 1780, he recorded their conversation:

> Robertson ... told me he had read the *Letter to Lord Braxfield*, and that it would do good, for it would show the judges they are not above censure. He thought it must be written by a man of business, well acquainted with the Court. I mentioned Gilbert Stuart. He said it had not the *bounce* of his style. I suppose Robertson had felt it like a boxer's head thump the pit of his stomach. 'It is a plain style', said he. 'But very well written,' said I. He agreed.[86]

'Bounce' was a reference to Stuart's critical remarks in the *Public Law of Scotland*. Here Boswell found himself the unsuspecting object of the humour of the Principal, who most likely knew that Boswell was the author, but gentlemanly honour required that Boswell remain silent and 'stomack' Robertson's remarks on the 'plainness' of his style.

In the other pamphlet Boswell warned of the dangers of autocracy which a diminution of the number of Session judges would cause for the public. It was an undemocratic reform which would further extend the powers of the Court and make the judges more susceptible to the influence of the government, particularly to the will of Dundas, or 'Harry the Ninth' as Boswell called him in the pamphlet. Boswell explained that the Court 'has acquired a kind of undefined arbitrary jurisdiction, called its *nobile officium*, for a full and bold account of which I refer you to Dr. *Gilbert Stuart*'.[87] Here, some six years after the publication of the *Public Law of Scotland*, at a time when Stuart was also engaged on a direct attack on Dundas as editor of the *Political Herald*, Boswell appealed to his argument for judicial reform.[88]

In the *Herald* Stuart argued that the diminution of Session judges 'would secure, in a manner, the most absolute, the ascendancy of the family of Dundas' (PH, I, 34)[89] and declared that it was 'in opposition to the Treaty of Union' (PH, I, 333).[90] His remarks were designed to rouse the spirit of rebellion in his fellow Scotsmen by comparing the danger of the bill with recent national events. Addressing himself to Ilay Campbell, the Lord Advocate and 'minion of Dundas', he wrote:

> We have lost America; and the fate of Ireland hangs in suspense. At this most critical of all times, you give a stab to Scotland. Do you imagine, that a people, who have been once so illustrious, and who even at the present moment are so remarkable for their fervid genius, will tamely submit to your insults? Is Scotland less attentive to its interests, and its character, than America, or Ireland? (PH, I, 35–6)

In the matter of legal reform and in politics generally Stuart and Boswell held similar views. The power base of Dundas and Buccleuch, which Stuart blamed for keeping him out of the establishment, to some extent prevented Boswell from succeeding in the political career he genuinely desired. Their efforts played a significant role in preventing the reform proposed by Dundas.

In its challenge to individuals in literary and political spheres, the *Public Law of Scotland* shows the extent of the interplay between antiquarian scholarship and contemporary events. The clash between the successful insiders who held professorships, pulpits, or both, and men like Stuart who were left to oppose them, emerges on religious, political and literary levels. The issues of Catholic relief, the American war, court patronage, historiographic methods and legal reform underpin the work. When it appeared in January 1779, Stuart was well aware that the controversial elements would not ingratiate him with the establishment. In a letter to William Jones, the orientalist and supporter of liberal political principles, Stuart clarified his fears about its reception:

> In two respects, I expose myself, very much to censure. I have attacked the *nobile officium* of the court of session; and I have vindicated the freedom of the Scottish government from the misrepresentations of Dr. Robertson, the historiographer of Scotland. With a thousand people, these things are the greatest of all crimes.[91]

Stuart knew that whether his criticisms of Robertson were just or not, he would probably not gain an ascendancy over his rival. Robertson himself remained powerful in political and literary spheres despite the defeat over the Catholic relief bill. An independent, adversarial role suited Stuart's nature best, although this was liberty of a different sort than he had envisaged for himself. In another letter to Jones he announced a new performance on 'a very remarkable period of the Scottish History'. In this work, the *History of the Establishment of the Reformation of Religion in Scotland*, Stuart set aside conjecture and controversy and appeared to have adopted the more popular narrative approach of which Robertson, Hume and Gibbon were then the undisputed masters. 'My former writings' he remarked, 'have been addressed chiefly to Men of research & learning. In this work I speak to the people.'[92] It was followed not long after by the *History of Mary Queen of Scots*.

5

Scottish Narrative History
A Reformation in Historical Writing 1780–1782

But it is a brave thing to be the Ecclesiastical Draw-Can-Sir.
Andrew Marvell, *Rehearsal Transpros'd* (London, 1672), I, 42

Stuart conceived his narrative *History of the Reformation* in a less overtly confrontational manner than was his wont. But John Murray feared that he would not, or could not, control his retaliatory spirit. He knew Stuart would 'encounter Dr. Robertson often, who occupies the same ground'.[1] To risk another financial failure was dangerous for Stuart's reputation and his own. He therefore begged for reassurance:

I trust you will be moderate in your refutation of his opinions. You have told me that your book contains not a word of controversy, and I rely that it does not ...

The sale of your work will be more certain with few notes & illustrations, than with many. If you want to be read you must address yourself to the capacity of the Multitude. This you are able to do without forfeiting the attention of Men of sense and learning.[2]

Murray offered Stuart sixty guineas for the first edition of 750 copies. It was a fair sum, but not as much as the author hoped for a popular narrative work. Murray clearly wished to publish and profit by the *History of the Reformation*, but with Stuart's own interest in mind, again insisted that if more money could be had, to 'make the most of your performance with another'.[3] To justify his offer, he explained that military defeats by the French had 'hurt Literary business'.[4] But to tempt Stuart into acceptance and to accommodate the more dignified nature of an historical narrative, Murray told of his plan to print the work in the large royal quarto format. He sent along a specimen of text (printed by Archibald Hamilton) boasting that the type was new and that 'it will make a handsomer volume than any produced from the London press for these ten years past.'[5] To indulge Stuart's vanity further, he offered to commission an engraved portrait of the author to be affixed to the work. The drawing for the print was executed by John Donaldson, a Scottish artist of considerable standing, who had done a head of Hume.[6] There were few precedents among Stuart's Scottish contemporaries for including a portrait in a first edition. But it was important in a work which would be associated with the events surrounding anti-Catholic activity in Britain to display the author of the views expressed. The authoritative image of 'Dr. Stuart at the age of 35' gave the public a figure from the republic of letters who would justify historically their opposition to reform. As a writer and as an individual Stuart now openly committed himself to the cause with which the work was inevitably connected.

In December 1779 the completed manuscript arrived in London. The three books into which Stuart divided the work covered a volatile half-century of Scottish history. The account began in the year 1517, when 'the conflagration which Martin Luther kindled in Germany ... extend[ed] itself to Scotland' (HR, 4). It concluded in 1561, when 'a convention of the estates gave its sanction to the Presbyterian scheme of government' (HR, 201). Essentially, Stuart told a story of politics and battles. The men and women who led the factions contending for power in Scotland and the military encounters in which they engaged dominate the historical drama. In Book I, the main players are James V, Henry VIII, Cardinal Beaton, the earls of Arran and Lennox and Mary of Guise (the Queen Dowager). The battles of Solway Moss (1542), the siege of St. Andrews (1546), the sieges of Haddington (1547 and 1549) and the battle of Pinkie (1547) receive due, though not minute, consideration. The book concludes with the rise of Mary of Guise to the regency of Scotland in 1553.

Book II contains an account of Mary's tumultuous six-year rule. John Knox and Lord James Stuart (Mary Queen of Scots' half-brother) emerge as the leaders of the 'Congregation'. Stuart recounted their efforts to advance the Reformation and the Queen's attempts to check its progress, vividly describing scenes of destruction and persecution on both sides. These paradoxically humanise the sentiments of the players and show the disruptive consequences for a country that was in the midst of political and religious transition. In Book III Mary Queen of Scots (with her husband, Francis II) and Queen Elizabeth enter the action. Battles at Leith and treaties at Berwick and Edinburgh reveal the extent to which Scotland's future was controlled by a variety of domestic but more often international influences. The successful establishment of the new religion and the abolition of the old, allow Stuart to reflect more generally on events which, 'while they excite, under one aspect, the liveliest transports of joy, create, in another, a mournful sentiment of sympathy and compassion' (HR, 204–5).

After reading the work, Murray found himself far from pleased with Stuart's effort. Together, the three books were far shorter than the bookseller expected; his calculations for the sale price and profits were necessarily lowered. He wrote a sharp reply, telling of his disappointment and asking 'how to publish with any degree of reputation a Quarto pamphlet under the name of a Quarto Volume and by the pompous Title too of a "History of the Reformation of Religion in Scotland". The event gives me concern both on your account and my own.'[7]

Murray's concern was somewhat abated when Stuart sent a substantial 'Collection of the Principal Records concerning the Establishment of the Reformation in Scotland' for inclusion in an appendix. These twenty-three original documents, Stuart explained to the reader, 'shew [sic] the actors in the Reformation of Scotland, under the dominion of great passions ... asserting their natural independency, and vindicating the political rights of their nation' (HR, iv). They are documents of religious and political significance, most of which he took from the works of earlier historians of the period.[8] Topics include an 'Act allowing the Bible to be read in the vulgar tongue' (HR, 209); the four Covenants of the Reformers (HR, 210, 218–19, 222 and 243–4); 'the treaty of peace at Edinburgh' (HR, 256–60); and accounts of the abolition of the mass and the authority of the Pope (HR, 263–6). Unlike a number of the articles in the appendices of the *View of Society* or the *Public Law of Scotland*, all these were in English (or Scots). While they added to the scholarly credibility of the work, the casual reader could easily skip over them as he progressed through the main narrative. This collection lengthened the work by more than a quarter and somewhat abated Murray's genuine concern. But he wrote again asking Stuart to introduce the work with remarks 'giving an account of the manner in which it is to be conducted, and your views in writing it'.[9] Stuart produced a short 'Advertisement' in which he declared his 'earnest endeavour to exert and exercise that precision which is not usually expected from the general historian; and that impartiality which is never to be found in the apologist of a faction' (HR, iii).[10]

The *History* appeared in February 1780 and received favourable reviews in the main London literary journals.[11] Murray was dubious about Stuart's reports that it was selling well in Scotland. Aware that his friend tended to exaggerate the success of his projects he wrote thus to John Bell, the Edinburgh agent for the work, to say that 'your not ordering more copies contradicts the Report more than 1000 tongues asserting it'.[12] Murray believed that the influence of the Edinburgh establishment, who saw in Stuart a bitter antagonist, had again been brought to bear to discredit the work. Two years later Murray told Bell: 'the sale of Dr Stuart's history ... was obstructed by your behaviour'.[13]

The relevance of contemporary events, although less obvious in the *History of the Reformation*, is no less important than in the *Public Law of Scotland*. Anti-Catholic sentiment in general and the Gordon riots in particular form a backdrop to the historical scenes Stuart described. In the months following publication anti-Catholic activity increased in London, and the public read the work as Protestant propaganda. Murray explained to Stuart that 'from the Protestant Association I expect nothing. Nor do I like to publish a book that has occasion for any artifice to push it. The work must appear impartial to avoid risk of censure.'[14] But the publisher was always a prudent marketer and therefore presented a copy on Stuart's behalf to Lord George Gordon. When the London riots broke out in June 1780, Murray told Stuart: 'The late Confusion of this City has been superior to any thing you can conceive. Nor is it yet over.'[15] Such unrest was hardly conducive to bookselling.

In *Barnaby Rudge*, Charles Dickens vividly recorded a scene from the Gordon Riots at Holborn, the part of London a short distance from Fleet Street where Stuart and Murray had spent much of their time:

> At Holborn Bridge, and on Holborn Hill, the confusion was greater than in any other part; for the crowd ... united at that spot and formed a mass so dense, that at every volley the people seemed to fall in heaps ... At this place a large detachment of soldiery were posted, who fired, now up Fleet Market, now up Holborn ... At this place too, several large fires were burning, so that all the terrors of that terrible night seemed to be concentrated in one spot.[16]

Stuart was in Scotland at the time of the Gordon Riots. Still, he supported the English 'No Popery' campaign as he had the Scottish. His low opinion of religious fanatics had been clearly expressed before, but he regarded the political significance of Protestant activism as more important. He viewed the affair as a secular event and as such, he could justify the principles on which the protesters acted, although it was more difficult to condone the violent consequences. Rioting could do little to promote democratic reform. The articulate and determined voice of 'the people', not the violence of the mob, would further the progress of liberty. In an anonymous review written two years after the riots Stuart reflected more coolly on the affair and on the 'gross illiberality of the Protestant Association': 'In a country which prides itself in its philosophy, and which boasts of being free, it is altogether horrid that any idea of intoleration and persecution should be prevalent.'[17]

At the outset of the *History of the Reformation* Stuart acknowledged the interdependence of politics and religion, but he gave precedence to the first as a source of human motivation. It was a struggle between political factions in Scotland and not the will of God, as some church historians claimed, that facilitated the establishment of Protestantism during the reign of James V. Scotland's unstable political situation 'furnished ... a peculiar source of encouragement' to the doctrines of the Reformation (HR, 4). Stuart returned to this point in the only critical note of the work, where he attacked David Hume and 'the despotical maxims he inculcates' in the *History of England*. In Stuart's opinion 'a writer may do complete justice to the actors in the Reformation, without being suspected of fanaticism, or even Christianity' (HR, 123n).

Stuart never questioned the 'natural propriety' (HR, 4) of Protestantism over the imperfections of Catholicism.[18] The attack on Popery with which the *History of the Reformation* opens recalls his remarks in the *English Constitution* and the *View of Society*, where, as a religion and as a political establishment, he denounced the priestcraft of the ancient church for imparting fear and superstition:

> Popery, as a species of religion, when examined by the principles of reason, appears to mock the judgment and capacity of men; and when surveyed as a political establishment, it seems intended to disturb the tranquility of society ... A priest, seated at Rome, claiming the prerogatives of a deity ... is a boundless violation of propriety. Prelates ... with interests opposite to those of the community of which they are members ... may justly be considered as an institution in hostility to all the maxims of civil government. (HR, 2)

An anti-Popish tradition was especially deep-rooted in Scotland, where there were few Catholics and a powerful reformed church.

Stuart's remarks connect the events of the sixteenth century with the anti-Catholic sentiment of his own day. He noted, for example, that in 1551 laws were enacted to keep people in 'the true and catholic faith, by forfeiting to the crown the moveable goods of all persons who ... should delay to reconcile themselves to the holy church' (HR, 70), which implied that the legal establishment of Catholic religious freedom in the mid-eighteenth century might lead to the repetition of such draconian legislation.

Riots themselves were a significant feature during the Reformation as they were in the later period.[19] John Murray drew a more overt parallel when he wrote of rising Protestant activism in 1780: 'It would appear that the bold and daring spirit of fanaticism wants only an object to rouse it to appear at this day as intrepidly as it did in the days of the beautious Mary.'[20] On the whole, Stuart's narrative contains an excess of persecution scenes and of violence wrought upon Catholics and Protestants alike. In the descriptions of the first Scottish martyrs to the Reformation he evoked sympathy for those who died in defence of their faith, but balanced this view with the reminder that some martyrs were too ready to lay down their lives for their opinions (HR, 44). Scenes of religious enthusiasm, scattered throughout, read like fictional vignettes and offer a contrast to the main political narrative. The burning of the palace and abbey at Scoon by the supporters of the Reformation is one example:

> It was in vain that their leaders interested themselves to save them. Even the rhetoric of John Knox was here ineffectual. An enraged multitude set fire to these stately edifices; and while the flames were ascending, an old woman was heard to exclaim, 'See how the judgments of God are just! ... This place, in my memory, has been nothing else but a sink of whoredom.'   (HR, 125)

Initially, Stuart focused on the policies of James V and, to a lesser extent, on his English rival Henry VIII. He portrayed James as an uncertain ruler, unable to play off the power of the nobility and the clergy either to his own advantage or on behalf of Scotland. The result of his ill-conceived policies was the defeat by the English at Solway Moss in 1542. Shortly after this event, the despairing king died, leaving as the heir to the throne the infant Mary Queen of Scots.

At this point in the narrative Stuart paused to reflect on the character of James. He had explained the importance of this technique a few years before when he commented in the *Edinburgh*

Magazine and Review that the historian's object is to 'exhibit the true character of every personage who appears in his composition [and to] discover the utmost care and penetration in investigating the most retired and latent motives of action' (EMR, V, 35).[21] Stuart's use of the character portrait emphasises the degree to which the examples of classical writers suited his literary approach. The Elder Seneca in the *Suasoriae* explained that 'whenever historians relate the death of a great man they ... give a summary of his whole life and pronounce a kind of funeral eulogy'.[22] Tacitus, Stuart's most important classical model, also contributed to the formulation of the historical obituary.

In these passages Stuart offered creative and deliberately judgemental reflections. By setting before the reader the qualities of an historical figure, without the necessity of reconciling contrary factors, he recreated an enduring, if paradoxical, image of the character.[23] Stuart's portrait of the king fits well within this model. He marked James' greatest fault as 'the respect he entertained for Cardinal Beaton and the clergy' (HR, 24), even though previously he had offered sound political reasons why James sought their support. In such comments the analytical eye of the historian freely assumes an intimate and retrospective view of the king and his times. James 'forgot that a good sovereign will not persevere in supporting ancient systems of theology, when they have become too gross and absurd for the understandings of his people' (HR, 24). Here Stuart added his own judgement to the historical record, making the point that any sympathy or association with Popery could not be condoned.

Stuart's account of the regencies of the earls of Arran and Lennox, which follows, demonstrates the extent to which the hope of political gain undermined seemingly steadfast religious principles (HR, 33–4). The idea of civic virtue as a force which promotes righteous behaviour by aligning the interest of the individual with society, seemed hardly to exist at this period when feudal institutions were in decay but modern commercial polity not yet in place. In such uncertain social and political circumstances, a strong leader was necessary to guide Scotland, but as Mary was a mere infant, Scottish, French and English factions made the country a political battleground. In the struggle for the regency, Mary of Guise eventually triumphed. At this point in the narrative (April 1554) the first book of the *History of the Reformation* draws to a conclusion.

The period from the beginning of the queen's regency in 1554 to her deposition by the Lords of Congregation in October 1559 makes up the second book. In contrast to the earl of Arran, she was capable of prudent leadership; and, as Stuart remarked, 'even her indifference on the subject of religion might, in a political view, be esteemed a virtue in times of controversy and disputation' (HR, 76–7). Ultimately, however, her close association with France and her unfamiliarity with the 'manners and genius' (HR, 79) of the Scots led to dissent and disruption. Following Buchanan, Stuart condemned her attempt to form a standing army by levying a tax on landowners, a plan which was antithetical to the mixed form of government which characterised Scotland. As if speaking to the queen herself, he explained that such a measure, if politically expeditious, threatened the liberty of the people:

> No necessity existed for a humiliating taxation and for bands of mercenaries ... Soldiers, allured with pay, had no sentiment of honour. It was a wild infatuation to confide in them in preference to men who fought for every thing that was most dear to them, their country, their reputation, their families, their fortunes ... From such innovations the most destructive calamities might proceed. They respected their constitution as sacred; and in its stability they acknowledged a decisive proof of the wisdom with which it had been framed.   (HR, 80–81)

Stuart employed republican rhetoric like a true militia man. The refusal of the people to accede to the queen's plan could serve as a reminder that a similarly independent martial spirit was still alive in 1780. Republicanism, conceived within the limits of a constitutional monarchy, was more than a hobby horse for Stuart and assertions that political authority belongs to the people are scattered through the work.

Stuart's narrative of sixteenth-century Scottish history is set in accounts of the increasingly violent activities of the reformers and their Catholic opponents. Emotive scenes in which 'the populace broke out in acts of outrage and violence' (HR, 86) characterised Scotland both in 1560 and 1779. In other places he related the more prudent, legal methods by which the reformers gained the sanction of the people. More often their influence extended beyond the bounds of 'natural propriety'. To advance their ideas (and themselves) they engaged in activities contrary to the tenets they were espousing:

> Design and art concurred with piety, novelty, and religion. The leaders ... encouraged the vehemence of the multitude.

The covenant to establish a new form of religion extended from the few to the many. Amidst the turbulence and discord of the passions, and interests of men, the soft voice of humanity and reason was not heard. The sharp point of the sword, not the calm exertion of inquiry, was to decide the disputes of theology. (HR, 99–100)

Stuart's language reflects an idiosyncratic combination of eighteenth-century ideas and literary conventions. The use of words which define the nature of human conduct, such as 'passion', 'interest' and 'reason', in combination with more emotive phrases, such as 'the soft voice of humanity' and the 'sharp point of the sword', mark a movement from the more dispassionate prose of Hume and Robertson to a more evocative brand of historical writing. By emphasising the language of the heart more than the language of reason at critical points in the narrative, Stuart sought to narrow the gap not only of understanding but of sympathy between the past and the present. His readers could imagine themselves transported in time and feel the spirit of historical characters within themselves.

Stuart's account of the activities of John Knox in Book II demonstrates his approach. Knox's return to Scotland heightened an already volatile situation. He 'inspirited' (one of Stuart's favourite verbs) the people into rebellion: 'Putting their swords into their hands, it was now their business to build up the fabric of their religion, or to fall like men' (HR, 119). Stuart viewed rather pessimistically the human condition in the time of Knox, as in his own day. He knew that philosophy might explain human behaviour, but it could do little to change or improve the scenes in which men and women acted. Religion, though a potentially beneficial force, was often detrimental to society.

In a manner which recalls the Gothic imagery found in such novels as Horace Walpole's *Castle of Otranto* (1765) or William Beckford's *Vathek* (1786), Stuart described the havoc which spread across Scotland as the reformers exerted themselves against the ancient church and events built up to a decisive military confrontation. The destruction of the Abbey of Cambuskenneth, unable to 'preserve itself from their fury', followed, and 'the gloomy Protestant walked over its ruins' (HR, 125). In another descriptive passage he wrote of the Romish religion: 'An immense and disproportioned structure falling to pieces, covered the ground with unseemly ruins.' (HR, 194.) The Gothic ruin is a fitting metaphor to describe the decline of feudal society.[24] Stuart pieced together

these fragments of an historical image much as he brought historical evidence into a unified narrative. He extended the metaphor to
introduce James Stuart, who rose up 'to erect the banner of the
Reformation upon the ruins of Popery' (HR, 142). The successes
which attended this man's actions Stuart acknowledged but criticised the means by which he achieved them. An attempt to understand the motivating principles of human behaviour led to this
judgement:

> The love of liberty ... was not, in him, the effect of patriotism,
> but of pride; his zeal for religion was a political virtue; and
> under the appearance of openness and sincerity, he could
> conceal more securely his purposes. Power was the idol
> which he worshipped; and he was ready to acquire it by
> methods most criminal.   (HR, 138)

On the other side, he acknowledged James Stuart's importance:
'To his talents, his genius, and his resources, Scotland is indebted
for the Reformation. But by this memorable atchievement [sic], he
meant nothing more than to advance himself in the road to greatness' (HR, 139).

The Protestant success in deposing the queen regent without
royal sanction was an act unprecedented in Scottish history. But
Gilbert Stuart, appealing to the 'democratical genius of the Scottish constitution' (HR, 148), justified it by referring to later examples in history (such as the execution of Charles I) when the
people, 'making [their monarch] a sacrifice to justice, and an
instruction to posterity, conduct him from the throne to the scaf-
fold' (HR, 148). On this note, similar in its defiant tone to the
conclusion of the Isle of Man history, Book II ends.

In the final book Stuart surveyed the beginning of a new era of
close interaction between Scotland and England. The reformers,
in their uncertain political state, turned to Queen Elizabeth, the
monarch of a powerful Protestant country, in the hope that she
might aid them against rival Catholic interests. They emphasised
the threat which France posed to England and insisted that only
'the extirpation of idolatry, and the preservation of their civil
rights motivated them to action' (HR, 155). The signing of the
Treaty of Berwick confirmed the mutuality of the English and
Scottish Protestant interest and effected a complete victory over
the queen regent.

The queen died shortly after her fall from power. Stuart's portrait of this woman is the most detailed in the work. While he
extolled the virtues of her character, he censured her political

attachment to France as 'her fatal error'.[25] The description is more sentimental, more finely drawn, than his male character portraits. Such topics as sexual morality fall within the bounds of 'natural propriety' and provided the reader with a moment of respite from the turmoil of the times: 'Though a widow, at an age when the soft passions have their full power, no suspicion was ever entertained of her chastity' (HR, 177). Stuart's interest in sexual morality became even more evident in the *History of Mary Queen of Scots*, especially in relation to Elizabeth and Mary. Such portraits, wrote a contemporary reviewer, 'we know to have been reprobated by some, as the *Splendida Paccata* of modern historians. But let us not listen to the voice of fastidious prudery ... It is the natural effusion of the mind, on the final dismission of a great actor.'[26] Stuart appealed not only to the morality of his readers but to their sensual nature. By sketching the personalities of historical figures who otherwise exist only as part of a scene, he made history relevant and alive.

In more sober prose, Stuart described the political events which led to the establishment of Protestant ecclesiastical government. He acknowledged the larger good of the Reformation in Scotland, but voiced regret that in the violent events surrounding its establishment, and especially in the severe punishment imposed upon Catholics, the enthusiastic will of the masses triumphed over reason and virtue:

> This fierceness ... did not suit the generosity of victory; and while an excuse is sought for it in the perfidiousness of the Romish priesthood, it escapes not the observation of the most superficial historians, that these severities were exactly those of which the Protestants had complained so loudly, and with so much justice. The human mind, in the warmth of tumult and agitation reconciles itself to violence of every kind ... The utter contempt and abhorrence of persecution, and the philosophical and unbounded toleration of opinion, have never distinguished the practice of nations, and are never to be expected from them.   (HR, 192–3)

Here Stuart voiced his approval of religious toleration, at the same time pointing out that even when the nature of society was understood, little could be done to remedy its faults.

The remarks with which the work concludes, offer a character portrait of the Reformation itself. Stuart was quick to associate its doctrines with the 'existence of civil liberty' and to praise its leaders for giving 'permanent security to the political constitution

of their state' (HR, 205). In essence the Reformation was a beneficial event. He also expressed popular fears about the threat of the
establishment of Catholicism as the state religion in his own day:

> In this enlightened age of philosophy and reflection it is
> difficult indeed to be conceived that any serious attempts to
> establish [Catholicism] shall be made; yet, if by some fatality
> in human affairs, such endeavours should actually be tried,
> and should succeed, it may be concluded…that all the
> boasted freedom which the Reformation has fostered would
> then perish for ever … Men would … renounce their natural,
> their religious, and their political rights; and be contented to
> creep upon the earth, to lick its dust, and to adore the ca-
> prices and the power of a tyrant.   (HR, 206)

William Robertson alluded to these emotive remarks in the
context of his own support for Catholic toleration: 'What above all
was detestable, at a time when I was fighting for a cause so sacred
as religious liberty, [Stuart] concluded his History of the Reformation with reflections evidently intended to expose me to popular
odium and personal danger.'[27] The distance of the events may
have led Robertson to exaggerate the effect of these remarks or to
conflate them with the overt criticisms against him at the end of
the *Public Law of Scotland*. Stuart had made no pretence of treating
Robertson with 'natural propriety' either in his conjectural inquiries or narrative histories.

The reception of the *History of the Reformation*, although modest,
encouraged Stuart to continue on the path he had set out in the
work. While the chaos caused by the Gordon Riots lessened,
Stuart remained in Scotland to prepare a continuation of his narrative of Scottish history. He was finally able to pursue his genuine
calling. The product of his labour, the *History of Scotland from the
Establishment of the Reformation till the Death of Mary Queen of Scots*,
appeared in 1782. It was offered to the public as an alternative to
Robertson's account of the period.

Since her execution in 1587 histories of the reign of Mary Queen
of Scots have been written by apologists and accusers. Over a four
hundred year period numerous plays, poems and novels, as well
as operas and works of art, have appeared in which she is the
central figure. Mary has become a colourful and contradictory
character. A Catholic martyr, a romantic heroine, an adulterous
wife, and a powerful monarch, she is likewise a symbol for Scotland as the country emerged 'from rudeness to refinement' (VS,
title). To this day she continues to be the subject of historical,

literary and artistic expression and a figure of general wonder. The renewed interest in Mary in the mid-eighteenth century gave impetus to further literary renderings of her story throughout the nineteenth century: Scott, Blake, Swinburne, Tennyson, Schiller and others conveyed the captivating interest of her life in their writings. Gilbert Stuart's *History of Mary Queen of Scots* has an important place in this Marian revival.

There were few educated men or women in Scotland in the eighteenth century who did not take an interest in Mary's reign. Hume's account in the Tudor volumes of the *History of England* (1759) and Robertson's *History of Scotland* (also 1759) achieved immense popularity and became centrepieces of Enlightenment historical writing.[28] Stuart sought to supplant their works with one not only more favourable to the queen but written in a different manner.

Even before her execution, Mary became a convenient vehicle for expressing a range of opinions. James Phillips, in *Images of a Queen* (1964) sets out the two contradictory characterisations of Mary and warns the reader that neither bears a close relation to the truth: 'One is the image of a sinister and adulterous murderess constantly plotting with every Machiavellian trick to destroy England and Protestantism. The other is that of a supremely beautiful woman, a devoted wife and mother, and an innocent martyr for the faith in which she died.'[29]

The production of anti-Marian literature began essentially with George Buchanan's *Detectio Mariae Reginae* (1571). Censure of Mary gradually decreased in the early decades of the seventeenth century as the political significance of her reign, deposition and execution lessened and the crowns of Scotland and England united under her son James. From this time her image began to improve until the accession of William and Mary. Then, Stuart wrote, it became 'the fashion of consequence to treat the House of Stuart with indignity' (MQS, I, 437n).[30] In 1760 Samuel Johnson observed:

> It has now been fashionable for near half a century to defame and vilify the house of *Stuart*, and to exalt and magnify the reign of *Elizabeth*. The *Stuarts* have found few apologists, for the dead cannot pay for praise; and who will, without reward, oppose the tide of popularity?[31]

Johnson's Jacobite sentiments were shared by many, including Stuart's mentor, Thomas Ruddiman. The appearance of his comprehensive edition of George Buchanan's works in 1715 spawned numerous controversies because he condemned Buchanan 'as an historian, who threw out reproaches against his sovereign, and benefactress, instead of recording truth, and of teaching morals'.[32] Ruddiman, like Johnson, disapproved of the revolutionary settlement, a fact which put him in the camp of Marian vindicators and led him to support the Jacobite cause. Gilbert Stuart was not a Jacobite, but the influence of his 'much esteemed relation' (MQS, II, 177), was significant. He therefore followed Ruddiman in condemning Buchanan on political grounds.

> His admiration of tyrannicide, and his contempt of royalty, betray a propensity to licentiousness and faction ... His activity against Mary ... was in a strain of the most shameless corruption; and the virulence with which he endeavoured to defame her by his writings, was most audacious and criminal. They involve the complicated charge of ingratitude, rebellion, and perjury.   (MQS, II, 176)

Yet in almost every other context Stuart saw in Buchanan a model for emulation. The character portrait of the historian, which appears near the end of the *History of Mary Queen of Scots*, reads like an autobiographical portrait of Stuart himself. It is speculation whether he wrote with a degree of self-conscious reflection. Nevertheless a few examples suggest a correspondence that illuminates his own character. Stuart wrote of Buchanan: 'Violent in his nature, he embraced his friends with ardour ... Against his enemies he was animated with an atrocity of revenge (MQS, II, 174–5). Stuart's interactions were much the same, and this polarity of emotion increased in the course of his life. 'From the uncertain condition of his fortune, or from his attachment to study, he kept himself free from the restraint of marriage; but ... he was no enemy to beauty and to love, and must have known the tumults and the langours of voluptuousness' (MQS, II, 174). 'A malignant keenness glanced in [Buchanan's] eye; and the persecutions of priests, and the oppressions of misfortune, served to augment the natural fretfulness of his disposition, and gave an edge to his spleen. His conversation was gay, ingenious, and satyrical' (MQS, II, 175). Stuart was also animated by conflict and his attacks were often directed at clerics. Many of the disappointments he suffered were the consequence of such encounters failing to have their intended effect. Among companions, as Thomas Somerville remarked, he was the centre of attention and source of entertainment.

Buchanan's 'zeal for the interests of mankind is worthy of the highest praise; yet in many places it is too eccentric and fierce, and too little under the controul of knowledge and ability' (MQS, I, 263n). As a political writer, Stuart upheld the voice of 'the people' against the authority of government, but at times so emphatically that rhetoric overshadowed principle. As if to anticipate the posthumous reputation he himself would have, Stuart remarked: 'Buchanan was pursued with reproaches while in his grave. Many writers have described him as a monster of impiety, as habitually besotted with wine, and as deluded with women' (MQS, II, 174). Yet with all these similarities, the impression Stuart left with his reader is that of Buchanan's relentless persecution of Mary, for which he, as the vindicator of the queen, could offer no apology.

Buchanan was not the only historian in whom Stuart found a mixture of qualities both worthy of emulation and necessary to challenge. More than any member of the house of Stuart, Mary was 'disturbed and persecuted in her grave by the most mercenary of all human creatures, the adorers of tyranny' (MQS, I, 438n). Stuart used the phrase 'adorers of tyranny' in his conjectural inquiries to describe those historians he believed were guided more by the prospect of court patronage than by historical truth. As a Scot he revitalised Mary's image on patriotic, though not overtly political grounds. As a Whig he vindicated her actions to an audience for whom Toryism and support for the Stuarts were no longer synonymous. As a writer he found in Mary a story the retelling of which demanded a new and tragically conceived narrative.

Stuart saw the reign of Mary re-emerge as a subject of contemporary political relevance and literary entertainment. The recovery of material relating to the period also encouraged historical revisionism. Numerous references in the histories of Hume, Robertson and Stuart indicate the importance of recently published evidence.[33] Of course, the additional information did not mean that at last an accurate and impartial account of Mary's reign could be written, and inevitably, politics and religion continued to influence writers. Whigs and Tories; Hanoverians and Jacobites; Presbyterians, Episcopalians and Catholics; Scotsmen, Englishmen and Frenchmen all had something to gain by promoting or suppressing certain accounts. A writer's claim to impartiality did not exempt him from party, religious or personal bias; it often was a rhetorical ploy, and consequently a warning of tendentiousness. Stuart was no exception in this regard.

After Ruddiman, Walter Goodall opened a new era of Marian

literature with his *Examination of the Letters, said to be Written by
Mary Queen of Scots* (1754). Goodall rectified many errors in earlier
accounts by making use of newly found documents relating to
Mary's reign to demonstrate that the famous 'Casket Letters' had
been forged. The letters between Mary and James Hepburn, the
Earl of Bothwell, were the primary evidence against the queen in
the murder of her husband, Lord Darnley. Though excessive in his
praise, Goodall established the precedent that a judgement of
Mary should be made on the basis of the authenticity of the letters.
Echoing the words of Macbeth, Goodall insisted that 'whatever
has been said, to the disparagement of that Princess, or whoever
said it, signifies nothing: For Mary ... so far excelled all other
sovereign Princes who ever yet appeared on the face of the earth,
that ... all the arts and contrivances of her numerous and malicious enemies have not availed to fix upon her one crime.'[34]

The initial popularity of Goodall's panegyric prompted him to
begin writing a full-scale life of Mary. Just how much of this
project he completed is not known, but it was rumoured at the
time by the antiquary George Paton that Gilbert Stuart 'picked
from Mr. Goodall's notes' in preparing the *History of Mary Queen of
Scots*. These notes, however, have not been traced.[35] Goodall's 1754
effort met with formidable opposition when William Robertson
presented his *History of Scotland* five years later. This account of
Mary, with its engaging narrative, systematic reasoning and
moral attitude, represented a generic shift away from the more
antiquarian and controversial tradition of Ruddiman and
Goodall. His calm and reassuring tone stands in contrast to the
exhortation of Goodall, which even Gilbert Stuart found 'excessive, and even romantic' (MQS, I, 383). Though sympathetic to
Mary as a suffering figure, Robertson asserted her guilt in the
murder of Darnley. Partly in response to Goodall but more, as he
said, 'to assist others in forming some judgment concerning the
facts in dispute', he appended to the *History* 'A Critical Dissertation concerning the Murder of King Henry, and the Genuineness
of the Queen's Letters to Bothwell'. If more impartial than the
main narrative, its effect nevertheless was to reconfirm the guilty
verdict. On the other main point of historical contention – Mary's
role in the conspiracy with Anthony Babington to depose Queen
Elizabeth – Robertson adjudged the Scottish queen to be innocent.

As a young man Gilbert Stuart had admired Robertson's work,
but he began to see it as yet another apology by the Protestant
clergy, not only for the leaders of the Reformation but for English

dominion in his own day. Then Stuart went further, rejecting the view implicit in Robertson's account that Anglo-Scottish relations should be described in 'glowing terms' when in fact the situation was far from ideal.[36] Though both men criticised the superstition and corruption of the Catholic church, Stuart refused to condone the zeal and intolerance of the Protestants in their efforts to establish new doctrines. He followed Hume in censuring the activities of those zealous Scottish Protestants who effected Mary's deposition and concurred with Hume's remarks to Hugh Blair that the 'godly Strain' in Robertson's work 'most expos'd [it] to Criticism'.[37]

Hume's account of Mary's reign appeared just months after Robertson's. Although it was only part of a larger history of the Tudors, and of Elizabeth's reign specifically, attention was mainly focused on his treatment of Mary. It was a matter of disappointment, however well concealed, that Robertson's *History* was more popular.[38] Hume was convinced of Mary's guilt in the Darnley-Bothwell affair. His investigation into the evidence surrounding the Babington Conspiracy, led him to return another guilty verdict. If to some extent sympathetic to Mary, though less so than Robertson, Hume's private feeling revealed in a remark to Lord Elibank that Mary was 'an old Strumpet, who had been dead and rotten near two hundred Years' is not altogether obscured in his work.[39]

In February 1760, shortly after the publication of Robertson's and Hume's accounts, William Tytler entered the controversy in defence of Mary. In the *Enquiry into the Evidence Produced ... against Mary*, he refuted a list of arguments put forward by Robertson and Hume. Tytler generally followed Goodall's argument, but as it was the subject of current controversy he enjoyed considerably more success. Both Robertson and Hume were displeased by Tytler's 'belligerency and unfairness'.[40] Hume, who rarely confronted his adversaries publicly, asserted in the 1770 edition of his *History* that the *Enquiry* was 'composed of such scandalous artifices; and from this instance, the reader may judge of the candour, fair dealing, veracity, and good manners of the Enquirer'.[41] The debate continued into the 1770s but resolved only a few minor points of historical argument. Hume, and later Robertson, did silently rectify some errors noted by Tytler, but neither moved away from his opinion about the guilt of the Queen of Scots. Robertson, in a private letter to David Dalrymple explained his approach: 'I mean not to take the field as a controversial writer, or to state myself in opposition to any antagonist. Whenever I am satisfied that I have fallen into error I shall quietly and without reluctance correct it.'[42]

Stuart saw in Tytler a scholar who had proved Hume and Robertson wrong on a number of facts. The *Enquiry* cleared the way for a new narrative of Mary's reign. In one of the few critical notes in the *History of Mary Queen of Scots*, Stuart aligned himself with Goodall and Tytler in 'refuting the able and hypothetic partiality' of Hume and in 'exposing the feeble and unargumentative pertinacity' of Robertson (MQS, I, 383–4n). He resisted the temptation of a full-blown attack on Robertson and instead, referred the reader to the *Public Law of Scotland*, where

> I have inquired attentively into the real abilities and merit of this writer ... stated the notions he inculcates ... with entire impartiality, and opposed them with argument ... While I have found no reason to retract the doctrines I advanced in it, I have discovered nothing that is too powerful, expressive, or unbecoming in the strain and manner with which I distinguished it.   (MQS, I, 385n)

These are the only references to either of his rival historians in the whole of the work. It was prudent of Stuart to leave these and let his *History* stand on its own merits. However, he remarked to the Earl of Buchan that he had hundreds of notes listing the errors in Robertson's work which he was tempted to publish.[43]

The Marian controversy appealed to Stuart's ambitious nature, while Mary's story captured his imagination. Much as the Roman Empire offered Gibbon ample scope for his innovative work, Stuart found in her a subject which contained the materials for a new way of writing history. His systematic examination of the evidence led him to conclude that the queen was innocent of the charges of murder and conspiracy. The injustice of her imprisonment and execution made her both an object of sympathy and an evocation of tragedy. There was tension between 'Tragic historiography' and the Enlightenment requirement of an historical narrative to be detached and sceptical which Stuart did not resolve in either direction. Nor did he neutralise it by an appeal to absolute morality (religious or otherwise). Instead it became a measure of Mary's own irreconcilable predicament and his own pessimism about the possibility of progress or justice.

The *History of Mary Queen of Scots* appeared in two nicely printed quarto volumes in the summer of 1782. Priced in boards at £1 and 5 shillings, it was by no means a cheap book. At over 800 pages it was about four times the size of the *History of the Reforma-*

tion. Stuart divided the work into eight books and followed an essentially chronological plan from the birth of Mary in 1542 to her death in 1587. Behind this ordering of events lay more subtle organisational themes. Rivalry is one of these. Mary's encounters with her half-brother, James Stuart (the Earl of Moray) dominate the first part of the work, while her relationship with Queen Elizabeth assumes prominence in the second. Rivalry also manifests itself on a social level, in the conflict between the monarchy and the nobility, as Stuart expanded his narrative of political events to include a general view of society. From these interactions, the Queen of Scots emerges as the heroine of the work. Moray and Elizabeth become guilty, power-hungry conspirators. Stuart imparted to other figures, such as Buchanan, Knox and Darnley, aspects which are less clearly defined. He reserved the role of villain for Bothwell. Others may be villanous, but Stuart portrayed this man as villainy incarnate.

Stuart's interest in the nature of the Scottish feudal kingdom is no less obvious in this work than in the *Public Law of Scotland* or the *History of the Reformation*. A series of minority reigns through the sixteenth century enabled the factious nobility to control political affairs. In England and France, by contrast, a powerful monarch made his court the centre of government and exerted his authority throughout his dominions. Stuart had surveyed the general causes which had produced this change in the government, laws and manners of European states before; in the *History of Mary Queen of Scots* he investigated the affairs of a country at a specific period, in the midst of such social change. A desire to write for 'the many' rather than for 'the few', the prospect of profit, the challenge to Robertson and Hume and a genuine interest in Mary were Stuart's primary motives. He aimed to describe the principles of change more precisely than Robertson, for whom 'rebellion follows rebellion, intrigue follows intrigue with no indication of successive stages of evolution and degeneration'.[44] Stuart sought to do more, and in a manner which would still appeal to a wide audience.

From a collection of contradictory evidence, he uncovered the principles which motivated individuals to action in the midst of political and religious turmoil. It was not enough to observe that the establishment of Protestantism in 1560 ultimately benefited the Scots. The events which led to that end were of interest. For example, he remarked of the New Covenant of the reformers:

This measure so formidable in itself, and so pernicious as a precedent, at a time when no real danger appears to have threatened the Protestant religion, ought to be considered as a factious device to excite the terrors of the people, and to inflame them against the administration and the person of their sovereign. It was a most wanton insult of government, and it was to lead to other insults and enormities.

(MQS, I, 53)

By rejecting the legitimacy of a religious justification for what he considered to be essentially political change, Stuart set himself against the traditional view of Scottish church history. His condemnation of the reformers, moreover, provided the background for the scenes in which Mary commenced her reign.

Stuart contended that when Mary arrived in Scotland, 'the majority of the people were confident of the good intentions of their sovereign, and placed the blame for the turmoil which ensued upon 'discontented nobles who were animated by the dishonourable motives of hatred, envy, and ambition' (MQS, I, 112–13). Further to complicate matters for Mary, vocal churchmen like John Knox objected to her own private Catholic worship and aroused public antipathy against her. Stuart himself criticised the superstitious practices of the Catholics even though his heroine was one herself, and her involvement in plots to re-establish Catholicism in England was an error he could not but condemn: 'In an unhappy and calamitous moment she became a party to a league the most disgraceful to virtue that had ever been devised by human craftiness'(MQS, I 126). Catholicism was a tragic flaw, but at the same time Mary's religious devotion showed model fortitude.

Mary's claim to the English throne, when 'a bull from Rome had declared Elizabeth to be the offspring of an illegal commerce' (MQS, I, 8), led the English queen to defend the threat to her power and the stability of the reformed religion in Britain and thus made the women natural rivals. In the first book of the *History* Stuart sketched a preliminary portrait of Elizabeth in the context of these affairs:

> These affronts made a deep impression upon her. It was her nature to feel with sensibility, and her hatreds did not diminish with time. To repress the ambition of the Scottish Queen, and to give check to the encroaching spirit of the court of France, she had joined her power to that of the Protestants of Scotland, and had enabled them to overturn Popery.

(MQS, I, 8)

Mary's claim 'drew the respect of all the princes of Europe' (MQS, I, 15), and therefore she rejected Elizabeth's plan to have her ratify the Treaty of Edinburgh, thus renouncing any right to the English throne in Elizabeth's lifetime. The intrigues in which both queens involved themselves, aggravated their personal rivalry and brought turmoil to the affairs of Scotland.

The dramatic murders of Mary's court favourite David Riccio and of her husband Darnley provide the intensity of the narrative of the first part of the *History*. These events threatened and ultimately ruined the queen's prospects of political stability. They precipitated a course of events that resulted in her deposition, imprisonment and execution. The murder of Riccio at Holyrood Palace by Darnley and other noblemen, in the presence of the queen, is among the most famous events of her reign. Stuart graphically described how he 'was torn and mangled with fifty-six wounds' (MQS, I, 136). Through the horror of the scene, however, he focused on Mary's response: 'In these agitated and miserable moments she did not lose herself in the helplessness of sorrow. The loftiness of her spirit communicated relief to her, and wiping away her tears, she exclaimed, that it was not now a season for lamentation, but for revenge' (MQS, I, 136–7). This description recalls the evocative picture Stuart quoted from Tacitus of barbarian women who 'soon dismiss their lamentations and tears, but slowly their sorrow and regret' (VS, 288).[45]

Stuart next addressed the topic of Mary's rumoured adultery with Riccio. In contradiction to the majority of seventeenth and eighteenth-century accounts, he affirmed that 'it is a wild absurdity to conceive that a Queen so young and so beautiful would submit to the caresses of deformity and old age. A common prostitute must be brought to endure this misfortune' (MSQ, I, 133n)[46] In a comment of a similar flavour, but concerning the sexual morality of Elizabeth, Stuart highlighted the differences between the two queens. He drew a Gothic portrait in which Elizabeth is seen to be an uncivilised creature, physically repulsive and morally depraved:

> In the main there is little reason to doubt the corrupt manners of Elizabeth ... Amidst the infamous calumnies which this princess was solicitous to fix upon the Queen of Scots, it must excite the highest indignation to consider her own contempt of chastity, and the unprincipled licentiousness of her private life. Even when palsied with age she was yet burning with unquenchable desires, and vain of her haggard

and cadaverous form, sought to allure to her many lovers.
(MQS, II, 211n)
It is a curious reversal of roles to show the so-called Virgin Queen
as a violator of the sexual manners of the age; and Mary, the
reputed 'Strumpet', as a model of virtue. By this shift Stuart
awakened his reader to the revolution in historical understanding
he was presenting. Hume offered rather more sober reflections on
Elizabeth's morality but similarly concluded that 'her extreme
fondness for Leicester, Hatton, and Essex ... render her chastity
very much to be suspected'.[47] Robertson adopted an opposite view
but made less of an issue of the subject.[48]

Although Stuart rejected the idea of a sexual alliance with
Riccio, he by no means denied Mary's sexuality. With Darnley she
surrendered to 'the bewitching tumults of joy' (MQS, I, 128) and
with Bothwell 'the seductions of softness and flattery ... was
stiring up in her bosom that playsome and dangerous pleasure
with which women, even of the most unconquerable chastity,
delight to enjoy' (MQS, I, 211–12). The frequent place of sexual
references in the *History* has a parallel in the contemporary novels
of romance. Stuart's use of excessively colourful language plays
on the moral (and immoral) sensibilities of his readers. Such
passages humanise, if in a somewhat forbidden sense, remote
historical figures, who in other respects are either canonised or
defamed. They contrast with the reasoned legalistic narrative he
employed when deliberating upon more general points of historical contention.

Stuart acknowledged Elizabeth's leadership abilities and described her political policies with objectivity. He built upon
Hume's characterisation of the queen as both 'a rational being,
placed in authority, and entrusted with the government of mankind' and as 'an excellent hypocrite'.[49] Robertson lauded Elizabeth
to a far greater degree, although he did accept that 'no apology can
be offered for her behaviour to Queen Mary; a scene of dissimulation without necessity; and of severity beyond example'.[50] Stuart's
descriptions are often defamatory and sensationalised. Duplicity
and deceitfulness, insincerity, insensibility and imprudence are
words most often attached to the English queen. Many of the
marginal notes which guide the reader are pejorative references to
these unfavourable characteristics.[51]

He also highlighted the contrary features of Mary's character,
such as her moderation, magnanimity, candour and prudence. He
did not deny that she engaged in intrigues, and even referred to

moments when 'the two Queens exasperate mutually their passions and disgusts' (MQS, I, 439). But as the narrative progresses
he focused on the indignities to which Mary was exposed and on
her suffering and distress generally. The description of events
leading up to her marriage with Darnley shows the mixture of
passion and determination in her character:

> The charm of his [Darnley's] accomplishments, the sensibili-
> ties of the Queen, and the unguarded openness of mirth and
> joy, were more powerful than intrigues and negociations.
> Love stole into her heart, and effaced every favourable
> thought of all her former suitors.
>
> Struck with the insolence, the selfishness, and the insincer-
> ity of the Queen of England [who opposed the match], and
> disgusted with the dealys in which she had been involved,
> Mary felt a burst of the keenest indignation. Yielding to her
> resentments, she resolved to be abused no longer by the
> tricks of negociation; giving way to the impulses of tender-
> ness, she determined to take an early opportunity of carrying
> her wishes into execution.   (MQS, 85–6)

Although the match seemed promising, Darnley's true nature was
soon apparent. Perfidiousness, levity and imprudence are the
terms often used by Stuart. In her husband Mary found only a
rival who from the start, was envious of her authority. Consequently, their first year of marriage was fraught with difficulties.
Darnley's object was to attain the Crown Matrimonial, by which,
in the event of Mary's death, he would assume the Scottish throne.
'The lust of dominion', Stuart remarked, 'was his ruling appetite;
and the prudence of the Queen had excluded him from power'
(MQS, I, 128). He conspired with the Earl of Moray and other
dissatisfied nobles to overthrow her and they openly killed Riccio,
a man whom they believed had gained too much of Mary's political (and sexual) favour.

The question of who planned the subsequent murder of
Darnley, however, was more doubtful. Stuart initially mentioned
the popular idea that Mary conspired in the act because she was in
love with Bothwell, but later retracted this argument and even
suggested that she and Darnley had become reconciled (MQS, I,
186). Having considered the reasons for believing Mary was
guilty, he defended her innocence. By accepting Bothwell's aid
against Darnley and his faction and then marrying him, Mary
acted imprudently. But Stuart opposed the view held by Hume
and Robertson, and generally accepted today, that this scandalous

marriage was the primary cause of her troubles.[52] Like Goodall and Tytler before him, he argued that Mary was coerced into marriage by Bothwell, who was himself a pawn of the rebellious Protestant nobility. Stuart also affirmed that the 'Casket Letters', which implicated her in the murder of Darnley, were forged. His sentimental and sensual description of Mary's condition at the time of her marriage reads more like contemporary fiction than historical fact.

> She was under the dominion of a young and agreeable, a daring, and an unprincipled profligate; skillful in seduction and accustomed to impose upon female frailty; who could read in her look the emotions of her heart, and the secret workings of forbidden desires; allure her mind to give itself up to the power of the imagination and the senses; take a pastime even in her pangs of remorse, and make them act as a zest to enjoyment; mark the conflicts and the progress of expiring virtue; and exult in the triumphs of sensibility over shame.   (MQS, I, 219)

Later in the work Stuart moved away from the position of Hume and Robertson, that Mary succumbed to the seductive temptation of Bothwell, and expressed the opinion that he plied her with 'amatorious potions' (MQS, I, 376). Here the border between historical speculation and romantic imagination was blurred. The hypothetical nature of the potion theory required that Stuart re-assert his impartiality: 'If I were professedly the panegyrist of Mary, I would dwell upon this topic, and use rhetorical arts to paint it in all the blackest colours. But ... it is my ambition to lay the truth simply before my reader' (MQS, I, 376n). In reality, though, it is at such points he most forcefully employed 'rhetorical arts' to evoke a picture of 'virtue in distress'.[53]

From the time of her seduction by Bothwell, Mary became less and less an important political figure who could only retain her centrality in the narrative by being reconceived in an idealised and sentimental form. The 'amatorious potion' argument recalls the fate of Samuel Richardson's fictional heroine Clarissa Harlowe, who yielded to the seductions of Lovelace in a similarly fantastic manner. Both women finally encountered the prospect of death with firm Christian devotion. Like Clarissa, Mary's life was a catalogue of imprisonments and escapes in the course of which she was increasingly cut off from those who might have helped her to regain her freedom.[54] Imprisonment is not only important as an historical fact but as a setting for the development of the queen's image in the literature that grew up around her. Stuart's use in the text of letters as historical documents, a feature not unrelated to the epistolary technique of Richardson, enlivens and lends empirical credibility to the narrative.

An account of the 'Casket Letters' occupies a central place in the *History*. Since Stuart's day the importance of this correspondence in making sense of the political events of the period has diminished, though their force in Marian hagiography remains important. Hume believed the correspondence to be authentic. He drew this conclusion from Mary's 'refusing to give an answer to the accusation of her enemies' at a time when the truth could have been made known.[55] Robertson's argument in favour of their authenticity reads more convincingly and benefited from the presentation of more detailed evidence in the 'Dissertation' with which his work concludes.[56] More recently, Gordon Donaldson asserted the likelihood of Mary's guilty role in 'schemes against her husband', but conjectured that 'some genuine letters from Mary to Bothwell were tampered with.'[57] Stuart rejected this first charge and categorically stated that the letters were a forgery devised by George Buchanan, Moray and Morton.

As an example of eighteenth-century historical scholarship, Stuart's analysis of the Casket Letters is quite persuasive. He is a sober and methodical advocate who traces the course of events surrounding the letters, considers the actions of the players involved and draws conclusions which it would seem could not be confuted. 'The letters', he argued, '... could not possibly give rise to events which were prior to their discovery. This is to reverse altogether the laws of nature. Previously to the period in which [the nobles] acknowledge that they first saw the letters, they affect to have been governed by them' (MQS, I, 363). Stuart's proof was built upon Goodall's philological evidence and is essentially a chronological deduction. The verdict was not only an assertion of Mary's innocence but an indictment of her adversaries.

> She was denied that common humanity and justice, which in rude as well as polished societies is due, and paid to the most abject and the most abandoned criminal. Nor were they [the Scottish nobles] contented with this wanton mockery of her sanctimonious rights as a Queen and as a human creature. They not only obtained from the three Estates a pardon of their past transactions to her prejudice, but engaged them to extend their impunity to the cruelties they might still commit against her. In the overbearing tyranny of their measures

they betrayed the lively consciousness of their own enor-
mous guilt, and of her injured innocence. (MQS, I, 279–80)
He then took his argument one step further by considering the
evidence 'in the light most favourable' to the Scottish nobles. This
rhetorical technique, patterned on the legal speeches of Cicero,
reconfirmed his original hypothesis. The account of the Casket
Letters concludes with a reiteration of Mary's innocence, Moray's
guilt, and an indictment of George Buchanan, Moray's 'tool and
vassal' in the fabrication of the letters (MQS, I, 398).

In our age of more clinical, less evocative historical scholarship,
writers have made no attempt to vindicate Mary on the charge of a
scandalous affair with Bothwell.[58] Stuart's contemporaries were
less inclined to make a judgement. Rather than speculate on the
matter, Hume merely mentioned the rumour spread at the time of
'particular intimacies between them'.[59] Robertson gave the topic
more consideration but was equally ambiguous:

> At what precise time, this ambitious Lord first allowed the
> sentiments of a lover to occupy the place of that duty and
> respect which a subject owes his Sovereign; or when Mary,
> instead of gratitude for his faithful services, felt a passion of
> another nature rising in her bosom, it is no easy matter to
> determine.[60]

Robertson then challenged Knox and Buchanan for their assertions against Mary which he regarded as 'rash, precipitate, and
inaccurate'.[61]

Mary's love for Bothwell has often been the subject of debate. If
it was in fact genuine and the spur to the murder of Darnley, then
little can be said in her defence. Stuart supported the opposite
view, that politically, her marriage to Bothwell was the only way
she could gain an advantage over Moray and his associates, and
morally, as a seduced woman, it was the only way she could
regain her lost virtue (MQS, I, 223).

For Bothwell, who 'was dreaming on the brink of a precipice'
(MQS, I, 210) and for Darnley, Stuart had no pity. Darnley had
acted the part of a selfish child and like Bothwell was merely a
pawn of more powerful and prudent noblemen. His death offered
Stuart an opportunity to present his first character portrait. These
colourful descriptions read with an energetic lyricism. They enable him to open himself to philosophical, though not entirely
detached, reasoning:

> Under the guidance of no regular principles, he was incon-
> stant and capricious ... His preposterous vanity and aspiring

pride roused the resentment and scorn of the nobles. His follies and want of dignity made him little with the people. To the Queen, his infidelity and frequent amours were most insulting and ungrateful. The admiration of the sex which in cultivated and superior men is an elegant passion and an amiable weakness, was in him a gross attachment and an unsentimental propensity ... But while our graver historians [Knox and Keith], are assiduous to reproach him with wantonness in the chamber of Venus, it ought to be remembered, that the murder of Rizzio, and his attempt to dispossess the Queen of her government are far more indelible stains upon his memory ... It is with pain that History relates such cruel events, but while she melts with human woe, it is her province to be rigorously just. Her weeping eye is the indication of an instructive sorrow; and while her bursting heart mourns over the crimes, the calamities, and the wretchedness of ages that are past, she records them with fidelity as a lesson to succeeding times.   (MQS, I, 191)

Stuart imbued his personified muse, History, with a dual capacity for sentiment and instructive reasoning. First she 'melts with human woe', then, perceiving that emotion, applies 'rigorous justice'; she weeps then instructs; she mourns then records the cause of her mourning as a lesson. Passages such as these were aimed not only at the impressionable female reader but also at the 'man of feeling'. Stuart's desire to experience the past followed a philosophical principle commonplace in the eighteenth century: that impressions precede ideas. In other words, feeling is prior to reasoning. Experience, the fabric of human understanding, weaves the past into the present. The weeping eye is an important symbol in eighteenth-century literature: 'The sentimental tribute of a tear exacted by the spectacle of virtue in distress was an acknowledgement at once of man's inherent goodness and of the impossibility of his ever being able to demonstrate his goodness effectively.'[62] The readers of the *History of Mary Queen of Scots* would have agreed with Stuart's pessimistic lament over humanity and implicitly acknowledged the idea that, though they may be unable to learn from their mistakes, at least they could hope to understand something of human nature.

Amidst such philosophical speculations and romantic descriptions of seduction, imprisonment and escape, Stuart did not neglect the progress of political affairs. With a more objective pen, he described the course of events as they built up to the confrontation at Carberry Hill. There Mary, supported by royalist troops under the command of Bothwell, stood against a field of Scottish nobles. She was at a military disadvantage, further aggravated by the refusal of her soldiers to fight under Bothwell. In this dire situation a negotiation took place, and Mary determined that her only course was to dismiss Bothwell and conclude a treaty with her rivals; but the hope of reconcilliation did not last long. Stuart inserted a part of the queen's own speech to dramatise the scene (MQS, I, 236).

> Her enemies ... exclaimed indignantly against her as the murderer of her husband. They reviled her as a lewd adulteress in the most open manner, and in a language the most coarse, and the most opprobrious. Her nobility forgot their promises, and seemed to have neither honour nor humanity. She had changed one miserable scene for a distress that was deeper and more hopeless. No eye wept for her; no heart melted with her anguish. They surrounded her with guards, and conducted her to her capital. She was carried along its streets, and shewn to her people in captivity and in sadness.
> (MQS, I, 237)

The Protestant nobility advanced to control the government of Scotland and compelled Mary to resign the Crown in favour of her infant son James. When her rival the Earl of Moray assumed the regency, it was necessary for the nobles to justify their actions to the people, and so they accused Bothwell of the murder of Darnley. But their situation remained a delicate one, for the guilt of Bothwell tended to implicate them in the regicide. To expedite matters and satisfy any inquiries, they found victims and through legal contrivances had them speedily convicted and executed (MQS, I, 245).

In the wake of such upheaval, many began to question whether affairs in Scotland had improved with the deposition of their queen. Stuart placed the issue in the context of political liberty and left little doubt about his interpretation of events.

> Now that a revolution in the government was actually accomplished, men thought of it with astonishment and terror; and their minds were preparing for the calm of despotism. The Regent had dethroned his sovereign; and a few companies of regular or standing troops were alone wanting to enable him to trample on the liberties of his country and to be a tyrant.   (MQS, I, 271).

Stuart's comments are not those of an entirely impartial historian;

for many, Mary was herself a threat to the liberty of the people and to the reformed religion. While he was determined to trace effects to their causes and thus uncover the reasons for political change; and while he did not mitigate the dangers which Mary's Catholicism posed to Scotland, he was constantly overwhelmed by the image of her as a victim. The moral injustice of her ill-treatment mitigated her part in political strategems. His vivid account of the events following Mary's escape from Loch Leven Castle demonstrates this point. When this news was announced, supporters from all parts of Scotland came to her side. She declared her abdication to be void, charging that it had been exhorted from her. Mary's reviving hopes came to an end at the battlefield of Langside, where Moray's army, though smaller, quickly defeated her men. Soon after, despite the pleas of remaining supporters, she 'determined to seek a refuge in England, and to court in person the protection of a Queen who had never ceased to disturb her reign' (MQS, I, 292). This trust in Elizabeth, as Stuart remarked in the final paragraph of the work was 'the most unpardonable error of her life' (MQS, II, 310).

Elizabeth watched the struggle between Mary and the nobility with interest. Although she aided Moray against her primary adversary, he and his circle were a potential threat: they had deposed their queen and thus challenged the authority of the monarchy. Stuart highlighted 'the selfish admiration with which Elizabeth regarded the condition of a sovereign' and showed how 'her politics as usual were prudent and crafty' (MQS, I, 250) to prevent this threat and win control of Scotland. In the meantime, with Mary out of the way, Moray gradually gained recognition and security for his government. Stuart placed blame on him for failing to see that his greatest danger lay to the south.

His murder no more than four years after his rise to power, and at a point when a plan for Mary's release into his custody was being finalised, gave an abrupt turn to Scottish history. Here Stuart paused to reflect on his character. Elaborating upon descriptions from Hume and other historians, he arranged the favourable and unfavourable qualities of the 'godly Regent' and contrasted the man with the times in which he lived.

> His abilities ... though extensive and various, were better calculated for the struggles of faction than the speculations of polity. ... To the great body of the Scottish nobles, whose consequence he had humbled, – his death was a matter of stern indifference, or of secret joy, but to the common people,

it was an object of sincere grief, and they lamented him long
under the appellation of the godly Regent. Elizabeth be-
wailed in him a strenuous partizan, and a chosen instrument
by which she might subvert the independency of Scotland;
and Mary ... wept over a brother, a heretic, and an enemy,
whom a sudden and violent destiny had overtaken in his
guilty career, with his full load of unrepented crimes.

(MQS, I, 474–5)

To the Earl of Buchan, Stuart offered a more personal opinion of
the 'Godly Regent', in response to Buchan's request for a fuller
biography: 'He is so abominable a character ... that I could not
have any pleasure in portraying him: and indeed I may possibly
have said enough about him in my History of Mary.'[63]

After Moray's death various domestic and foreign powers contended with each other in the hope of settling the affairs of Scotland in their favour. With the election of the Earl of Morton to the
regency in November 1572, Mary's own hopes were severely
depressed. A long imprisonment in England had impaired her
health and spirit, and, sensible that 'she could have no hope to
survive Elizabeth ... the cares and the anxieties of a mother,
induced her to be earnest to preserve and secure her titles to her
son' (MQS, II, 152). Like all of Mary's appeals to Elizabeth, this
was not only disregarded but served to animate the English queen
'in her habits of cruelty and vengeance' (MQS, II, 153). Stuart's
portrait of Mary, enhanced by pathetic anecdote and passionate
language, became increasingly romantic. Even her guards, he
wrote, 'refused to her the exercise of the Christian duty of dispens-
ing an alms; and they would not allow her the soft consolation of
moistening her eye with sorrows not her own' (MQS, II, 218).

Stuart interposed such dramatic scenes with more straightforward accounts of political and ecclesiastic affairs during the Earl
of Morton's ten-year regency. However abhorrent Stuart found
the regent, he gave him due credit. Morton drew up the Pacifica-
tion of Perth, a treaty which brought the queen's adversaries into
an alliance with the young king's party and thus gave stability to
the Protestant religion, sanction to his regency and authority to
James' succession. Stuart acknowledged that this treaty, removed
'the troubles and civil wars which had disfigured the kingdom'
(MQS, II, 87) but it reduced the affairs of Mary 'to the most
wretched extremity'; and Morton 'found himself in the plentitude
of power, and was giddy with it' (MQS, II, 93).

Five years later James, though only twelve years old, assumed control of Scotland under the guidance of a council of peers, appointed on a rotational basis to advise him. It was not long, however, before the king developed an association with the Earl of Lennox which worried not only Morton but the clergy and Elizabeth. To test his authority, James found it expedient to charge Morton in the murder of his father (Darnley). To counter this plan Elizabeth 'engaged in intrigues' to liberate Morton and effect the ruin of Lennox. Once again, forged letters appeared (as they would later in connection with the Babington Conspiracy), which implicated Lennox in abetting 'foreign powers to invade England' (MQS, II, 135). Upon the discovery of Elizabeth's duplicity, James asserted himself more forcefully. Stuart applauded the king for remaining 'true to his friends, and attentive to uphold his dignity ... . He commanded all the ... militia to be in readiness to attend upon the royal standard' (MQS, II, 137). This threatening strategy was sufficient to avert a military encounter. Morton was put on trial, found to be a guilty party in Darnley's murder and then executed. The indictment of Morton, according to Stuart, further lifted the accusation of guilt from Mary, thus refocusing the image of an imprisoned though innocent queen (MQS, II, 141).

Subsequent events, such as the Raid of Ruthven of 1582 and later the Gowrie Conspiracy of 1601, in both of which James was taken prisoner, reflected, in Stuart's view, the chaotic state of government. As a constitutional historian he questioned whether the parliamentary approbation of the king's imprisonment could confirm the legality of a treasonable act. He did not deny that factious nobles like Lennox had exerted a prejudicial influence on James, but it was more important to see that the confinement of the king (though it was hardly the first time in Scottish history a king had been kidnapped) directly challenged the foundations of government.

These events also offered Stuart an opportunity to return to Mary, the central character. Although a prisoner herself, she was all the while engaging in plots to reassert her power. The tears which Stuart shed for her position may call into question the impartiality of his account, as Mary could not at one turn engage in wild plots to regain the throne and at another display total ignorance of why Elizabeth wisely kept her captive. At the same time they reveal a compelling moral sympathy which overrides all other considerations.

The Babington Conspiracy is the last major political event in the work. It was a plot by dissatisfied English Catholics to assassinate

Elizabeth and put Mary on the throne of both kingdoms. The conspiracy failed because Elizabeth's spies learned of the plan from its inception. Stuart asserted Mary's innocence on the basis that she did not have prior knowledge of the attempt, but he did not stop there. In his view there was a greater conspiracy at work. He showed that Elizabeth and her advisors had letters forged to ensure that there would be sufficient evidence to establish Mary's guilt.

> They ardently desired to involve the Queen of Scots in the guilt of Babington and his associates in order to create a pretence or occasion for executing against her the last act of severity and vengence ... It was contrived that answers in the name of the Queen ... should be found in the hole of the Castle wall. By this method it was easy to multiply evidences to her prejudice.   (MQS, II, 250–2)

Stuart founded his argument on documents to which previous historians, such as Robertson and Hume, apparently did not have access. 'These particulars,' claimed a writer in the *Critical Review*, 'are in a great measure, supplied by Dr. Stuart ... and the conspiracy of Babington now displays a consistency, which bears the strongest resemblance of truth.'[64] Stuart is to be credited with establishing the essential facts of the conspiracy and arriving at an opinion with which historians ever since have largely agreed.

When the public trial of Mary was about to commence, she argued that her peers, the monarchs of Europe, should be her judges, not a commission of English legal officers. Though certain of her innocence, Mary had no hope of freedom but by consenting to the trial. 'This sacrifice to her honour', Stuart remarked, 'she thought might be excused from the peculiarities of her situation. The confidence of virtue induced her to detract from her own grandeur, and to tarnish the glory of her predecessors and her nation' (MQS, II, 264). Stuart commended Mary for her attempt to defend monarchical prerogative just as he criticised Elizabeth for paying it little regard. The English queen further undermined her authority by insisting upon parliamentary confirmation of the guilty verdict (MQS, II, 277).

Stuart described the trial with dramatic coolness. Mary's own quoted defence occupies the central place. In editorial notes, which stand in contrast to the impassioned tone of Mary's own defence, Stuart cited various procedural and factual irregularities of the trial. It was a prelude to the final picture of the queen at the hand of the executioner. Between these two events, he recounted the general political situation in Great Britain and the situation of the young king. James had been won over to Elizabeth's side by the prospect of his succession to the English Crown. But the approach of Mary's death led him and the Scottish people to realise the extent to which they had been subjugated by Elizabeth.

His subjects entered into his passions; and did not brook the disgraces and insults which had been heaped upon Mary, with a prodigality so systematic, and so unfeeling. Her long and unexampled sufferings, were stinging reproaches of their tameness; and while they conjectured the future from the past, they were seized with foreboding apprehensions.

(MQS, II, 282)

Attempts by James to stay his mother's death sentence proved futile as did similar applications from her foreign relations. These efforts nevertheless preyed on Elizabeth's mind and made her irresolute about signing the death warrant. 'Corrupted by her passions, and lost to the sensibilities of virtue, Elizabeth had now reached the last extremity of human wickedness. Though a sovereign princess ... she blushed not to give it in charge to her ministers to enjoin a murder' (MQS, II, 294–5). A plan to assassinate Mary was contemplated but abandoned. At last Elizabeth sealed the warrant; and then only Mary's execution remained. Here Stuart placed his heroine centre stage. Her religious devotion and the inhumane treatment to which her captors subjected her – were the two contrasting images he presented. Not only was Mary denied a confessor of her own faith, but she was harangued by zealous Protestant clergymen to renounce Catholicism. To the last, however, she asserted her dignity as a queen. The scene of her death itself reflects a concentrated visual grandeur. As Mary spoke her final words, the executioner, 'with design, from unskillfulness, or from inquietude, struck three blows before he separated her head from her body' (MQS, II, 306).

In this last character portrait Stuart reiterated the two tragic flaws of the queen: first, the incompatibility of her adherence to the Catholic faith with the leadership of a reformed country; and second, the 'imprudence with which she ventured into England, and entrusted herself to the power of Elizabeth' (MQS, II, 310). The portrait itself brings to a climax the tension in the narrative between rational rhetoric and romantic ideals . The reader is left with a powerful sense of tragedy. Mary's

> virtues were great; her misfortunes greater ... Her understanding was clear, her judgment penetrating, her spirit

lofty, her application vigorous. But she was called to the
exercise of royalty, in an unhappy and most critical period.
The troubles of the Reformation had confirmed the turbulence of her nobles; and she had been accustomed to the
orderly government, and the refined and seducing manners
of France. The zeal of her people for the new opinions was
most passionate; and she was attached to the antient religion
with a keenness that excited their fears ... With the happiest
intentions, with public spirit and the love of justice, with
moderation, liberality and splendour, she attained not the
praise of true glory. Circumvented by the treachery of smiling and corrupted counsellors, and exposed to the unceasing
hatred and suspicions of turbulent ecclesiastics, she perpetually experienced the miseries of disappointment, and the
malignity of detractions.   (MQS, II, 308)

Stuart humanised his subject by praising her cheerful temper, easy
conversation, and polite wit, on the one hand, and criticising her
capacity for dissimulation, and the unbounded confidence she
placed in her advisors, on the other (MQS, II, 309). At the same
time he canonised Mary by recasting her flaws as virtues. He
called upon his female readers to see in themselves the qualities of
the heroine of the *History*. They should weep for the queen but also
be instructed by her example.

   After the appearance of the work Stuart took pleasure in noting
that 'many of her own sex have approved my researches, have
been convinced by me of her innocence, and have revolved her
misfortunes, in my narration of them, with anguish and tears'.[65]
Stuart's characterisation of Mary reveals more than his sympathy
for the queen. It marks his identification with her tragic plight and
it reflects tension in his own historiographic method. He was
probably too immersed in his subject and too spontaneous a writer
to see these parallels. Only through an iconic account of an historical figure like Mary could he depict the complex forces which
composed his own tragic sense of reality. The *History* was a vindication of Mary and a statement of his own will to write in accord-
ance with the spirit of his vivacious mind, unfettered though
guided by reason.

   This was popular narrative history of a different sort – less
ironic than Gibbon's, less systematic than Robertson's and less
sceptical than Hume's. As a consequence it was more rhetorical,
more pessimistic, impressionistic and above all more tragic. Yet
while moving in new directions, it was still a product of the

Enlightenment. 'It is my wish', wrote Stuart at the outset, 'not to raise a monument to my prejudices, but to build a Temple to Truth'. (MQS, I, iv)

This re-creation of the queen was at once the catharsis of the writer and the destruction of the man. Stuart could write little else of significance after the *History of Mary Queen of Scots*. He could not find, or did not have the opportunity to find an equally enthralling subject. Over the course of his literary career, he modified and to some extent rejected the features which generally characterise the historical literature of his age. He transformed its rationalism and politeness, scepticism and detachment, into a force for re-vitalising the emotive power of the written word. Notions of sympathy and sentiment, which were also a part of his literary inheritance, took on more heightened significance in his writing. The *History of Mary Queen of Scots* shows the extent to which the Blakean conflict between the freedom of feeling and the tyranny of reason could express itself in narrative history and in so doing reflect the dynamic capacity of the creative mind.

Today, the *History of Mary Queen of Scots* is forgotten, despite the renewed interest in eighteenth-century historiography and the four hundredth anniversary of Mary's execution. At the time, however, the critics identified it as the definitive account of sixteenth-century Scottish history. *The Encyclopaedia Britannica*, in the second edition (1783), reprinted almost verbatim not only this work but also Stuart's *History of the Reformation* for their 'Scotland' entry.[66] Thus, even greater numbers of people than the steady sale of the works suggests, read his accounts. Murray, as the original publisher, brought the proprietors of the *Encyclopaedia* to law and won a decision in the Scottish Court.[67]

Interest in Mary's story was increasing. The popular appeal of a vindication of her character was evident not only in England and Scotland, but on the Continent and in North America. When other historians offered their reflections on the subject, Stuart's views were not neglected, if only for a short time.[68] A second edition *of Mary Queen of Scots* in the cheaper octavo format appeared in 1783. Editions of *An Abridgement of the History of Scotland, from Robertson, Stuart, &c* in 1793 and 1805 show further the attempts that were made to recast his ideas 'for the use of schools'. In 1786 John Wesley wrote in his journal: 'I read over Dr. Stuart's *History of Scotland*. He is a writer indeed! as far above Dr. Robertson as Dr. Robertson is above [John] Oldmixon. He proves beyond all possibility of doubt that the charges against Queen Mary were totally groundless; that she was ... one of the most blameless, yea, and the most pious women! [69]

The appearance of the Stuart's *History* also rekindled a public rivalry with William Robertson. Shortly after publication a number of notices, letters and pamphlets appeared in addition to the usual reviews.[70] These pieces were a part of a well-planned campaign in which Stuart and Murray used their literary connections to attract attention to the work and discredit Robertson's long-standing account. In the introductory remarks to a public letter which Stuart wrote for the leading newspapers and periodicals, Robertson was called upon to 'defend what he has written to the prejudice of the honour of Mary Queen of Scots'. This 'Literary Challenge' was written in military metaphors typical of the age:

> The ground for the encounter is marked out; the subject is a beautiful Queen; and the judges are appointed ... If Dr. Robertson enters the lists, and is successful, he will acquire new reputation. If he refuses...or enters them and is defeated, he will lose many laurels. This dispute will probably be an æra in the history of Scottish literature.[71]

As well as a vindicator of Mary, Stuart presented himself as a champion of women generally. Mary's virtue was of especial interest to 'fine ladies' as the 'glory of the female character is concerned'.[72] In the letter itself, Stuart begged the favour of presenting a copy of his work to the Earl of Buchan's newly formed Society of Antiquaries of Scotland. With modesty characteristic of the Advertisement to the *History*, he asserted a willingness to change his opinions about Mary should they be proven wrong. The tone of the letter shows that mixture of pride and humility typical of Stuart and of reason and romance which characterises the *History of Mary Queen of Scots*:

> If it shall be demonstrated that Mary was not so perfect and so innocent as I have represented her, I will yield to the controlling power of evidence and argument. Though I shall weep over the misfortunes, the frailties, and the crimes of this beautiful princess, I will yet pay my devotions to truth, and submit to the law of the victor.[73]

Stuart employed rather less humility and more satire in an anonymous pamphlet attack on Robertson which appeared around the same time. The lengthy title reads more like a table of contents: *Critical Observations concerning the Scottish Historians: Hume, Stuart, and Robertson: including an Idea of the Reign of Mary Queen of Scots, as a Portion of History; Specimens of the Histories of this*

Princess, by Dr. Stuart and Dr. Robertson; and a Comparative View of the Merits of these Rival Historians: with a Literary Picture of Dr. Robertson, in a contrasted Opposition with the Celebrated Mr. Hume.[74]
The pamphlet shows Stuart's calculated attempt to group himself among the two most successful Scottish historians of his time, or rather to place himself beside Hume in place of Robertson. Here even more severely than he had in the *Public Law of Scotland*, he attacked his rival by drawing a 'formal comparison' on the subjects of 'originality', 'narration', 'the drawing of characters' and 'composition or style'. Robertson, he wrote, 'has collected with industry the observations of others ... but he has never in one instance extended the sphere of historical or philosophical discovery' (CO, 34). 'He attempts to *dazzle*, not to *fill* the eye; and would rather please the ear by a harmonious period, than convey instruction to the mind ... Dr. Robertson writes to the many; Dr. Stuart to the few.' (CO, 41–3.)

The pamphlet concludes with another 'formal' comparison, this time between Robertson and Hume. Stuart's attack recalls his scathing 'Character of a Certain Historian' by a philosopher lately deceased. While he acknowledged Robertson's literary success, he argued that such popularity would not be of long duration. Hume's reputation, though slowly achieved, would endure.

While the sturdy oak rises slowly to its greatness and its honours, the transitory flower glitters in the sun, droops and perishes. The dying Hume foretold his bursting fame. The living Robertson bewails his decaying reputation.
(CO, 46–7)
Robertson is a puny stream losing itself in its mind; Hume is the voice of history speaking to ages, ... In posture and learning, genius and the want of it, cannot long be confounded. The operations of caprice and party are passing and transient. Truth and justice ever vindicate their rights.
(CO, 52)

On several occasions Stuart publicly denied the authorship and attributed the pamphlet to Robertson and his Moderate associates. In one public letter Stuart argued that 'it would ... be a far more honourable conduct in my adversaries, if, instead of opposing me by inventions and calumnies, they would take the field in an open and honest manner.'[75] Robertson clearly had little to gain from a public confrontation with a rival whose point of view was gaining considerable public approval. The appearance of dignity and impartiality in Robertson's writings carried over to his behaviour.

Publicly, he could remain aloof from the challenge while probably pursuing a strategy to minimalise the effect of Stuart's wrath.[76]

Stuart's aim was to make the debate about Mary Queen of Scots more than just a parochial literary squabble. There was something to be gained from winning public opinion about Mary to his side. His father entered with characteristic paternal support into the struggle. The anger he expressed at Robertson and his circle indicates the direction the encounter was taking:

> The puffing band, those pretenders to Literature, those Enemies of Liberty & Sticklers for prerogative who would engross everything to themselves to the disgrace of the Country have done everything in their power to crush the reputation of a young man who justly holds them all in sovereign contempt.[77]

The five hundred copies Murray published of the first edition of the *History of Mary Queen of Scots* sold out within a year. This contrasted with Stuart's other works, significant numbers of which remained in Murray's stock. However, with the recent success and renewed advertising, these also became in demand. Murray and Stuart planned a less expensive second edition priced at 14 shillings and with a newly engraved portrait of 'the beauteous Mary' after a drawing by John Donaldson. In this edition they mounted an even more determined attack on 'this chosen band [who], smiling at one another and calling themselves men of Letters, decide magisterially upon writings ... of every kind'[78]

Stuart planned to have copies available in the Edinburgh bookshops by May 1783, in time for the annual meeting of the General Assembly. He relished the thought of embarrassing Robertson before his fellow clerics. To his regret, the delays in printing and transporting the edition from London prevented it from appearing until August of that year. Under Murray's attentive management, a more timely strategy was employed in London for the autumn meeting of Parliament, where Stuart was confident the authority of Henry Dundas, by his close association with Robertson, would be weakened. Stuart told the Earl of Buchan: 'I hear good tidings of my second Edition at Edinburgh', and added rather sensationally of Robertson: 'I am told the Historiographer is imploring pity, & giving himself up to lamentation.'[79] Typically, Stuart's expectations were not entirely realised. Robertson could shelter himself from the passing storm, while Dundas could avoid it completely.

Stuart added two appendices to the second edition. The first contains the whole of the *Public Law of Scotland*. By reorganising the work, he gave the criticisms of Robertson a more equal status with the text. What was once the note section now became a separate book; and each note an individual chapter. The second appendix includes a collection of letters challenging Robertson to defend his historical views on the Queen of Scots. In one letter, Stuart explained to Buchan how Robertson had been 'zealous to erect a sort of literary despotism; and ... thought to wreck my reputation on the tide of their obloquy'.[80] The tone of this lengthy letter recalls his description of a letter in the *History*, which Mary wrote to Elizabeth 'in which she maintains her dignity while she yields to her resentments; and in which she has intermingled ... the most fervent protestations of innocence, and the boldest language of expostulation and reproach' (MQS, II, 164). Buchan's printed reply hailed Stuart as a vindicator of Mary and attacked the Moderates' control of Scottish political and literary affairs: 'I suppose the fear of offending the high presbyterian party, [and] the desire of pleasing the English by an extenuation of the ungenerous conduct of Elizabeth ... induced your antagonist to avert his eye from the proofs which you have produced in vindication of the unfortunate Mary'.[81] Buchan placed the encounter between Stuart and Robertson in the context of Anglo-Scottish politics. He used the language of republicanism to affirm his views. The constitutional and patriotic principles which Stuart expressed in the *History of Mary Queen of Scots* were antithetic to those held by the powers controlling the flow of patronage from London to Scotland. The chain of influence from Henry Dundas to Robertson found itself challenged at a critical period by a faction led by Buchan and his influential brother Henry Erskine. The second edition appeared just as the Fox–North coalition had formed a new government, in which Erskine replaced Dundas as Scotland's Lord Advocate. But as Dundas' control of Scottish politics was still considerable, he continued to be a worthy object of attack. As it was, he reassumed power soon afterwards.

There may seem to be a paradox implicit in Stuart's whiggism and his defence of Mary. Historically it had been those he called 'the advocates of tyranny' who supported the House of Stuart. William Thomson made this point in a political satire he wrote at the time when he said of Stuart: 'He is distinguished by a strange mixture of prejudices apparently inconsistent, violent whiggism, and no less violent attachment to the family of *Stuart*.'[82] From Stuart's point of view there was a common ground between the two 'attachments'. Both could be employed as effective artillery with which to challenge those in positions of authority. Political history showed that the same rhetorical devices and the same sets of facts could serve opposite ends, if used judiciously. Thus, in the context of post-Union Scottish patriotism, Buchan and Stuart adopted Mary as a symbol for their own age: she was Scotland oppressed by its powerful southern neighbour; she was the victim of the alliance between the Earl of Moray and Elizabeth; she was an historical personification of the suffering inflicted by men such as Henry Dundas on Scottish autonomy and identity. Dundas was a contemporary Moray, and Robertson a pandering leader of the Reformation like George Buchanan.

The challenge to the establishment further manifested itself when Buchan sought to obtain a royal charter for the Society of Antiquaries, which he founded in 1780.[83] Buchan's genuine interest in preserving the antiquities and recording the history of Scotland, motivated him to promote the new society. But this was also a time when the political situation was unfavourable to his own ideas and family interest, so that the Society was a means of recovering his influence. The application for a royal charter met with formal opposition from three Edinburgh civic bodies: the Senatus Academicus of the University, the Faculty of Advocates and the Philosophical Society. Robertson, the leader of the first, argued in an official memorial to the Lord Advocate (at that point still Henry Dundas) that only one organisation (i.e. the Philosophical Society) dedicated to the advancement of learning was practical in Scotland. He declared further that the Advocates' Library was a sufficient 'repository of everything that tends to illustrate the History, the Antiquities and the Laws of this Country'; and that the Society of Antiquaries' museum was superfluous because the museum at the University could accommodate all of Scotland's public artifacts. Robertson's aim was to subsume Buchan's society into a newly planned Royal Society of Edinburgh. His further assertion that 'narrow Countries' like Scotland could not establish with advantage 'a considerable Variety of Literary Societies', angered patriotically-minded men like Buchan and Stuart.[84]

James Boswell likewise was critical of Robertson's plan. When the Faculty of Advocates decided to oppose Buchan's application for a charter, he 'was vexed that there was such a majority on the illiberal side'.[85] Ultimately, both societies received royal charters. It was a compromise of sorts for Robertson, necessary at a time when politics were in a state of flux. Buchan opposed the trend towards specialisation and elitism towards which the new Royal Society was heading.[86] He, like Stuart, sought to perpetuate the tradition of gentlemanly scholarship and antiquarian inquiry inherited from Napier of Merchiston, Pitcairne, Ruddiman and other Scots who promoted the humanist pursuit of learning. Both men confronted their opponents with the patriotic resolve of Scotsmen who did not want to see the resources and individuality of their country further compromised by English dominance.

In the midst of the charter controversy, Buchan listed reasons why he met with opposition from the Edinburgh establishment. The first he gave was that 'we have had the audacity and want of taste in admitting Doctor Gilbert Stuart the Asserter of the Principles of Liberty and the opponent of the great Robertson to be a member of our Society'.[87] After the controversy, Buchan defined the nature of the patriotism which he shared with Stuart:

> I considered Scotland ... as a rude but noble Medallion of antient Sculpture, which ought not to be defaced or forgotten in the Cabinet of Nations because it lay next to one more beautiful and splendid, richer & larger, more polished and elegant, *but of less relief. As a Man* I felt myself a Citizen of the World, as a friend to peace, to liberty, and to science ... I considered myself as an Inhabitant of an united Kingdom, but as a Citizen, *I could not help remembering that I was a Scot.*[88]

In the course of the affair Stuart moved to London and was writing for John Murray's new periodical, the *English Review*. In the May 1783 issue he prepared a lengthy article on a 'dispute which happened between the Society of the Scottish Antiquaries on the one hand, & Dr. Robertson, the celebrated Historian, with his friends on the other' (ER, I, 425–35). To Buchan he wrote privately that 'your victory will be a Lesson of humility to the Historiographer, & to his obedient vassals in the university'.[89] The victory was satisfying to Stuart. It was an affair of national consequence in which he and the *History of Mary Queen of Scots* played a supportive and public role. In his mind he had gained a moral and scholarly ascendancy over Robertson, however short-lived or superficial it might have been.

6

Acrimonious Endings 1783–1786

A very Drawcansir of political debate, a swashbuckler, and
soldado of Parliamentary Conflict.

Justin McCarthy, *History of our own Times* (London, 1880), IV, 6

The relative success of the *History of Mary Queen of Scots* encouraged Stuart to plan a 'History of Scotland from the earliest accounts of time till the Rebellion in the year 1745'.[1] He also pledged himself to contribute a number of literary portraits of eminent Scotsmen for the Earl of Buchan's 'Biographia Caledoniead'. He began to write a life of John Knox, supplementing it with 'some reflexions upon religious establishments' and planned another of the jurist Thomas Craig, to which he intended to add 'some thoughts upon the feudal & Canon laws'.[2] But he never completed any of these projects.

The expense of living in London made it difficult for Stuart to continue his historical studies. To return to Scotland, however, was not an appealing prospect because of the control which Robertson and his 'literary band' continued to hold in civic and literary spheres. Stuart therefore remained in London where his *History of Mary Queen of Scots* was making a considerable impression on the public. The reputation of the queen had long suffered in England, but it was now beginning to improve. John Logan noted this shift in sentiment when he told Alexander Carlyle: 'We English have taken her under *our* protection and are resolved to defend her … The truth is an impression of Mary's innocence prevails universally here.'[3] These factors compelled Stuart to settle permanently in London and once again take up the pen of a journalist. His reputation as such had always been considerable despite his absence from the metropolis for over eight years. One contemporary said of Stuart as a critic, that he held 'great influence over the periodical dispensatories of fame, and by them over public opinion'.[4] This was the role he aspired to upon his return, and went a considerable way towards achieving in the three years before his death.

In a letter to David Dalrymple, thanking him for a complimentary copy of Dalrymple's own contribution to the Earl of Buchan's series, Stuart expressed regret that he had not been able to contribute something further himself to show the progress of Scottish culture. He also reflected generally on his own state of mind:

> Disappointments, which I have never merited, by calling me to reside in London, have given a different direction to my cares. When it is in my power to live easily in my own country, I shall return to it [and] renew my Historical & Literary occupations. In this World, we must often yield to circumstances & accident. But, if Fortune has been frequently unkind to me, my claims upon her, I consider, to be the greater ... At all events, it becomes me to act my Part with propriety & fortitude.[5]

This modest, if somewhat despondent self-appraisal characterised the way Stuart wished to be seen by others, particularly men of superior standing, like Dalrymple and Buchan. In one of the letters to Buchan published in the second edition of the *History of Mary Queen of Scots*, he acknowledged similarly that 'fortune may delude me with smiles, or fill me with hopes that are destined to perish'.[6] Those individuals with whom Stuart was intimate probably witnessed more resentful expressions of his unhappiness and behaviour that was harmful to his physical and mental well-being. Stuart rejected overt sympathy, but at the same time it was important that his friends knew the circumstances behind his 'disappointments'.

Once settled into his old lodgings at 13 Southampton Buildings, Stuart resumed his connection with Ralph Griffith's *Monthly Review*. In an article on Lord Monboddo's *Ancient Metaphysics* he renewed the attack on Monboddo's sweeping condemnation of modern writers: 'He speaks contemptuously of Newton, Locke, Shaftesbury, and Hume. Yet how infinitely preferable to his writings are the works of these great men!'[7] In other reviews Stuart turned his attention to national politics, an area which more and more dominated his writings in this last London period.

When John Murray established the *English Review, or An Abstract of English and Foreign Literature* in January 1783, Stuart left the *Monthly* and began to play an active role as writer and advisor for the new periodical. The publisher was determined to moderate Stuart's controversial inclinations to increase the chances of producing a successful work in the competitive London market. Not only did he find that certain articles by Stuart and others 'frequently required the pruning knife' but in general it was his policy 'firmly to maintain a controul over [his] own property'.[8] According to Samuel Smiles, the periodical 'was by no means a paying production'.[9] But the fact that it continued for over ten years under Murray's management and for some time after his death, indicates that it was at least a moderate financial success. On a practical level the periodical assured him of ample and usually favourable exposure for his own publications.

Murray believed that the ever increasing British reading public sought genuinely independent literary and political news. Therefore he promoted his journal not so much as a rival but as a complement to the *Monthly* and the *Critical*. When Dr Johnson saw a copy of the *English Review*, he remarked to Boswell that he doubted the survival of such an '"irregular review" (in opposition to the regular established ones)'.[10] After Murray's death in 1793 it was incorporated into the *English Analytical Review*. The work was popular enough, and Stuart's role well enough known, to be included in a satirical poem called the *Patriad* (1786):

> The *Monthly* – whisper: on my life
> Is wrote by Griffiths, and his wife.
> The *Critical*, it is well known,
> Is scribbled all by Hamilton.
> As for the *English*, all its stock
> Of knowledge issues from the Loch.[11]

To ensure the appeal of the work, he and Stuart planned to offer something more than the 'regular' reviews. They added to the main critical portion one section surveying the London theatre and another recounting national and international affairs. The editors built upon the growing political awareness of society at large and claimed 'a reciprocal action of government on literature, and of literature on government' (ER, I, 4). They ambitiously marked their intention of commenting on the affairs of the Empire and on 'every book and pamphlet which shall appear in England, Scotland, Ireland, and America' (ER, I, 3). The critical section, which formed the main part of the periodical, was divided into two sections: the first included about ten to fifteen reviews of important new books; the second, entitled the 'Monthly Catalogue' contained short articles (twenty on average) on less important works, pamphlets, poems, translations, novels and foreign publications.

Murray did not depend on Stuart's talents alone. He brought in an able group of literary men. William Thomson, formerly a Scottish minister, was one of the main contributors. His literary skills were such that he later became the proprietor of the periodical. Murray also enlisted a number of contributors with expertise in their given fields: Thomas Holcroft wrote a regular section on the London theatre; Robert Liston transmitted reviews of foreign books; the Reverend John Logan wrote articles on Scottish church politics; John Whitaker reviewed literary and historical works; Alexander Hamilton, Thomas Beddoes and John Hellins reviewed new medical and scientific works; and William Godwin wrote political articles. Other contributors were James Currie, J. O. Justamond, Edmund Cartwright and John Moore.[12]

Murray paid his contributors between two and four guineas a sheet (sixteen printed pages), which was as much as any other London review. He was an authoritarian editor, emphasising that articles 'should be done with the utmost impartiality, for I must avoid violence & party spirit in my publication'.[13] When Murray found, for example, that Godwin's political articles were not meeting this standard and that Godwin would not alter his views, he found another writer for this section. Godwin was given this characteristic explanation:

> As sole proprietor of the English Review and as responsible for what it contains, I cannot admit matter foreign to my sentiments. Your principles ... are as unbending, and no doubt you will think it impertinent in an illiterate fellow of a bookseller to attempt in any shape to control or to dictate in these matters.[14]

William Thomson subsequently wrote the piece, but he too was challenged by Murray for 'prostitut[ing] the National Article'.[15]

When Murray was out of town Stuart managed the periodical. Rumours circulated, however, that he was 'the despotic ruler of the English Review'.[16] Although this was untrue, his influence with the publisher was such that solicitous authors and their friends would often beg the favour of a good review. To this end John Logan wrote to Stuart on behalf of Hugh Blair, whose *Lectures on Rhetoric and Belles Lettres* appeared in the early part of 1783:

> Dr Blair, hath I confess one deplorable fault. From inveterate and incurable habits he is too much connected with a literary Imposter, whom you have completely stripped of his borrowed plumes. He has never with pedantic authority op-

posed the career of other Authors ... I cannot help wishing
Success to Fingal in the last of his fields ... Your influence to
give Dr Blair his last passport to the public will be very
agreeable to the Literati.[17]

Logan asked Stuart to respond to his request and 'quiet the fears'
of Blair. He even offered to write the review. It may be that Stuart
detected not only opportunism but insincerity in Logan's rather
too determined attack on Dr Robertson. In any case he reserved
the article for himself.

In his review Stuart praised Blair's logical arrangement and
expressive language but added more critically that a short treatise
might have done more to advance his reputation (ER, II, 95). 'No
new discoveries are to be made; and the discerning inquirer is
somewhat scandalized, to be deluded with grand preparations
that are to lead only to old and established truths' (ER, II, 19).
Stuart's anti-clerical opinions resurfaced when he criticised the
author for giving what he considered to be an unbalanced survey
of oration. Blair, he wrote, 'was eager to leave the bar to examine
the eloquence of the pulpit' (ER, II, 82). An expressed preference
for the sermons of the French clergy rather than those produced in
England or Scotland met with Stuart's censure on patriotic
grounds. He regarded Blair's opinion as artificially cosmopolitan,
an odd criticism of Blair, whose own sermons were extremely
popular. Stuart failed, or perhaps chose not to see Blair's deliberate modesty. He also scrutinised Blair's views on historical composition and challenged the assertion that historians before
Hume, Robertson and Gibbon were 'little more than dull compil-
ers' (ER, II, 88). He cited Bacon, Herbert and Raleigh as counter
examples and noted with rather self-effacing immodesty that history is 'a subject infinitely beautiful ... and not perhaps to be
completely understood, except by those who have actually distinguished themselves by historic works' (ER, II, 86). The review, on
the whole, was more severe than the 'master of rhetoric' or his
servant, Logan, might have hoped, but the *Lectures* were immensely successful just the same.[18]

Stuart's hand in the political department of the *English Review* is
more difficult to detect. Nevertheless, the views expressed are
interesting and indicate his concerns at the time. The most important political event of 1783 was the establishment of the coalition
government of Charles Fox and Lord North. This 'fourth change
of ministers in the course of twelve months' (ER, I, 183) was
surveyed with scepticism and concern. The prediction proved

correct that 'this extraordinary conjunction will whet the public appetite for censure, will sharpen the jealous eye of opposition ... and give the very worst colour to every error in their administration' (ER, I, 357). Fox was called 'the man of the people', but his association with North compromised his policy of reform and lessened his popularity (ER, II, 269). The actions of both men were 'grounded not on political principles, but on private interest and ambition' (ER, I, 268). The *English Review* welcomed the fall of the coalition in December 1783 and the consequent rise of William Pitt. 'Public Spirit', it declared, 'is the ruling power in the British Constitution' (ER, II, 476).[19]

The lack of political reform in Scotland was often compared with its more progressive southern neighbour. The archaic method of electing Scottish parliamentary representatives favoured the rule of the aristocracy and required reform. Even a landowner like James Boswell could not vote in parliamentary elections.[20] The undemocratic method of electing city magistrates also came under fire. Articles, which Stuart undoubtedly had a share in writing, roused the public spirit of the Scots and warned Westminster of what was to come: 'If the Scotch obtain not the redress for which they wish, there is not a doubt, that matters must be decided by superior force' (ER, I, 527). The demand for a Scots militia, a familiar appeal in Stuart's writings, was added to the list of reforms (ER, I, 359). These were not abstract demands; they were placed in an intentionally threatening context of recent political events. 'The Americans and Irish having successfully claimed the power of sovereigns, the Scotch nation ventured at length to think of arming itself in its own defence, and to claim the privileges of loyal subjects' (ER, I, 87). In addition to commentary in political articles, the editors furthered their objectives in reviews of pamphlets which advocated Scottish reform. Stuart probably had a hand in the account of the *Letters of Zeno, Addressed to the Citizens of Edinburgh on the Present mode of Electing a Member of Parliament*. The anonymous author was Thomas MacGrugar, the secretary of the Edinburgh Committee for parliamentary reform.[21] In the pamphlet he directed the reader to remarks in the *Public Law of Scotland* and described it as 'a book which for important information, and the liberal spirit in which it is wrote, is a very considerable acquisition to the republic of letters, and the interests of civil liberty'.[22] MacGrugar reiterated Stuart's assertion that the inhabitants of cities originally possessed the right to elect officials. In the review it was lamented that Scotland, unlike England, had 'not been distinguished by any great and steady efforts for civil liberty' (ER, I, 498). The piece ended with the more optimistic expectation of 'the rising spirit of the Scottish Nation' (ER, I, 501).

The Scottish reform movement was gaining momentum from the example of English extra-parliamentary groups, the most important of which at the time was the Reverend Christopher Wyvill's Yorkshire Association. Wyvill knew the strategic importance of Scottish support; he also realised that a well connected political commentator with a considerable reputation as an historical writer could help to promote his aims. He therefore wrote to Stuart asking for assistance in the cause of constitutional reform.

> Having been long accustomed from the general spirit of your writings, to consider you as a warm and decided friend to the Constitution of our Country, I take the liberty to transmit to you the inclosed Proposal of the Yorkshire Committee for a general correction of abuses in the frame and duration of Parliament, and for the extention and better regulation of the Right of Election to Parliament throughout the kingdom.[23]

Stuart was flattered to have been approached by Wyvill. It was gratifying, he replied, that his works had 'a title to be not indifferent to the friends of Liberty and Mankind', and with becoming modesty claimed that he had 'not sufficiently the command of Language to express ... the extreme happiness with which I received your communications'.[24] That Wyvill wrote to everyone remotely interested in the cause of reform did not matter. In the principles of the Yorkshire Association Stuart could see the political themes of his historical works translated into direct action.

While in London, Stuart could do little directly for the Edinburgh Committee. He did, however, write to the Earl of Buchan (as Wyvill had done) to enlist his patron's support. Stuart placed the necessity for Scottish reform in the context of his own encounter with those who controlled Scottish affairs. He told Buchan, who had long campaigned for reform: 'There exists in Scotland, an inclement faction of men, who are enemies to the freedom of our Constitution, & who would gladly seek for the true order of government in the dead calm of despotism.'[25] Stuart was alluding to Henry Dundas and the Duke of Buccleuch, who opposed the reforms proposed by Wyvill.

Dundas' authority in Scotland met with a challenge as Fox and North rose to power, when in July 1783 Henry Erskine replaced him as Lord Advocate of Scotland. Now there was an opportunity for the side Stuart supported to make its mark. An account of this change appeared in the *English Review* which, if not written by Stuart, clearly expressed his view.

Civil, ecclesiastical, and literary preferment ... was generally understood to be very much under the direction of Mr. Dundas and his friend Dr. Robertson. The public curiosity is not a little excited to know the various effects that may arise, in a country that is now animated by a passion for reformation, from the late appointment of the office of Lord Advocate, of a gentleman [Henry Erskine] who ... has uniformly maintained the claims of the people ... over that of the Duke of Buccleugh [sic], and the House of Arniston [Dundas].

(ER, II, 160)

Stuart's satisfaction in seeing his enemies fall from power was short-lived, for with the fall of Fox and North, Pitt rose to power and with him, Henry Dundas. Ilay Campbell, a loyal supporter of Dundas, replaced Erskine as Lord Advocate. In reality Dundas had never completely lost power. Stuart therefore contemplated other strategies for undermining 'Harry the Ninth's' ever increasing authority.

He found his confrontational manner somewhat constrained by Murray's cautious control of the *English Review*. Scottish political affairs were important but could not justifiably command the amount of space Stuart required. Consequently, Stuart sought a forum where he could directly attack Dundas and promote reform in Scotland. The opportunity arose when leaders of the party who opposed Pitt – namely Fox, Burke and Sheridan – approached Stuart to ask him to edit a new periodical. It was a flattering opportunity which could not be lost. Backed by these influential men, he established the *Political Herald and Review; or, a Survey of Domestic and Foreign Politics; and a Critical Account of Political and Historical Publications* in July 1785. The regular salary Stuart received from party funds gave him the security he had so long desired.

Where Murray strove for political impartiality in the *English Review*, the *Herald* was an emphatically factional vehicle for Opposition propaganda. It appeared at a time when Ministry and Opposition as political institutions were becoming more securely entrenched as adversarial elements of the parliamentary process.[26] Stuart called in two of the most able journalists to assist him: William Thomson and William Godwin. He had worked with both at the *English Review* and was in a position to know and capitalise on their talents. There were undoubtedly other contributors, but almost nothing is known of their identities.[27]

The *Political Herald* was not specifically a monthly production but a 'periodical pamphlet' appearing at irregular intervals. During Stuart's tenure as editor, twelve numbers came out between July 1785 and the summer of 1786, when he fell ill. Afterwards, a further six numbers were published under the editorship of Godwin. It was published by the Robinsons and printed by Millan.

Stuart chose a conventional format for the *Herald*. It was divided into two basic parts: the first was headed 'Political and Historical Speculations'; and the second, 'A Review of Political and Historical Publications'. Each issue was eighty pages (five octavo sheets). On average three to four articles appeared in the first part, some of them of considerable length and not infrequently continued over more than one issue. Godwin's 'Critique of the Administration of Mr. Pitt' appeared in a considerable number of issues; and Thomson's 'The Present Times', a survey of political events in various countries, was a regular feature. Irish affairs, which were then at a critical juncture, were regularly discussed and many pamphlets on the subject reviewed. Pseudonymous authorship was not uncommon. Godwin chose 'Mucius' (PH, I, 182; II, 183, 249 and 411), after Mucius Scaevola and Stuart returned to his favourites 'Brutus' (PH, I, 278) and 'Lucius' (PH, II, 21).

The number of review articles varied considerably, depending on how many suitable publications had appeared in the interval between issues. Seven articles was the average, though as few as four or as many as twelve publications might be given attention. Annotations in the Bodleian copy suggest that Stuart was more involved in writing reviews, although his pen was by no means absent from the 'Political Speculations'. A few of the more interesting works reviewed are *Burke's Speech on the ... Nabob of Arcot's Private Debts* (PH, I, 219–32); Boswell's *Journal of a Tour to the Hebrides* (PH, I, 394–400); Charles Wilkins' translation of the *Bhagvat-Geeta* (PH, II, 155–60) and Hester Piozzi's *Anecdotes of the late Samuel Johnson* (PH, II, 370–9).

From the outset the *Herald* emphasised the importance of public opinion in shaping government policy. Stuart asserted that 'to the People this undertaking addresses itself' (PH, I, 3). After the election of 1784 this appeal signified something more than commonplace political rhetoric. The task before the writers of the *Herald* was to convince 'the People' that Pitt was now the wrong man to lead the government. The journal sought 'to instruct, to please, and to reform' (PH, I, 3). This last addition emphasised the periodical's political immediacy and support for the Opposition.

Shortly before publication, Stuart wrote in confidence to the Earl of Buchan to announce that 'the Attack against the Dundas faction commences in the first number'.[28] He planned to recount the deteriorating political situation in Scotland in order to 'shake the power of a very corrupt family'. The secrecy of his role in the project was essential because 'the idea to be inculcated is, that the publication is conducted by Englishmen; & on that account it will be proper to abstain carefully from any mention of my name.'[29] If the work had the appearance of English authorship the censure of Dundas would be more effective.

As treasurer of the Navy Dundas held considerable power. He was portrayed as a man of unsteady principles who was motivated by self-interest. His political attachment to Lord North in the 1770s placed him among those politicians who opposed parliamentary reform and conciliation with America. When the loss of the Colonies brought down North's government, and 'power and emolument were no longer to be disposed of by the same hands, Mr Dundas accordingly … choice [sic] to cooperate with those [namely Pitt], by whom his patron [North] had lately been opposed' (PH, I, 402). In the political camp of Pitt he became an advocate of reform. A man such as this, who abjured the values of civic virtue, was unfit to play such a formative role in government. When Dundas speedily pushed a bill through parliament, Stuart attacked him for 'insulting the legislature of England' and 'convert[ing] it into an humble instrument to destroy your adversaries' (PH, I, 277). 'Your behaviour … has been pressed against you by Mr. Burke, with a force that carries conviction to every reader. Nor have you ventured to contradict his charges and reasonings by any acknowledged or legal declaration' (PH, I, 278).

In an article entitled 'The Political Situations of the Scots at Different Periods', Stuart presented an abbreviated constitutional history of Scotland from 1603 to his own day. It was another attack on Scotland's corrupt electoral system and the ministers who kept it in place:

> The high qualification requisite to vote at a county election, checks the industry as well as emulation of the inferior ranks … The method of splitting votes, too, introduced and practised though contrary to law, has thrown the influence …

almost entirely into the hands of the great families ...
The mode of election in burghs is still more degrading and
deplorable. The magistrates and members of councils are not
chosen by the community which they represent. They elect
one another ... and hold the exclusive management of all
public affairs.   (PH, II, 196)
About the reforms which Dundas did propose for Scotland Stuart
was equally condemnatory. He asserted that the reaction of the
Scottish people would be such that war might be the consequence,
and even threatened that a renewal of 'their antient alliance with
France' would be the means by which England would be invaded
and the Union dissolved (PH, I, 36). Stuart expressed increasing
doubt about the advantages Scotland could gain from the Union.
Public opinion and political reform, though dynamic features of
English politics, had made slower progress in Scotland. He attributed this to Dundas and to the aristocratic influence which held
sway in his day much as it had in the corrupt period of feudalism.
But though the *Political Herald* pointed out the faults of Dundas
and Pitt in a seditious and often satirical manner, it could not get
them out of office. As it turned out, they remained in power for
over twenty years.

The onset of illness in the spring of 1786 prevented Stuart from
performing his editorial duties. Godwin was asked by the Opposition leaders to take his place. The journal was not a paying publication; and Godwin's refusal to receive a salary directly from
party funds was an important factor in the decision to cease
publication before the end of 1786.[30]

The factional emphasis of the *Political Herald* 'excited great
indignation' in Scotland.[31] In remarks to the Society of Antiquaries
not long after Stuart's death, the Earl of Buchan justified Stuart's
attacks on Dundas.

> Let it be remembered, that the worst that can be said of Stuart
> is, that he was a violent satyrist, and stopped at nothing to
> pull down a man whom he considered as a chief advocate for
> absolute power in this country and nation, whilst at the same
> time he continued the integrity of his political creed. But of
> the sycophants of D[undas], it may be affirmed, that they
> support a man who despises them in his heart, derides them
> in his conduct, and has taught them to expect that he will
> leave them in penury and contempt whenever another *Tem-
> ple* shall be erected on the platform of royal favour.[32]

In the same article Buchan referred to the 'misfortunes' and 'disappointments' which 'pressed upon [Stuart's] genius, his temper, and his character'. He also said it was regrettable that a man of Stuart's 'eminent abilities should have been forced to lend himself to occupations of so inferior a nature' as writing for the *Political Herald*.[33] William Godwin took exception to both these remarks and came to Stuart's defence in the pages of the *Herald* itself.

> He undoubtedly did not bask in the smiles of fortune, and he was not entirely at his ease in his personal situation. But with respect to the world, for whom he laboured, and to which he devoted all his talents, he did not miscarry – No! he succeeded, in a manner that lays an everlasting claim to their admiration, and creates an immeasureable debt upon their gratitude.
> ... As an author and as a citizen, his claim was of the highest order: – but he condescended to write in the Political Herald ... You have uttered strictures on the character of doctor Stuart; and though we did not intent to celebrate, we know how to defend it.   (PH, III, 280–2)

In vindicating Stuart's public character, Godwin confirmed Buchan's description of a very unhappy and unfortunate man. What made Stuart so uneasy in his 'personal situation' at a time when he was at the height of his profession? Was it, as Buchan believed, 'his misfortune to miss a situation at the university of Edinburgh for which he was highly qualified'?; was it the difficult choice either to leave Scotland 'or to submit to be pointed at in the street as literary Drawcansirs'?[34] Was it misfortune in love or the death of his brother which made him despondent? Was it the fact that his ambitions as an historian were not fully achieved? Was it the realisation that his political writings were making little impact? It would seem that all these factors weighed upon his mind and led him increasingly to seek solace in drink.

Stuart's constitution was robust, but he took little care of himself. Jaundice, asthma and worsening dropsy brought him to a condition where John Murray felt compelled to warn George Stuart of the tragedy towards which his son was heading if something was not done soon. Difficulty in breathing prevented him from sleeping properly; a yellowish pallor replaced his once ruddy complexion; and his legs began to swell and cause discomfort. These were the classic signs of the latter stages of alcoholism.

'He is much emaciated,' reported Murray and 'water is suspected to have got into his chest.'[35] Though on closest terms with his ailing friend, Murray hesitated to confront him about his

declining condition, fearful that 'it might ruffle his temper & hurt
him'.[36] Murray suggested that George and Jean Stuart come immediately to London as their 'joint authority might perhaps save a
life that is precious to his friends'.[37]

When Stuart was healthy and writing for the *Herald*, he could
readily support himself. Illness, however, prevented him from
working and debts began to mount. His landlady, Mrs Wait, cared
for him with maternal regard, but even she inquired to Murray
about arrears in the rent.[38] Reports of Stuart's poor state came to
Scotland from other sources. John Logan remarked to Alexander
Carlyle that '*Gilbert* has been at the gates of death, but is getting
better'.[39] The improvement was only temporary. Despite the concern
of his friends and regular visits from physicians, Stuart behaved as if
unaware of his dangerous condition. He even spoke of going abroad.
Violent pains in his side puzzled medical advisors, but even these
signals did not bring Stuart to care for himself.

He was usually the centre of activity, but offensive bodily
smells, another consequence of his ailments, reduced him to a
state where he shunned company. Confinement and illness made
him short-tempered and more and more unreceptive to advice
from those who had his interest alone at heart. The prospect of his
own death, of his own fallibility, was not something he could
easily bear.

In the meantime, medical advisors thought the fresher air of
Hampstead might be beneficial. He was transported there at the
end of April but showed little improvement. Latterly, Murray had
sensed Stuart's unspoken desire to return to Scotland. During the
first days of August, accompanied by William Thomson, Stuart
boarded a ship for North Berwick. The publisher, so often at his
bedside during the illness and for nearly twenty years his closest
friend, missed the opportunity to bid him farewell and thus wrote
in haste, fearful that Stuart would die before receiving a final
communication: 'This is not a letter of news,' he explained, 'but of
solicitous enquiry after you.' He asked Stuart to reply, adding
'you will greatly oblige a man who since the commencement of
our acquaintance always had your reputation and real welfare at
heart'.[40] Stuart had written a great deal in his short life but he
would write no more.

Warmly wrapped and sitting on the ship's deck, what thoughts
must have passed through his mind, now confronted with the
grim prospect of his own demise? As the ship entered the Firth of
Forth and the familiar landscape of Scotland's coastline came into

view, the gamboling of seals captured Stuart's attention, and he inquired of the captain: 'Tell me, Sir, upon what diet do these creatures feed?' To the answer 'Salmon and saltwater', Stuart quickly replied, 'Very good meat but very bad drink.'[41]

After a short journey by land, he settled into the home of his parents at Fisherrow. The dramatic change in his appearance caused grave concern. His father immediately called in Alexander Bruce, a local surgeon married to his daughter. Bruce could see that his brother-in-law had only a few days to live. To relieve the painful swelling, Bruce 'tapped' him at the abdomen. As the draining began, Stuart exclaimed: 'Bottle these fluids and send them to Principal Robertson to use as a purge.'[42] The truth was that Robertson was about to be purged of his most ardent adversary.

Word of Stuart's death on 13 August 1786 shook Murray, though it could not but be expected. Passing the news on to John Millar, he pointed out an important aspect of Stuart's personality:

> You have lost a friend in Dr. Stuart, indeed he was the greatest enemy to himself. He could not endure to be thought subject to human infirmities; he was confident to the last in his constitution, and this confidence killed him, for he would not take care of himself.[43]

Murray also sent condolences to Stuart's parents, while at the same time attempting with the utmost propriety to obtain funds sufficient to settle outstanding financial obligations. As Stuart had written of George Buchanan: 'Careless of the future, he made no provision for the season of ... helplessness. His money and his life terminated in the same moment' (MQS, II, 175).

George Stuart had been instrumental in developing his son's native talent and took an immense paternal pride in those literary achievements which he believed were an indication of greater things to come. He was also a loving parent, and very much involved in his son's life. For these reasons he felt the tragedy more sensibly than any other. Just hours after witnessing Gilbert's death, he wrote to the Earl of Buchan:

> The fatal hour is now come. That masterly hand, which could paint beauty & deformity, virtue and vice in so lively & durable colours, is now languished and will fill the canvas no more. To lose a child ... is something to a feeling mind, but to lose a man of such talents – of such hopes – is a Stroke even to one who knows his duty, too severe for the frailty of human nature to bear.[44]

The next day Stuart was interred at Inveresk churchyard. Family members, Buchan, Dr James Gregory, William Smellie and a collection of other Edinburgh literati attended. Alexander Carlyle probably officiated at the burial. In the following months short accounts of his life appeared in many of Britain's leading magazines and newspapers. On the whole the London press offered more favourable obituaries than the Scottish. The *Daily Universal Register* referred to Stuart as 'a gentleman well known in the literary world for the learning, ingenuity, and elegance of his historical and periodical compositions'. The writer described his *History of Mary Queen of Scots* as 'a celebrated historical production ... [which] hath restored probability and truth to this part of our annals, and vindicated the honour of the Scottish Queen from the aspersions of all her enemies'.[45] The *Gentleman's Magazine* concluded its account in a manner which typified the dismissive view of Stuart which was to be passed down: 'He was a boon companion; and, with a constitution that might have stood the shock of ages, he has fallen premature, a martyr to intemperance.'[46]

A Latin inscription also appeared in print which commemorated Stuart and summarised his contributions to intellectual culture. The setting was his arrival in the Elysian fields, where he was welcomed with a 'blithe spirit' by Mary Queen of Scots, 'victim of her own country and of the savage Elizabeth', and by the great Scottish patriots, Fergus, Wallace and Bruce as one 'who defended the kings of Scotland from the charge of poverty and the clan chiefs from the charge of eternal treason'. The welcoming party also included classical heroes such as Cicero, 'chief of orators' who 'recognised his own style in Gilbert's writing'. The poem concluded with a claim for the enduring quality of his writings: 'He is not completely dead; the better part survives, and his fame will fly by the faces of men until the world breathes its last in the avenging flame.'[47]

Nearly ten years later an advertisement in the *Edinburgh Evening Courant* offered for sale a life sized bust of Stuart, modelled by R. Cummins.[48] The other busts which could be obtained were Copernicus, Mary Queen of Scots, Napier of Merchiston, David Hume, William Robertson, William Smellie, and John Brown. Before casting each figure Cummins required ten subscribers, at one guinea each. Apparently this number could not be raised for the bust of Stuart. The bust of Robertson, however, was already cast and selling well. Even at a period after both men had died, Stuart could not hope to displace his rival, or even share space atop the bookcases of a new generation of Scotsmen.

From the youthful challenge to Hume in the *English Constitution* to the attack on Dundas in the *Political Herald*, Stuart confronted opponents with confidence and vigour. In real terms he had little chance of success, but this did not lessen his determination. The likelihood of failure made the distant prospect of triumph all the more desirable. Stuart's career was not entirely a catalogue of defeats. There were some victories, and he made the most of them. The shift in public opinion in favour of Mary Queen of Scots may have been his most significant contribution, but it brought disagreeable consequences along with it: Stuart could no longer live comfortably in Scotland, where, in any case, the views of Robertson and Hume on Mary still held sway.

Disputatious by nature, he took the field as an adversary, an antagonist or even an assailant. To men in positions of authority, he made himself available as a propagandist, but his patrons could not be certain of a successful attack. This may explain why the 'Memoirs of the Isle of Man' were never published. Patrons were also fearful that he would turn against them. This may explain why Robertson could not risk bringing so unequivocal a man into the Moderate fold. Stuart was too independent by nature to work with or fight for others. To his own cause he was adamant and true, even if its justice was questionable, and in his historical and journalistic writings his determination predominates, at times to a fault. Even the collective involvement of talented and prudent men could not save the *Edinburgh Magazine and Review* from decline after initial success. Stuart compromised the scholarly integrity of the *View of Society* and the *Public Law of Scotland* by a too insistent attack on rivals and rival ideas.

It would be an ill-conceived panegyric to turn Stuart's faults into virtues. It is more interesting to look into the motives behind his actions, drawing out the peculiarly embattled contexts in which they were performed rather than justifying them. Had Stuart lived longer, the story might have been very different. As editor of the *Political Herald* he was at the forefront of radical political ideology. What scope the French Revolution would have given him is not difficult to imagine. He was friends with Godwin and Holcroft in London, and an ardent campaigner for electoral and judicial reform in Scotland. His antipathy towards the government and his growing awareness of the power of the people had already fueled his radical views. Like so many others in the early 1790s, he might have stood on trial for seditious libel, been found guilty and been transported to Botany Bay; or, with the majority, watched with increasing indignation, as the Revolution betrayed its ideals, forcing him to question, and perhaps to change his view. Would he have remained true to his principles, yet ever more pessimistic, like his colleague Godwin, or might he have moved to the Right, with Gibbon and Pitt, Wordsworth and Coleridge?

One thing is certain: he would not have been silent. He would not have been like 'the bulk of men ... deceived into the highest admiration; and forgetful of their natural rights, and of the privileges of citizens' (EC, 150–1); rather like the noble Saxons, for whom 'the honour of their nation, the rivalship of their equals, the hopes of renown, all conspired to inflame their minds with the most generous ardour to excel' (EC, 5).

Notes

Introduction

1. S. Austin Allibone, *A Critical Dictionary of English Literature, and British and American Authors Living and Deceased*, 3 vols (London and Philadelphia, 1859–71), under 'Stuart', II, 2292.
2. Isaac D'Israeli, *The Calamities and Quarrels of Authors; with some Inquiries respecting their Moral and Literary Characters*, A new edition edited by Benjamin Disraeli (London, 1869), pp. 138–9.
3. Ernest Mossner, 'Hume as Literary Patron: A suppressed Review of Robert Henry's *History of Great Britain* 1773' in *Modern Philology*, 39 (1942), 373 and 366.
4. Attribution of this article to Godwin is found in William St Clair, *The Godwins and the Shelleys: The biography of a Family* (London, 1989), p. 36.
5. James Boswell, *The Applause of the Jury, 1782–1785*, edited by Lustig and Pottle (London, 1981), p. 305 (1 June 1785).

Chapter 1

1. Old Parish Records, Parish of Edinburgh, Edinburgh Parish Record Office.
2. Ibid. The names of the children who died were James (born 24 March 1747) and Jean (born 9 September 1749). Walter was born on 28 May 1746; Mary on 9 August 1748; and Agnes on 3 October 1750.
3. George Stuart to Charles Stuart (a grandson of Thomas Ruddiman), 30 May 1792, NLS, Adv. MS 21. 1. 12, f. 66. George Stuart explained in the same letter: 'My grandmother was his aunt'.
4. George Chalmers, *The Life of Thomas Ruddiman* (London, 1794), p. 289.
5. Two useful studies of Thomas Ruddiman are Chalmers, *The Life of Thomas Ruddiman* and Douglas Duncan, *Thomas Ruddiman: A Study in Scottish Scholarship of the early Eighteenth Century* (Edinburgh, 1965). See also George Davie, *The Democratic Intellect: Scotland and her Universities in the Nineteenth Century*, paperback edition (Edinburgh, 1981), pp. 223–9.
6. Joseph Addison, *Tatler*, Number 165 (29 April 1710).
7. George Stuart was christened on 24 August 1711. The parish record book for Forglen is so faded that the date of his birth cannot be determined, although it was most probably a matter of days or weeks before the christening date. His father was named John Stuart, but nothing is known of his mother (Old Parish Records, Edinburgh).
8. George Stuart's university education cannot be confirmed. He is not

listed in Edinburgh University or Aberdeen University matriculation
rolls.

9. Evidence of this concern is found in a letter from Lady Minto to Lord
    Minto, 18 Jan. [1764], NLS, Minto Papers, 11008, ff. 30–1.
10. George Stuart to Charles Mackie, 22 Aug. 1739, EUL, La. II, 91.
11. Edinburgh Town Council Minutes, 11 Dec. and 16 Dec. 1741, vol. 62,
    ff. 230–3. From this time Stuart became secretary to the Senatus
    Academicus, the governing body within the University. This was a
    task usually given to junior members of staff. His neat hand recorded
    the Minutes for nearly twenty years.
12. Charles Mackie to Lord Bolgonie, 7 Jan. 1742, Scottish Record Office,
    Leven and Melville Papers, XIII, 615.
13. Ibid. The ballad begins: 'I sing of electors but not of a king,/ An
    Emperor, Pope, or any such thing./ But of a Professor who now wears
    a gown/ In spite of the Ladys, in spite of ye Town.'
14. George Stuart relayed information about Elliot's prospects for
    returning as parliamentary member for Selkirkshire and kept him up-
    to-date on Edinburgh politics: George Stuart to Gilbert Elliot, 27 Jan.
    1756, NLS, Minto Papers, 11008, f. 240 and 22 Nov. 1760, 11015, f. 75.
15. George Stuart to Gilbert Elliot, 20 Oct. 1772, NLS, Minto Papers,
    10019, f. 49.
16. *Gentleman's Magazine*, 63 (July 1793), 672.
17. The children of Stuart's sister Anne, (Gilbert Stuart Bruce and George
    Stuart Bruce) won a considerable degree of fame and fortune through
    the patronage of Gilbert Elliot (1751–1814), the 1st Earl of Minto.
    Antonia Raeburn has written a study of these men, *The Stuart Bruce
    Family 1710–1907* (Privately printed, [1988]). Descendants of this line
    of the family (named Bowen) live in Cornwall.
18. Old Parish Records, Parish of Dunbarton; James Duncanson's parents
    were Robert Duncanson and Isobell Porterfield. See also George
    Stuart to John Mackenzie, 19 Jan. 1776, NLS, 1480, f. 98. The full story
    of Stuart's relationship with the Smolletts is told in Chapter 2.
19. *Matriculation Rolls of the University of Edinburgh: Arts, Law, Divinity*, I, 232.
20. Ibid., I, 239–41.
21. John Ramsay, *Scotland and Scotsmen in the Eighteenth Century*, edited
    by Alexander Allardyce, 2 vols (Edinburgh, 1888), I, 231.
22. George Stuart to Charles Stuart, 16 and 19 June 1792, NLS, Adv. MS
    21. 1. 12, ff. 91 and 92.
23. Lady Minto to Lord Minto, 18 Jan. [1764], NLS, Minto Papers, 11008,
    ff. 30–1.
24. See 'An Account of the Late Duke Gordon M.A. including Anecdotes
    of the University of Edinburgh', *Scots Magazine*, 64 (Jan. 1802), 23–6
    and Jeremy Cator, 'James Robertson 1720–1795: An Anti-
    Enlightenment Professor in the University of Edinburgh'
    (unpublished Ph.D. dissertation, New York University, 1976), pp. 219
    and 239.
25. Edinburgh Town Council Minutes, Petition of George Stuart, 9 March
    1748, Vol. 67, ff. 115–18. The Catalogues are found in EUL, Da. 1. 2–4.
26. Ibid. The rooms (Numbers 26–31) were on the east side of the upper
    college buildings. Stuart paid ten guineas per annum for the rental.
    Matthew Stewart, the Professor of Mathematics and father of Dugald
    Stewart, obtained rooms on the same day.
27. Gilbert Elliot to his father, 28 Oct. 1766, NLS, Minto Papers, 11008, f.

281. George Stuart had been instrumental in arranging for Robert Liston to be tutor to the Elliot boys prior to their attendance at the University. Gilbert became Governor-General of India. Hugh Elliot (1752–1830) had a distinguished military career.

28. *European Magazine,*10 (Oct. 1786), 235–6.

29. *Matriculation Rolls of the University of Edinburgh : Arts, Law, Divinity,* I, 267 and 284.

30. An account of Sheridan's lectures is found in the *Scots Magazine,* 23 (July 1761), 389–90. The published version appeared as *A Course of Lectures on Elocution* (London, 1762).

31. George Stuart to Gilbert Elliot, 6 Oct. 1757, NLS, Minto Papers, 11014, f. 73.

32. George Stuart to Gilbert Elliot, 24 July 1762, NLS, Minto Papers, 11016, f. 39; the 'Memorial Relating to Newspaper', f. 34.

33. Ibid.

34. John Mackenzie to Gilbert Elliot, 21 Dec. 1766, NLS, Minto Papers, 11008, f. 283.

35. Henry Mackenzie, *The Anecdotes and Egotisms of Henry Mackenzie 1745–1831,* edited by H. W. Thompson (Oxford, 1927), p. 174.

36. *Encyclopaedia Perthensis; or Universal Dictionary, of Knowledge,* 23 vols (Perth, 1796–1806), XXI, 499.

37. *Monthly Review,* 47 (Nov. 1772), 361–2, in a review of *A Collection of Curious Discourses by Eminent Antiquaries.*

38. Boswell, *The Ominous Years, 1774–1776,* edited by Ryskamp and Pottle (London, 1963), p. 228 (2 Feb. 1776).

39. *Monthly Review,* 47 (Nov. 1772), 362.

40. *Daily Universal Register* (precursor to *The Times*), 2 Sept. 1786.

41. EUL, Student Borrowing Ledger, Da. 2. 8–10; Library Receipt Books, Da. 1. 34 and La. II. 247.

42. George Stuart to Gilbert Elliot, 23 Nov. 1767, NLS, Minto Papers, 11012, ff. 91–2.

43. By 'historiography' I mean simply the study of the writing of history. By 'Enlightenment' I mean a tradition in western intellectual culture taking place mainly in the eighteenth century which had, in the words of Peter Gay, 'a program of secularism, humanity, cosmopolitanism, and freedom, above all, freedom, in its many forms – freedom from arbitrary power, freedom of speech, freedom of trade, freedom to realize one's talents, freedom of aesthetic response, freedom, in a word, of moral man to make his own way in the world'. Gay, *The Enlightenment: An Interpretation,* 2 vols (New York, 1966–9), I, 3: a useful starting point for understanding the period in a thematic context.

44. David Hume to William Strahan, [August 1770] *The Letters of David Hume,* 2 vols, edited by J. Y. T. Greig (Oxford, reprinted 1969), II, 230 (Letter 449).

45. Henry St. John, Viscount Bolingbroke, *Letters on the Study and Use of History,* Letter II, 'Concerning the true use and advantage of it'. Bolingbroke was himself quoting loosely from Dionysius Halicarn (London, 1779), p. 15.

46. Dugald Stewart, *Biographical Memoirs, of Adam Smith, LL.D. of William Robertson D.D. and of Thomas Reid D.D.* (Edinburgh, 1811), p. 47. Stewart's 'Life of Smith' was first read to the Royal Society of Edinburgh in 1793.

47. Ibid., p. 46.

48. Roger Emerson, 'Conjectural History and Scottish Philosophers', in *Historical Papers 1984 Communications Historiques*, Canadian Historical Association, p. 82. For a sample of other articles on conjectural history see H. M. Höpfl, 'From Savage to Scotsmen: Conjectural History in the Scottish Enlightenment', in the *Journal of British Studies*, 17 (Spring 1975), 18–40. Duncan Forbes, '"Scientific" Whiggism: Adam Smith and John Millar', in the *Cambridge Journal*, 7 (Aug. 1954), 643–70. Alice Wheeler, 'Society History in Eighteenth-Century Scotland' (unpublished Ph.D. dissertation, Emory University, 1966); and Roy Pascal, 'Property and Society: The Scottish Historical School' *Modern Quarterly*, 1 (1938), 167–79.

49. *Edinburgh Review*, III (Oct. 1803), 163, in a review of a new edition of John Millar's *Historical View of the English Government* (first edition, London, 1787).

50. Murray to John Whitaker, 6 March 1783, Murray's Copybooks.

51. Hayden White, *Metahistory: The Historical Imagination in Nineteenth-Century Europe* (Baltimore, 1973), pp. 47 and 66 and Chapter 1 generally. Another useful work concerning Enlightenment historiography is J. C. Hilson, 'Hume: Historian as Man of Feeling', in *Augustan Worlds*, edited by Hilson, M. M. B. Jones and J. R. Watson (Leicester, 1978), especially pp. 218–19.

52. White, *Metahistory*, p. 66.

53. Barbara Shapiro, *Probability and Certainty in Seventeenth-Century England* (Princeton, 1983), is a useful general study of the legacy of Bacon and Newton.

54. Duncan Forbes, '"Scientific" Whiggism: Adam Smith and John Millar', p. 646.

55. Alexander Fraser Tytler, *Memoirs of the Life and Writings of the Honourable Henry Home of Kames*, 2 vols (Edinburgh, 1807), I, 160.

56. David Hume to Adam Smith, 12 April 1759, *The Letters of David Hume*, I, 304 (Letter 165).

57. In a review of *Eumonus; or Dialogues concerning the Laws and Constitution of England*. F. T. H. Fletcher, *Montesquieu and English Politics 1750–1800* (London, 1939), p. 84, called Dalrymple's Essay 'the first of real importance devoted to the study of constitutional and legal origins'.

58. Gibbon, *The Decline and Fall of the Roman Empire*, edited by J. B. Bury, 7 vols (London, 1896), I, 213 (Chapter IX).

59. The title quotation is found in Montesquieu, *De L'Esprit des Loix*, 2 vols (Edinburgh 1750), I, 229 (Liv. XI, Ch. VI); the second quotation, I, 215 (Liv. XI, Ch. V). This is the first British edition and the one Stuart used.

60. *Scots Magazine*, 61 (Oct. 1799), 661–4 and (Nov. 1799), 734–5.

61. H. T. Dickinson, *Liberty and Property* (London, 1977), p. 69. Another useful discussion of the term 'the people' is found in J. A. W. Gunn, *Beyond Liberty and Property: The Process of Self-Recognition in Eighteenth-Century Political Thought* (Kingston and Montreal, 1983), pp. 73–88.

62. Samuel Johnson, *A Dictionary of the English Language*, sixth edition (London, 1785), under 'whiggish'. Johnson, true to his Tory sentiments, defined 'Whig' as 'the name of a faction'.

63. In a review of Alexander Gerard's *Essay on Genius* (EMR, II, 588–97), Stuart came closest to showing his understanding of the association of ideas and other important aspects of Hume's philosophy. His remark that there is difficulty in 'throwing new light on any philosophical subject which has been illustrated by Mr Hume' (EMR, II, 591)

indicates the extent of his regard for Hume as a philosopher.

64. 'Of the Parties of Great Britain', in *Essays Moral, Political, and Literary*, Liberty Classics edition (Indianapolis, 1987), p. 64.

65. Nicholas Phillipson, *Hume* (London, 1989), p. 138.

66. Ibid., p. 139.

67. Hume, *History of England from the Invasion of Julius Caesar to the Revolution in 1688*, 6 vols, Liberty Classics Edition (Indianapolis, 1983), II, 525.

68. Ibid., I, 4.

69. Stuart to David Hume, 2 May 1768, NLS, 23157, f. 74.

70. David Hume to Gilbert Elliot, July [1768], *The Letters of David Hume*, II, 184, (Letter 420).

71. For a recent collection of essays see *Ossian Revisited*, edited by Howard Gaskill (Edinburgh, 1991).

72. Nicholas Phillipson notes that during the eighteenth century the type of assimilation with English society that was initiated by the Scots themselves 'was regarded not so much as a threat to Scottish life as a stimulus to it'; 'Scottish Public Opinion and the Union in the Age of the Association', in *Scotland in the Age of Improvement*, edited by Phillipson and Rosalind Mitchison (Edinburgh, 1970), pp. 142–3. For a more general study see Gerald Newman, *The Rise of English Nationalism: A Cultural History 1740–1830* (London, 1987).

73. Dugald Stewart, *Life of Robertson*, pp. 259–65, provides a useful summary of the manner in which Robertson, Smith, Hume and Gibbon integrated the note into their historical narratives.

74. William Smyth, *Lectures on Modern History*, 2 vols (London, 1840), I, 77, remarking on the scholarly utility of Stuart's extensive notes, pointed out that they are 'the only way in which any estimate can be given of the situation of society at any particular period'.

75. The influence of Tacitus on eighteenth-century historical writing cannot be over emphasised. The translation by Thomas Gordon (London, 1728–31) was the standard edition of the day. It is one of the few books Stuart is known to have purchased (Murray's Account Ledgers, Murray Archive, I, 102). On the continent Hume was called the English Tacitus.

76. John Pocock, *The Ancient Constitution and the Feudal Law. A Study of English Historical Thought in the Seventeenth Century* (Cambridge, 1957), pp. 17–18, elaborates on the kind of 'constitutional antiquarianism' which engaged historians like Stuart who appealed 'to the existing "municipal" laws of the country concerned and to the concepts of custom, prescription and authority that underlay them, as well as to the reverence which they enjoyed by reason of their antiquity'.

77. William Hayley, *An Essay on History in Three Epistles to Edward Gibbon* (London, 1780), Note XII (to lines 327–30).

78. Robert Heron [John Pinkerton], *Letters of Literature* (London, 1785), p. 368.

79. This topic is discussed further on pp. 81 and 168–71.

80. Adam Ferguson, *An Essay on the History of Civil Society*, edited with an introduction by Duncan Forbes (Edinburgh, 1966), p. 105.

81. Pocock remarks that 'to admit of [a Norman] conquest was to admit an indelible stain of sovereignty upon the English constitution. *The Ancient Constitution and the Feudal Law*, p. 53.

82. Hume, *History of England*, IV, 22–51. See also the essay 'Of Super-

stition and Enthusiasm' in the *Essays Moral, Political, and Literary*, pp. 73–9.
83. *Critical Review*, 25 (June 1768), 452.
84. *Monthly Review*, 39 (Dec. 1768), 452; by Andrew Kippis.
85. The German translator is unrecorded, though the publisher C. G. Donatius, is known to have had a share in the translations of English works. Boulard translated many English works of the period, including Johnson's *Rambler* (1785), Stuart's *View of Society* (1789), Robert Henry's *History of Great Britain* (1788) and Adam Smith's *Dissertation on the Origin of Language* (1796).
86. Fletcher, *Montesquieu and English Politics*, p. 87.
87. George Lyttleton (1709–73) was an historian and an important political figure. Charles Jenkinson (1727–1808), later Lord Liverpool, was Lord of the Treasury at the time. Stuart's letter accompanying the presentation copy to Jenkinson, 23 Jan. 1770, is in the British Library, Liverpool Papers (20), 38209, f. 259.
88. John Mackenzie to the Duke of Atholl, 23 March 1772, Blair Castle Archive, Box 54, III, f. 84.
89. Alexander Grant, *The Story of the University of Edinburgh*, II, 314.
90. Richard Sher, 'Professors of Virtue: The Social History of the Edinburgh Moral Philosophy Chair in the Eighteenth Century', in *Studies in the Philosophy of the Scottish Enlightenment*, edited by M. A. Stewart (Oxford, 1990), pp. 113–16.
91. George Stuart to Gilbert Elliot, 15 Jan. 1767, NLS, Minto Papers 11012, ff. 86–7.
92. Ibid.
93. EUL, Senatus Minutes, 16 Nov. 1768.
94. George Stuart to Gilbert Elliot, 15 Jan. 1767, NLS, Minto Papers, 11012, ff. 86–7.
95. *European Magazine*, I (Feb. 1782), 128.
96. For a volume of articles on Brown see *Brunonianism in Britain and Europe*, Medical History, Supplement No. 8, edited by W. F. Bynum and Roy Porter (London, 1988).
97. William Cullen Brown, *The Works of Dr John Brown, to which is prefixed a biographical account of the author*, 2 vols (London, 1804), I, ciii-civ.
98. John Murray to John Brown, 10 May 1787, Murray's Copybooks.
99. [John Armstrong], *The Oeconomy of Love: A Poetical Essay* (London, 1736) pp. 8–10. See also Christopher Fox, 'The Myth of Narcissus in Swift's *Travels*', in *Eighteenth-Century Studies*, 20 (Fall 1986), 18.
100. Kerr, *Life of Smellie*, I, 502–3.
101. Stuart to Murray, 6 July 1769, Murray Archive.
102. Andrew Dalzel to Robert Liston, 6 Sept. 1787[6]. Quoted in Andrew Dalzel, *History of the University of Edinburgh from its Foundation*, 2 vols (Edinburgh, 1862), I, 72.
103. H. S. Corran, *A History of Brewing* (London, 1975), p. 151.
104. Though Stuart certainly agreed with this view, it is not clear whether he or William Thomson wrote these remarks.
105. Donald Grant to Murray, 3 Sept. 1774, Murray Archive.
106. *The Book of the Old Edinburgh Club*, (Edinburgh, 1906–present), III, 163.
107. Ibid., III, 164.
108. Kerr, *Life of Smellie*, I, 503.
109. Murray to William Thomson, 28 August 1786, Murray's Copybooks.

Chapter 2

1. Stuart made this comment about London in a character sketch of Arbuthnot.
2. William Robertson to David Hume, 31 Jan. 1769, NLS, Robertson–Macdonald Papers, 3942, ff. 75–6. Published in 'William Robertson and David Hume: Three Letters', edited by R. B. Sher and M. A. Stewart, *Hume Studies*, Tenth Anniversary Issue, (1985) pp. 76–7.
3. Thomas Somerville, *My Own Life and Times, 1741–1814* (Edinburgh [1861]), p. 149.
4. Ibid.
5. Ibid., pp. 149–50.
6. Murray to William Lothian, 5 April 1779, Murray's Copybooks.
7. Murray to Stuart, 22 Nov. 1774, Murray's Copybooks.
8. Murray to Hugo Arnot, 19 March 1779, Murray's Copybooks.
9. *The Repository*, 2 vols (London, 1771), I, 'The Editors to the Reader'.
10. Murray's Account Ledgers, I, 102, Murray Archive.
11. John Millar to Stuart, 17 March 1771, Murray Archive; John Murray to David Dalrymple, 16 Oct. 1775, NLS, Newhailes Papers, Acc. 7228/23, f. 90; Stuart to William Cullen, 4 Aug. 1782, Royal College of Physicians at Edinburgh, MS Cullen, C 32.
12. W. C. Lehmann, *John Millar of Glasgow, 1735–1801* (Cambridge, 1960), p. 1.
13. John Millar to Stuart, 17 March 1771, Murray Archive. See also Millar to Stuart, 14 April 1771, Murray Archive.
14. Murray to Thomas Ewing, 22 March 1771, Murray's Copybooks.
15. *Monthly Review*, 45 (Sept. 1771), 188–9.
16. Millar wrote: 'The same people who talk in so high a strain of political liberty ... make no scruple of reducing a great proportion of the inhabitants into circumstances by which they are not only deprived of property, but almost of every right whatsoever' (*Observations concerning Ranks*, London, 1771, pp. 241–2). Millar revised considerably for the third edition and renamed the work *The Origin of the Distinction of Ranks ...* (1779).
17. John Craig, 'An Account of the Life and Writings of John Millar, Esq.' prefixed to *The Origin of the Distinction of Ranks*, fourth edition, (Edinburgh, 1806), p. lxxvi.
18. Ibid.
19. 'The nobles', Millar wrote, 'maintained their independence during the time of the Saxon princes, and were reduced to be the vassals of the crown in the reign of William the Conqueror' (*Observations concerning Ranks*, p. 173).
20. Millar, *Observations concerning Ranks*, second edition (London, 1773), p. 248n.
21. Phillipson, *Hume*, p. 138.
22. Stuart to Murray, 20 May 1774, Hughenden Papers, G/1/927.
23. In an obituary notice Stuart expressed his regard for John MacMillan, 'an active critic, a bold asserter of civil liberties, an elegant poet, an agreeable novelist, who died at age twenty-eight', (EMR, I, 334).
24. *London Magazine*, 38 (March 1969), 156–7. In the following months further excerpts from the work appeared, probably at Stuart's instigation (July, pp. 248–52 and Oct., pp. 523–5).
25. *London Magazine*, 41 (April 1772), 151–2.
26. *Boswell for the Defence, 1769–1774*, edited by Wimsatt and Pottle

(London, 1960), p. 95 (3 April 1772).

27. *London Magazine*, 41 (June 1772), 281–3. For the attribution see *Boswell for the Defence*, p. 132 (18 April 1772).
28. Corran, *A History of Brewing*, p. 151.
29. B. C. Nangle, *The Monthly Review First Series 1749–1789: Indexes and Contributors and Articles* (Oxford, 1934), p. viii, remarked of its contributors and specifically of Gilbert Stuart, that 'the miserable hacks of legend thus prove to be in fact among the most eminent scholars in the kingdom'. See also Derek Roper's remarks on the *Monthly Review* in *Reviewing before the Edinburgh 1778–1802* (London, 1978), pp. 29–35.
30. Nangle states that Griffiths 'was himself a staunch but fair-minded Whig and Dissenter, but saw no reason why political or theological views should influence criticisms of such subjects as science or literature' (p. xi). Griffiths' papers on the *Monthly Review* are in the Bodleian Library. For wages, see Bodleian MS Adds. C. 89, f. 369.
31. Percival Stockdale, *Memoirs of the Life and Writings of Percival Stockdale*, 2 vols (London, 1809), II, 59.
32. Nangle, *The Monthly Review First Series*, p. 43.
33. *Monthly Review*, 45 (Dec. 1771), 432, in a review of William Guthrie's *New Geographical Grammar*.
34. *Monthly Review*, 45 (July 1771), 73, in a review of *The Generous Husband*, and (Aug. 1771), 156, in a review of *Pro and Con*.
35. *Monthly Review*, 45 (Aug. 1771), 144.
36. *Monthly Review*, 43 (Aug. 1770), 157, in a review of *The New Present State of Great Britain*.
37. Ibid.
38. *Monthly Review*, 44 (May 1771), 418.
39. Ibid.
40. *Monthly Review*, 44 (April 1771), 331–2. The *London Magazine*, 40 (Oct. 1771), 505, in an article entitled 'Reviewers Reviewed', reprinted a portion of Stuart's review along with a contrasting favourable article from the *Critical Review*.
41. In a review of William Thomson's *The Man in the Moon*. Stuart reiterated this view the following month (July 1983) when he reviewed Blair's *Lectures on Rhetoric and Belles Lettres*, but he criticised Blair for 'suppressing with design his real opinion' of Johnson, and printed extracts from a manuscript of the actual lectures (ER, II, 91).
42. The first volume of Hooke's *Roman History* was published in 1738. For an account of this work see Addison Ward, 'The Tory View of Roman History', in *Studies in English Literature*, 4 (1964), 443–52.
43. *Monthly Review*, 45 (Sept. 1771), 173.
44. Ibid.
45. *Monthly Review*, 46 (Jan. 1772), 1–2.
46. *Critical Review*, 36 (Sept. 1772), 213.
47. Stuart to John Mackenzie, 14 April 1772, Blair Castle Archive, Box 54 III, f. 81.
48. Stuart to John Mackenzie, 14 Aug. 1772, NLS, 1480, ff. 102–3. Appendix Number I is headed 'A Chronicle of the Kings of Man'. The other appendices (referred to in the text) are not extant.
49. Ibid.
50. Ibid.
51. In a review of Thomas Leland's *History of Ireland, from the Invasion of*

Henry II.
52. 'Memoirs of the Isle of Man', Manx Museum, Douglas, Atholl Papers, AP X 43/4.
53. Stuart to John Mackenzie, 14 April 1772, Blair Castle Archive, Box 54. III, f. 81
54. Ibid.
55. The Duke of Atholl to John Mackenzie, 7 Aug. 1774, printed in the *Chronicles of the Atholl and Tullibardine Families*, 5 vols, collected and arranged by John, the 7th Duke of Atholl (Edinburgh, 1908), IV, 14.
56. Parliamentary Act, 5 Geo. III, c. 39.
57. 'Memoirs', ch. 5, p. 22.
58. The exact sum demanded was £249,373 for customs, duties, land property and manorial rights; £42,000 for regalities and £8,400 for the patronage of the bishopric and ecclesiastical benefices.
59. 'Memoirs', ch. 5, pp. 33–4. To balance this emotional appeal, he then referred to instances in the history of Britain and of other less democratic countries when it was proper that 'the state may call for the Land of a Proprietor' (ch. 5, p. 34). One example was the abolishment of heritable jurisdictions in Scotland after the 1745 Rebellion for which the government paid the nobility £150,000 'not for visible & corporeal inheritances like those of the Duke of Athol but for pride, custom of living, trains of followers & Highland-dress' (ch. 5, p. 36).
60. John Mackenzie to the Duke of Atholl, 20 April 1772, Blair Castle Archive, Box 54, III, 80. Atholl's answer on 16 May 1772 (NLS, 1406, f. 182) stated: 'As to the History of the Isle of Man, I should wish to see the present intended Publication and upon that we may Judge if any other steps should be taken and what.'
61. John Mackenzie to the Duke of Atholl, 20 April 1772, Blair Castle Archive, Box 54, III, f. 80.
62. The Duke actually paid Stuart £52.18s.9d on 28 November 1772. NLS, 1409, f. 128.
63. 'Memoirs', ch. 1, p. 1.
64. Hume, *History of England*, I, 3–4. Hume wrote: 'The history of past events is immediately lost or disfigured, when intrusted to memory and oral tradition ... the sudden, violent, and unprepared revolutions ... disgust us by the uniformity of their appearance; and it is rather fortunate for letters that they are buried in silence and oblivion.'
65. Stuart to John Mackenzie, 15 July 1772, Blair Castle Archive, Box, 54 III, f. 149.
66. Stuart to John Mackenzie, 29 Dec. 1773, NLS, 1480, f. 104–5. Stuart went on to explain his comment: 'You will easily perceive that I allude to the papers of Junius.'
67. John Mackenzie to Stuart, 15 July 1772, Blair Castle Archive, Box 54, III, f. 149.
68. 'Memoirs', ch. 5, p. 42.
69. Stuart to Murray, 16 Nov. 1772, Hughenden Papers, G/1/908.
70. Stuart to Murray, 2 March 1773, Hughenden Papers, G/1/911.
71. Ibid.
72. Stuart to Murray, 3 Dec. 1775, Murray Archive. This information is new; for an overview see Paul-Gabriel Boucé, 'Eighteenth- and Nineteenth-Century Biographies of Smollett'; in *Tobias Smollett Bicentenial Essays Presented to Lewis M. Knapp* (New York, 1971), edited

by G. S. Rousseau and P. G. Boucé, pp. 201–30.

73. Ibid. Stuart included a short notice of the Commissary's death (EMR, IV, 672).
74. Stuart to John Mackenzie, 20 Feb. 1777, NLS, 1480, f. 112.
75. Ibid. In a letter to Murray, dated 2 March 1773 (Hughenden Papers, G/1/911), Stuart wrote regarding the gathering of anecdotes: 'Hamilton, with whom I find his [Smollett's] relations are at mortal variance, will be able to give you many curious particulars. This consciencious printer has advanced a very extravagant claim against the Doctor on an open account.' But what role Archibald Hamilton, an executor of Smollett's will, had in the affair is not known.
76. George Stuart to John Mackenzie, 19 Jan. 1776, NLS, 1480, f. 98.
77. George Stuart to John Mackenzie, 19 March. 1777, NLS, 1480, f. 100. 'I wrote a long Latin inscription to be put on Tobie's monument.'
78. Ibid. The inscription was 'broken into pieces by mischievous boys throwing stones', wrote J. Mawe to John Pinkerton on 6 July 1800. *The Literary Correspondence of John Pinkerton*, 2 vols (London, 1830), II, 173. According to Lewis Knapp in *Tobias Smollett, Doctor of Men and Manners* (Princeton, 1949), p. 334, the inscription was written jointly by George Stuart, John Ramsay of Ochtertyre and Samuel Johnson. Gilbert Stuart printed the Latin inscription 'intended for the pillar' (EMR, II, 420).
79. Boucé, 'Eighteenth- and Nineteenth-Century Biographies of Smollett', p. 207.
80. *Plays and Poems Written by T. Smollett, M. D.* (London, 1777), pp. xiii–xiv.
81. Luella F. Norwood, 'The Authenticity of Smollett's Ode to Independence', in the *Review of English Studies*, 17 (Jan. 1941), 55–64.
82. *Plays and Poems*, pp. 267–8.
83. Murray to John Moore, 5 May 1777, Murray's Copybooks.
84. Murray to Stuart, 17 May 1777, Murray's Copybooks.
85. *Boswell for the Defence*, p. 21 and p. 147 (editors' comments) and Murray's Preface to the 1786 edition of the *Poems of Mr Gray*.
86. Murray's Account Ledgers, I, 102, 115 and 123, Murray Archive.
87. Translator's Advertisement, *Elements of the History of England*, 2 vols (London, 1771), I, v.
88. *Monthly Review*, 45, (Oct. 1771), 269.
89. Ibid.
90. *Monthly Review*, 45 (Nov. 1771), 368.
91. Stuart to Murray, 5 March 1773, Hughenden Papers, G/1/912.
92. Murray to Stuart, 13 March 1773, Murray's Copybooks. The complete work in translation was published in five volumes by Strahan and Cadell (London, 1778–9).
93. Murray to Stuart, 13 March 1773, Murray's Copybooks.
94. Ibid.
95. Stuart to Murray, [nd] April 1773, Murray Archive.
96. Stuart to Murray, 20 April 1773, Murray Archive.
97. The work was published by George Kearsley, who bought a share from Murray For editions see Jean-Pierre Machelon in *Les Idées Politiques de J. L. De Lolme* (Paris, 1969), pp. 6–7.
98. Stuart to Murray, 7 Sept. 1774, Hughenden Papers, G/1/934. In choosing the title of the introduction he may have had in mind Thomas Hobbes' *Discourse on the Laws of England* (1681).
99. *Lectures on the Constitution*, p. xii, note.

100. Hume, 'My Own Life', prefixed to the *History of England*, I, xxx.
101. *Lectures on the Constitution*, p. xxx, note.
102. *Monthly Review*, 46 (June 1772), 584; continued in vol. 47 (July 1772), 38–47. The title of the first edition was *An Historical Treatise on the Feudal Law, and the Constitution and Laws of England*, which became the half-title of the second edition.
103. *Lectures on the Constitution*, p. vii.
104. Stuart to Murray, 17 June 1774, Hughenden Papers, G/1/930.
105. Stuart to Murray, 15 April 1775, Hughenden Papers, G/1/938.
106. *Lectures on the Constitution*, pp. v–vi. Stuart paid £1. 4s. for a finely bound copy of the *Lectures* which he presented to Lord North (Murray's Account Ledgers, I, 102).
107. Stuart to Murray, 17 June 1774, Hughenden Papers, G/1/930.
108. *Caledonian Mercury*, 27 November 1773.
109. Murray to William Creech, 29 Aug. 1774, Murray's Copybooks.
110. Hugo Arnot to Murray, 28 Nov. 1775, Murray Archive.
111. *Monthly Review*, 55 (May 1779), 354–62.
112. Appendix I dealt with one of Stuart's favourite subjects: an 'Account of the Misfortunes of Queen Mary, from the Death of … Darnley, till her flight into England.' As in Stuart's *History of Mary Queen of Scots*, we find a sympathetic and indeed romantic picture of her condition at that time. But the similarities are more specific. Compare, for example, passages from the two works on the subject of the Reformation in Edinburgh:

> The Magistrates of Edinburgh, to show their zeal on this occasion, with great readiness subscribed the bond of concurrence, which appeared to them to be *godly* and *honourable*. Sir Simon Preston, the Lord Provost, was desired to put his name to it, in testimony of the assent of all the Magistrates; and this injunction, with the bond itself, were ordered to be inserted in the Council Register, as a memorial to posterity. (Kincaid, *History of Edinburgh*, p. 243)

> It appeared to them [the Magistrates] to be a godly and honourable bond. They approved of its purposes and shewed an anxiety to pursue and advance them. They enjoined Sir Simon Preston, their provost, to put his name to it in testimony of their concurrence; and this injunction and the bond itself were ordered to be inserted in the council register, as a memorial to posterity. (MQS, I, 248)

113. Murray's Account Ledgers, I, 102.
114. Stuart to Murray, 16 November 1772, Hughenden Papers, G/1/908.
115 Stuart to Murray, no date, Hughenden Papers, G/1/943.
116. In a review of James Anderson's *Account of the Present State of the Hebrides*.
117. Stuart to Murray, 22 April 1773, Murray Archive.

Chapter 3

1. Lehmann, *John Millar of Glasgow*, p. 177.
2. Charles Elliot, an Edinburgh bookseller, was first offered Murray's share, but he declined it. A draft copy of the co-partnery agreement assigned one of the shares to William Kerr, a surveyor at the Post Office 'to furnish all the Assistance that his office allows him' (Draft of

Co-partnery, Library of the Society of Antiquaries of Scotland, Smellie Papers, III, f. 31). However a letter from Stuart to Murray (1 Sept. 1773, Hughenden Papers, G/1/919) stated that 'several booksellers here have applied for the share which Kerr refused & have offered money for it. And perhaps we may deign to induce some one of them with it, if he bleed freely. You stare at this and so do I too.'

3. Murray to Bennett and Hake, Booksellers at Amsterdam, 24 Nov. 1773; Murray to Robert Millar, Bookseller at Williamsburg, Virginia, 5 Dec. 1773, Murray's Copybooks.

4. Kerr, *Life of Smellie*, I, 401–8.

5. The original manuscript in Carlyle's hand is in the NLS, Carlyle Papers, 23920, ff. 15–28. A letter from A. Murray to Archibald Constable, 2 July 1806 reads:

> Dr. [James] Muirhead [minister of Urr] was the boon companion of Gilbert Stuart, Mr. [James] Naysmith, Mr. Smellie, and the club which wrote in the Edinburgh Magazine and Review ... He is the author of many of those bitter papers which are ascribed to Stuart and tells some anecdotes of this historian of the Reformation which would not have obtained the approbation of John Knox.

> (Thomas Constable, *Archibald Constable and his Literary Correspondents*, 2 vols, Edinburgh, 1873, I, 247)

   Unfortunately, these anecdotes are not extant.

6. Stuart to Murray, 13 Dec. 1773, Hughenden Papers, G/1/922.

7. Roper, *Reviewing before the 'Edinburgh' 1788–1802* (London, 1978), p. 44; see also pp. 42–4.

8. Stuart to Murray, November 1773, Hughenden Papers, G/1/921.

9. The amount of interesting research into the critical writings of these and other prominent writers is considerable. See generally: Roper, *Reviewing before the* Edinburgh (especially his Bibliography); James Basker, *Tobias Smollett, Critic and Journalist* (London, 1988), St Clair, *The Godwins and the Shelleys* (especially Chapters 3 and 4).

10. Harold Thompson remarked: 'It is tardy praise to state that Stuart was the ablest periodical writer that Scotland boasted – or did *not* boast – before Jeffrey'; in *A Scottish Man of Feeling: Some Account of Henry Mackenzie, Esq. of Edinburgh and of the Golden Age of Burns and Scott*. (London, 1931), p. 341.

11. *Edinburgh Review*, 1 (1755), iii.

12. Sher, *Church and University*, p. 70.

13. *Edinburgh Review*, 1 (Oct. 1802), i.

14. *Edinburgh Review*, 2 (1756), 63.

15. Murray to Stuart, 21 March 1774, Murray's Copybooks.

16. *Edinburgh Review*, 1 (Oct. 1802), [ii]. See also Roper, *Reviewing before the* Edinburgh, pp. 45–6. .

17. Thomson, *A Scottish Man of Feeling*, p. 344.

18. The comparison between Wedderburn and Jeffrey is taken from Nicholas Phillipson, 'The Scottish Whigs and the Reform of the Court of Session' (unpublished Ph.D. thesis, Cambridge University, 1967), p. 81.

19. Quoted in *Public Characters of 1798–99* (London, 1799), p. 538, in the article on Lord Monboddo.

20. Alexander Gillies to William Smellie, no date [Autumn 1773], printed in Kerr's *Life of Smellie*, I, 419–20. Gillies also suggested that rather than a monthly publication, the editors 'should publish sooner or later

just as you have exquisite materials'. But his suggestion was not adopted.

21. Stuart to Murray, 1 June 1773, Hughenden Papers, G/1/917.

22. Stuart to Murray, 6 Sept. 1773, Hughenden Papers, G/1/919.

23. There is an inconsistancy among extant sets of the five-volume periodical, probably the consequence of the delay in sending copies to London. Some sets (British Library and NLS) have two initial November 1773 issues. Another (EUL) has both the second and third numbers dated December 1773; and a further (in the Glasgow University Library) begins with an October first number. After the seventh number all three different sets become consistant. In references where dates are given, I have followed the NLS copy to avoid confusion.

24. For each number Smellie printed seven sheets in fours. The signature and pagination run continuously for volumes I (pp. 1–392) and II (pp. 393–786, + 6 page index) and for volumes III (pp. 1–392) and IV (pp. 393–784) and volume V (pp. 1–392). Title pages were printed for each volume.

25. No copies in original wrappers are extant. But Murray's correspondence gives a clear idea of what was printed on the covers. See, for example, Murray to William Smellie, 10 March 1775, Murray's Copybooks.

26. Murray to William Smellie, 31 Aug. 1775, Murray's Copybooks.

27. Some rather crude engravings of these figures by Andrew Bell complemented the written portraits.

28. Stuart to Murray, Sept. 1774, Hughenden Papers, G/1/934.

29. Kerr, *Life of Smellie*, pp. 442–98.

30. Stuart to Murray, 4 March 1774, Hughenden Papers, G/1/936.

31. In connection with the affair the editors printed in the 'Magazine' section 'The Correspondence of Dr Priestley with Dr Oswald and Dr Beattie' (EMR, II, 628–39).

32. Stuart to Murray, 4 March 1774, Hughenden Papers, G/1/923.

33. *Remarks on the History of Scotland* (EMR, I, 46); *Annals of Scotland* (EMR, IV,759–68); *Huberti, Langueti, Galli Epistolae ad Philippum Sydneium*, (EMR, V, 31–5). All reviews were by Stuart.

34. *Weekly Magazine, or Edinburgh Amusement*, 22 (18 Nov. 1773), 243.

35. In a note at the conclusion of Stuart's 'Sketch of the Character of John Knox'.

36. In a review of *Religious Correspondence; or the Dispensation of Divine Grace Vindicated*.

37. In a review of John Whitaker's *History of Manchester*. The publication of MacQueen was the *Letters on Mr Hume's History of Great Britain* (Edinburgh, 1756).

38. *Weekly Magazine*, 23 (6 Jan. 1774), 45. The *Caledonian Mercury* for 20 November 1773 printed a poem 'To the Conductor of a New periodical Publication'; and on 5 Feb. 1774 appeared another attack entitled 'Extempore, On seeing a certain periodical Publication in a double Cover in this severe weather'.

> A Storm so hard – What flesh and blood can bear it?
> Nay, things *inanimate* begin to fear it:
> *Sense*, quite froze up, lies scatter'd in our streets,
> Whilst *Nonsense* must be wrapt in double Sheets.
> Nor let the *Doctor* wonder, that he find
> A Colic should arise from too much *wind*.

Another attack was *A Specimen of the Scots Review* to which Stuart and Smellie replied with scorn in May 1774 (EMR, II, 447–8).

39. Stuart to Murray, 25 Nov. 1773, Hughenden Papers, G/1/921.
40. There is a useful biography of Laurence Dundas by Edith, Lady Haden-Guest in *The History of Parliament: The House of Commons 1754–1790*, edited by Namier and Brooke (London, 1964), II, 357–61.
41. In a review of Robert Walker's, *Sermons on Practical Subjects*.
42. Ernest Mossner, 'Hume as Literary Patron', p. 361. At the end of this article, Mossner published the review for the first time.
43. D'Israeli took these letters from John Murray junior to prepare his article. They have ended up in the Bodleian Library among the Hughenden Papers.
44. D'Israeli, *Calamities and Quarrels*, p. 130–1.
45. *Monthly Review*, 45 (July 1771), 30–9. Stuart wrote: 'The first volume of this work ... will be allowed to be full of erudition, and to contain many curious particulars ... that are not generally to be met with in our historians' (p. 32). Henry's *History* on a 'new plan' was very popular. He divided British history from Roman times until the death of Henry VIII into six parts, each comprising a volume. Each volume was in turn divided into seven subjects: 1) civil and military history; 2) religion; 3) government; 4) learning; 5) arts; 6) commerce; and 7) manners.
46. Mossner, 'Hume as Literary Patron', p. 363.
47. In an attack on the *Edinburgh Magazine and Review* in the *Weekly Magazine*, 22, (25 Nov. 1773), 267.
48. Stuart to Murray, 13 Dec. 1773, Hughenden Papers, G/1/922.
49. William Smellie, *Literary and Characteristical Lives of John Gregory, M.D. Henry Home, Lord Kames, David Hume, Esq. and Adam Smith L.L.D.* (Edinburgh, 1800), p. 203.
50. Hume, review of Henry's *History*, quoted in Mossner, 'Hume as Literary Patron', pp. 381–2. The review can also be found in *David Hume: Philosophical Historian*, edited by D. F. Norton and R. H. Popkin (Indianapolis, 1965), pp. 377–88.
51. Mossner, 'Hume as Literary Patron', pp. 374–82, notes these changes in his footnotes (pp. 374–82).
52. David Hume to [Stuart], 22 Dec. 1773, in *New Letters of David Hume*, edited by Kilbansky and Mossner (Oxford, 1954), p. 202.
53. Stuart to Murray, 4 March 1774, Hughenden Papers, G/1/923.
54. Murray to Stuart, 21 March 1774, Murray's Copybooks. On 2 April 1774 the publisher reported to Stuart that 'Henry has retailed *Humes* criticism in a couple pages quarto printed by itself which he personally distributes. It has however had no effect.' No copies of this piece are extant.
55. Malcolm Laing, 'Life of Robert Henry', prefixed to the fourth edition of the *History of Great Britain*, 6 vols (London, 1814), I, xi. See also Allibone's *Critical Dictionary of English Literature* under 'Henry', I, 825–6.
56. Stuart to Murray, 3 April 1775, Hughenden Papers, G/1/937.
57. Murray to William Smellie, 28 April 1774, Murray's Copybooks.
58. Murray to Stuart, 5 May 1777, Murray's Copybooks.
59. *Critical Review*, 44 (July 1777), 2. In the *Monthly Review*, 57 (Aug. 1777), 101–7, William Rose praised the work.
60. Murray to Robert Henry, 17 May 1777, Murray's Copybooks.
61. *Critical Review*, 44 (Oct. 1777), 316–20.

62. Scottish Record Office, RH4/26A/2–3. Quoted with the permission of Laurence Blair Oliphant.
63. Stuart died before the sixth volume was published.
64. Stuart to Murray, [Sept.] 1774. Hughenden Papers, G/1/934.
65. Murray to John Whitaker, 24 Aug. 1774, Murray's Copybooks.
66. Stuart to Murray, 2 March 1775, Hughenden Papers, G/1/936.
67. Stuart to Murray, 4 March 1774, Hughenden Papers, G/1/923.
68. Alexander Murdoch, *'The People Above': Politics and Administration in Mid-Eighteenth-Century Scotland* (Edinburgh, 1980), pp. 127–8.
69. Stuart to Murray, 4 March 1774, Hughenden Papers, G/1/923.
70. For general background see A. J. Youngson, *The Making of Classical Edinburgh*, chapters 1–4; Frederick W. Bedford, *History of George Heriot's Hospital*, second edition (Edinburgh, 1859), pp. 114–22. Also the Walter Ferguson affair, EMR, I, 110, 167 and 333.
71. Youngson, *The Making of Classical Edinburgh*, p. 98. The result of another cause against the city magistrates was the preservation of the gardens on the south side of Princes Street (Youngson, pp. 86–90).
72. *Address to the Citizens of Edinburgh*, p. 9.
73. The presentation copy of Stuart's *Address* is in the Edinburgh Central Library (Edinburgh Room).
74. *Considerations on the Management of George Heriot's Hospital*, p. iii. The dedication title ('To the Most Impudent Man Alive') may allude to an attack on William Warburton attributed to David Mallet (and sometimes Lord Bolingbroke), likewise entitled 'To the Most Impudent Man Alive'. Lucius Junius Brutus expelled the last of the Roman Kings (Targuin the Proud) in 507 BC.
75. Stuart to Murray, 2 Dec. 1775, Hughenden Papers, G/1/935.
76. Hugo Arnot, *The History of Edinburgh* (Edinburgh, 1779), pp. 566–7.
77. See Sher, *Church and University*, pp. 138–9 for an account. Stuart reviewed Ferguson's *Institutes of Moral Philosophy*, second edition, (Edinburgh, 1773), EMR, I, 103.
78. See also reviews of Josiah Tucker's *The Respective Pleas of the Parent-State and of the Colonies Examined* (EMR, III, 186–91) and John Wesley's *A Calm Address to our American Colonies* (EMR, IV, 632–6).
79. Sher, *Church and University*, p. 267.
80. These remarks concluded a review of John Erskine's pamphlet *Shall I Go to War with my American Brethren?*
81. *Caledonian Mercury*, 27 December 1773.
82. Stuart to Murray, 17 June 1774, Hughenden Papers, G/1/930. The inclusion of some 'Verses occasioned on the death of Dr. Hawkesworth' (EMR, I, 308) was probably an attempt to remedy the situation.
83. *Dictionary of National Biography*, III, 482, under 'Busby'.
84. Stuart to Murray, 1 Sept. 1773, Hughenden Papers, G/1/919. Adam is probably best remembered for the praise bestowed upon him as an educator ·by Walter Scott in the autobiographical 'Ashestiel Manuscript', prefixed to John Lockhart's *Life of Scott* (Edinburgh Edition), I, 32–5. See Alexander Henderson's *Account of the Life and Character of Alexander Adam, LL.D.* (Edinburgh, 1810), pp. 35–56, for an account of the affair with Stuart.
85. Stuart to Murray, 16 April 1773, Murray Archive.
86. EUL, Senatus Minutes, 14 Nov. 1772. The committee included Daniel MacQueen, Hugh Blair, John Erskine and James Robertson.
87. Ibid., 17 Nov. 1772.

88. Stuart to Murray, April 1773, Murray Archive.
89. *Animadversions on Mr. Adam's Latin and English Grammar*, p. 3.
90. Ibid., p. 4.
91. Stuart to Murray, 1 May 1773, Murray Archive.
92. *Weekly Magazine*, 19 (18 Feb. 1773), 245. 'In hac Urno jacet quod reliquum est/ Libelli inauspicati,/ Numquam resurrecturi,/ Invita et irate Minerva editi.'
93. George Davie, *The Democratic Intellect*, pp. 218–19.
94. *Political Herald*, II, 240.
95. Ibid.
96. Stuart to Murray, 17 June 1774, Hughenden Papers, G/1/930.
97. Ibid.
98. Stuart to Murray, 12 July 1774, Hughenden Papers, G/1/929.
99. Murray to Stuart, 24 Nov. 1774, Murray's Copybooks.
100. Murray to William Smellie, 25 Sept. 1775, Murray's Copybooks. Officials were demanding two shillings per sheet.
101. Stuart to Murray, [Sept. 1774], Hughenden Papers, G/1/934.
102. John MacLaurin to William Smellie; no date; in Kerr's *Life of Smellie*, I, 424.
103. Murray to William Smellie, 25 June 1776, Society of Antiquaries of Scotland Library, Smellie Papers, I, f. 36.
104. *Public Characters of 1798–9*, article on Lord Monboddo, p. 534.
105. David Hume to Adam Smith, 24 Feb. 1773, *The Letters of David Hume*, II, 277 (Letter 487). Monboddo believed the severe remarks in the *Edinburgh Magazine and Review* had been written by, or under the direction of Hume. Boswell reported that

> 'David seemed irritated, and said, "Does the scoundrel ... say so?" He then told me that he had observed to one of the Faculty of Advocates that Monboddo was wrong in his observations ... and gave as a proof a line in Milton. When the review came out, he found this very remark in it, and said to that advocate, "'Oho! I have discovered you".'
> *Boswell in Extremes*, p. 14 (7 July 1776).

106. Lord Monboddo, *Of the Origin and Progress of Language*, preface to volume 3, second edition (London, 1786), p. xx. See pp. xxi–xxii for Monboddo's further diatribe against the reviewers.
107. Stuart to Murray, 11 June 1773, Hughenden Papers, G/1/918.
108. Murray to William Creech, 11 July 1776, Murray's Copybooks.
109. Murray to John Balfour, Bookseller at Edinburgh, 25 June 1776, Murray's Copybooks.
110. See E. L. Cloyd, *James Burnett, Lord Monboddo* (Oxford, 1972), p. 49 and 54.
111. Monboddo's decision on literary property was printed in the *Caledonian Mercury*, 12 Feb. 1774. Boswell remarked after the decision that he 'had tea with Monboddo to triumph over him'. *Boswell for the Defence*, p. 215 (26 Feb. 1774).
112. Murray to William Creech, 21 March 1774, Murray's Copybooks.
113. Murray to William Smellie, 29 April 1776, Murray's Copybooks. A few months later the London bookseller wrote an uncharacteristically formal letter to the owners of the periodical demanding recompense for his outlays on advertising the work. It had been an unprofitable venture, and he was determined to minimalise his losses. See Murray to William Creech, 17 Aug. 1776 and to William Smellie, 17 Aug. 1776; and a letter to William Kerr, 28 Feb. 1777; all in Murray's Copybooks.

114. Stuart to David Dalrymple, NLS, Newhailes Papers, Acc. 7228/23, f. 169. Dalrymple's library is now part of the National Library of Scotland.

Chapter 4

1. Stuart's short conclusion did not appear in the posthumous editions of the work.
2. Murray to Stuart, 29 July 1777, Murray's Copybooks.
3. Stuart to Murray, 25 Sept. 1775, Hughenden Papers, G/1/941.
4. Murray to Stuart, 4 Oct. 1777, Murray's Copybooks. As part of the bargain Stuart arranged with Bell to have Murray's name on the title-page. Murray, in exchange, agreed to affix Bell's name to John Gillies' *Orations of Lysias and Isocrates* (1776), which he was about to publish.
5. Ibid.
6. 'Decree Arbitral', May 1785: NLS, MS 583, no. 855.
7. A 'Fief', also termed a 'fee', 'feud' or 'manor' is a possession, usually in the form of land, held by an individual in acknowledgement of a superior or in return for some service (such as military service) to that superior.
8. This bill is discussed by John Robertson, in *The Scottish Enlightenment and the Militia Issue* (Edinburgh, 1985), pp. 130–9.
9. The topics of the appendices include: the 'Charter of Dowry which Folradus, granted to his wife, Helegrina'; 'Fines made to Kings, that they would remit their Resentments and Indignation'; and 'An Injunction not to Tourney, by Henry III'.
10. Millar discussed the subject in Chapter 1 of the *Observations concerning Ranks*, 'Of the rank and condition of Women in different ages'. Kames discussed the subject in the *Sketches of the History of Man*, Book I, Section 6, 'Progress of the female sex'. Robertson's remarks are found in the *History of America*, Book IV. See also William Alexander's *History of Women* (1779). This account differs from the others in that it was 'composed solely for the amusement and instruction of the Fair Sex' (Author's Advertisement).
11. Stuart to Murray, 7 Sept. 1774, Hughenden Papers, G/1/934.
12. Ibid.
13. Ibid.
14. Robertson, *History of Charles V*, 3 vols, (London, 1769). He acknowledged the use he made of Voltaire's *Essai sur l'histoire Générale*: 'I have often ... followed him as my guide in these researches.' (I, 392.)
15. Robertson, *History of Charles V*, I, 124.
16. Ibid., 372.
17. Ibid., 27.
18. *Boswell for the Defence*, p. 102 (6 April 1772).
19. Somerville, *My Own Life and Times*, p. 275.
20. Stewart, *Life of Robertson*, pp. 223–4.
21. William Smyth, in his *Lectures on Modern History*, I, 77, wrote in this context: 'After Robertson, the work of Gilbert Stuart should be diligently searched. And here ... the reader will meet with observations injurious to the fame and authority of Dr. Robertson; yet that fame and authority are, on the whole, rather confirmed than weakened by the animadversions of Stuart.'

22. NLS, Carlyle Papers, 3464, f. 110.
23. EUL, Chalmers Papers, La. II, 451/1. Adam Smith folder. Smith's lectures were not published in his lifetime but did circulate in manuscript. Stuart mentioned Smith and 'his most ingenious Inquiries concerning the Wealth of Nations' on one occasion only in the *View of Society*, where he challenged Smith's opinion about the jurisdiction of property (VS, 265).
24. Murray described it as such in a letter to Robert Liston, 13 April 1778, Murray's Copybooks.
25. Grant, *The Story of the University of Edinburgh*, II, 315.
26. Murray to Stuart, 17 May 1777, Murray's Copybooks. Dr Johnson defined 'reversion' as: 1) 'The state of being to be possessed after the death of the present possessor; 2) 'Succession to; the right of succession to' (*A Dictionary of the English Language*).
27. Murray to Stuart, 17 May 1777, Murray's Copybooks.
28. Stuart told Murray in a letter:

> I am glad, that you had the Principal so long to yourself. And that he explained himself of ye subject of the book ... Get a letter from the principal ... and, if you like his plan, & are ascertained about the extent of his papers, form your opinion. And then I think, the conclusion of the affair may be left to ye principal & me. For, unless I am exceedingly deceived, the book from ye variety of its parts, must be a property.
>
> (2 Nov. 1775, Murray Archive)

29. Carlyle's unpublished 'Character of Robertson and Blair', NLS, Carlyle Papers, 3464, f. 112.
30. [William Thomson], *European Magazine*, I (Feb. 1782), 128.
31. Henry Brougham, *Lives of Men of Letters and Science who Flourished in the Time of George III*, 2 vols (London, 1845–6), II, 306–7.
32. [Alex. Maconochie], *Memoir of the late Hon. Allan Maconochie* (Edinburgh, 1845), p. 6. Robertson became the guardian of Maconochie, 1748–1816 (later Lord Meadowbank) after the death of the latter's father in 1762. Maconochie was also the pupil of Adam Smith at Glasgow University. It was not unusual to try to obtain such posts for one's friends or relations. In 1786 Robertson wrote to Henry Dundas in the hope of procuring another law chair for his son:

> Our Professor of Municipal Law lies ill of a very dangerous fever, from which ... there is hardly any chance of his recovering. Some of my Son's friends have thought him as a proper person to supply that Chair ... Nothing will make me more happy than he shall have the honour of your countenance & protection.   (EUL, MS, Phot. 1716)

33. *Memoir of Maconichie*, p. 11, for an outline of the course of lectures he prepared in 1779. The two divisions of the course were: 'State of Nature' and 'Political State'.
34. Murray to Stuart, 28 Dec. 1779, Murray's Copybooks.
35. Grant, *The Story of the University of Edinburgh*, II, 367–8.
36. For an account of Smellie's attempt to win a professorship see Kerr, *Life of Smellie*, II, 90–109; for Brown's attempt see Christopher Lawrence, 'Cullen, Brown and the Poverty of Essentialism', in *Burnonianism in Britain and Europe*, p. 4; and William Cullen Brown, *The Works of Dr John Brown*, I, lvii–iii.
37. The affair is described in Alexander Murdoch, 'The Importance of being Edinburgh: Management and Opposition in Edinburgh

Politics, 1746–1784', in *Scottish Historical Review*, 62 (April 1983), pp. 1–16. See also a volume of pamphlets and broadsides relating to the affair: NLS, RB.m.262.

38. It was not a coincidence that Stuart should refer to the 'Drysdale Bustle' in *Faction Displayed* to make the point that 'A [Moderate] clergyman, being at that time admitted into the city by presentation from the council, and not by the method of a popular call, an outcry was made against the measure, and a plan was conceived to overturn the administration of the borough' (FD, 10). For an account of this affair see Richard B. Sher, 'Moderates, Managers and Popular Politics in Mid-Eighteenth Century Edinburgh: The Drysdale 'Bustle' of the 1760s', in *New Perspectives on the Politics and Culture of Early Modern Scotland*, edited by Dwyer, Mason and Murdoch (Edinburgh, [1982]), pp. 179–209.

39. On the title page he placed a quotation from Cicero: Nobilitas sine potestate, Munus Publicum sine judicio, nihilo aliter aesti mande sunt ac Faex Civitatis. It translates: 'Nobility without power, public office without legal jurisdiction is nothing else but the dregs of the city.' I have not been able to locate the passage in Cicero's works.

40. See John Dwyer and Alexander Murdoch, 'Paradigms and Politics: Manners, Morals and the Rise of Henry Dundas, 1770–1784', in *New Perspectives on the Politics and Culture of Early Modern Scotland*, pp. 210–48.

41. Murray to Stuart, 6 Dec. 1777, Murray's Copybooks.

42. Arnot attacked Henry Dundas in *A Letter to the Lord Advocate* which he is seen holding in the scurrilous frontispiece engraving to the pamphlet.

43. *A Plan for Discharging the Incumbrances of the City of Edinburgh*, p. 22.

44. Ibid., pp. 35–6.

45. *Critical Review*, 45 (March 1778), 161–173 and 173. For the attribution of the review to Richardson, see Murray to Richardson, 2 Feb. 1778, Murray's Copybooks.

46. Murray to Stuart, 30 May 1778, Murray's Copybooks. *Monthly Review*, 58 (March 1778), 198–207.

47. The Aberdonian James Dunbar referred to the *View of Society* in his *Essays on the History of Mankind in Rude and Cultivated Ages* (London, 1780), pp. 53–4, and marked Stuart as 'a writer who has illustrated the liberal genius of feudal associations, and vindicated, in some material points, the character of our remote ancestors'. William Richardson in his *Anecdotes of the Russian Empire* (London, 1784) also cited the work, pp. 367, 387–8, 394). For instances of the *View of Society* in university curricula see David Hoffman, *A Course of Legal Study* second edition, 2 vols (London, 1836), II, 143–4; and Smith, *Lectures on Modern History* I, 45–7, 109 and 139.

48. Murray to Stuart, 16 Nov. 1780, Murray's Copybooks.

49. On Murray's death in 1793, there were 28 copies of the original edition in his stock ('List of Stock at Mr Murray's Death', Murray Archive).

50. *European Magazine*, I (Feb. 1782), 127.

51. Hoffman, *A Course of Legal Study*, I, 144. He added that the work 'contains many opinions which an acquaintance with the rise and progress of the British constitution forcibly contradicts, and much learning and research misapplied, or wilfully prostituted by party prejudice'.

52. Alexander Garden to an unnamed recipient, 13 July 1780. Garden

wrote the letter from Charlestown, North Carolina (*View of Society*, Edinburgh 1792, p. ii–iii).

53. Stuart to Dalrymple, no date [1778], NLS Newhailes Papers.
54. Ibid.
55. *Scots Magazine*, 41 (Jan. 1779), 43, advertised the book and reprinted the preface.
56. Horace, *Odes*, II, 1, 7–8.
57. Livy, *From the Founding of the City*, xxxix, 5, 3.
58. Stuart had made this point before in the *View of Society*, where he wrote:

    'When Dr. Brady ... Mr. Hume, and a multitude of writers, enlarge on the low and insignificant state of the towns, and, treating their inhabitants as little better than slaves, infer thence, the original despotism of our government, they are only active to betray their inattention. It is strange that men of genius and talents should take so lame a survey of this subject. Of the two states ... of society which prevailed, they have no conception. They knew only the history of towns in their last situation.'   (VS, 389)

    In the *English Constitution* he wrote: 'Men talk of the oppression of the people, and of the poverty of the boroughs: but the people were rather flattered than oppressed' (EC, 285).
59. Stuart's argument on this subject was criticised by Alexander Wight, *Inquiry into the Rise and Progress of Parliament, Chiefly in Scotland* (Edinburgh, 1784), p. 49.
60. George W. T. Ormond, *The Lord Advocates of Scotland*, 2 vols (Edinburgh 1883), II, 95.
61. Sher, *Church and University*, p. 277 and generally the section entitled 'The Cry of Intolerance' pp. 277–97. Eugene Black, *The Association: British Extra-Parliamentary Political Organisation, 1769–1793* (Cambridge, Mass., 1963) is a useful introduction to the topic as is Robert Kent Donovan, 'Voices of Distrust: The Expression of Anti-Catholic Feeling in Scotland 1778–1781' *Innes Review*, 30 (1979), 62–76.
62. *Political Herald*, I, 185, in an article headed 'Scots Reform'.
63. See Christopher Hibbert, *King Mob. The Story of Lord George Gordon and the Riots of 1780* (London, 1958) and an interesting contemporary biography by Robert Watson, *The Life of Lord George Gordon with a Philosophical Review of his Political Conduct* (London, 1795).
64. See Ian Christie, *Wilkes, Wyvill and Reform: The Parliamentary Reform Movement in British Politics, 1760–1785* (London, 1962), p. 115, on the subject of this hostility.
65. Murray to Stuart, 19 Sept. 1778, Murray's Copybooks.
66. Stuart to William Creech, 17 Nov. 1778, Scottish Record Office, RH4 26A/1–3.
67. Murray to William Creech, 27 July 1779, Murray's Copybooks.
68. Murray to Stuart, 11 March 1779, Murray's Copybooks.
69. *Critical Review*, 47 (April 1779), 84. The *Monthly Review*, 60 (April 1779) 269–81; by John Gillies.
70. Murray to Stuart, 11 March 1779, Murray's Copybooks.
71. NLS, Carlyle Papers, 23920, f. 49.
72. 'Character of a Certain Popular Historian', 3118, f. 199. Murray informed Stuart that 'the Character was republished ... in the Morn[ing] Post & was much spoken of' (18 Feb. 1778, Murray's Copybooks). It appeared in the *Post* on 18 Jan. 1778 as No. 1 of a new

section entitled 'Portraits of the Great and Eminent'. The title of the broadsheet which appeared in Edinburgh may have been taken from Alexander Pope's attack on the Duchess of Marlborough, 'A Character of a certain great Duchess deceased, by a certain great Poet lately Deseased' *Harleian Miscellany*, (1746), VIII, 212).

73. EUL, Chalmers Papers, La. II. 451/1.
74. Sher, *Church and University*, p. 102.
75. This is a point elaborated on by Mark Duckworth in 'Technique and Style in the Works of the Historian William Robertson: Story-Teller, Researcher and Theorist' (unpublished M.A. thesis, University of Melbourne, 1983), p. 111: 'He gives the impression that he has done a great deal more than he has done, and that he is thereby departing from former historians more than he actually does. He does to some extent therefore "affect" erudition.'
76. William Adam, *Sequel to the Gift of a Grandfather*, (Blair Adam, 1839), p. 53. Adam concluded his account of this incident with the comment: 'Dr. Robertson's reputation as an historian remains untouched, and … Stewart, if not entirely forgot, is rarely heard of' (ibid.).
77. Stuart to David Dalrymple, no date [1778], NLS, Acc. 7228/24, f. 51.
78. Brougham, *Lives of Men of Letters and Science*, II, 308.
79. The metaphor is also found in the same context in the *View of Society*, where the feudal association and chivalry 'were plants which were destined to take root … to sympathise in their growth, and in their decline. The seeds of them had been gathered by the barbarian in his woods; and, to whatever soil or climate his fortune was to carry him, there he was to scatter them with profusion' (VS, 37).
80. Robertson, *The Scottish Enlightenment and the Militia Issue*, p. 8, notes that 'The militia issue called upon the Scots to reconsider the two themes historically embodied in their martial heritage, the structure of landed society and the national identity, in the light of their eighteenth-century achievements of political stability and economic development.'
81. Boswell, *The Ominous Years*, p. 130 (6 April 1775).
82. Boswell, *The Life of Johnson. Together with the Journal of a Tour to the Hebrides*, edited by G. Birkbeck Hill, revised and enlarged by L. F. Powell, 6 vols (Oxford, 1934–65), II, 431.
83. In a review of Adam Smith's *Wealth of Nations* (third edition). The reference was to Lord Kames' praise of Smith.
84. Henry Cockburn, *Life of Lord Jeffrey*, 2 vols (Edinburgh, 1852), I, 82.
85. Boswell, *Laird of Auchinleck 1778–1782*, edited by Reed and Pottle (London 1977), p. 211 (11 May 1780).
86. Ibid., pp. 212–3 (15 May 1780).
87. *A Letter to the People of Scotland, on the Alarming Attempt to Infringe the Articles of Union, and Introduce a Most Pernicious Innovation, by Diminishing the Number of the Lords of Session* (London, 1785), p. 5.
88. Boswell's pamphlet was reviewed (possibly by Stuart) in the *English Review*, 5 (June 1785), 441–4 and in the *Political Herald*, I, 150–1.
89. In 'An Address to Ilay Campbell, Esq. Lord Advocate for Scotland'.
90. In 'Intelligence concerning Scots Reform'.
91. Stuart to William Jones, 12 Feb. 1779; quoted in Lord Teignmouth *Memoirs of the Life, Writings and Correspondence, of Sir William Jones*, second edition (London, 1806), p. 169. In the *Edinburgh Magazine and Review* Stuart praised Jones as the only English author 'who has been able to treat of the actions of men, with … masterly discernment and

sagacity' (EMR, I, 18–19).

92. Stuart to William Jones, 26 August 1779; transcribed in Murray's Copybooks.

Chapter 5

1. Murray to Stuart, 2 Oct. 1779, Murray's Copybooks.
2. Ibid.
3. Murray to Stuart, 7 Sept. 1779, Murray's Copybooks.
4. Ibid.
5. Murray to Stuart, 2 Oct. 1779, Murray's Copybooks.
6. Ibid. See W. H. Tapp, 'John Donaldson: Enameller, Miniaturist and Ceramic Artist' in *Apollo*, 36 (Aug. and Dec. 1942), 39–42 and 55; 37 (Jan. 1943), 4–7 and 22. The portrait was engraved by John Keyse Sherwin.
7. Murray to Stuart, 28 Dec. 1779, Murray's Copybooks.
8. The texts Stuart most frequently borrowed from for the appendix and the work itself are: John Knox, *The History of the Reformation of Religioun with the Realme of Scotland* (1587); John Spottiswood, *The History of the Church of Scotland* (1655); Robert Keith, *The History of the Affairs of the Church and State in Scotland* (1734).
9. Murray to Stuart, 1 Jan 1780, Murray's Copybooks.
10. For 'the general historian' Stuart would have had in mind William Guthrie's *General History of Scotland, from the Earliest Accounts to the Present Time*, 10 vol. (London, 1767–8). Knox, Spottiswood and Keith (mentioned above, note 8) would be included in the category of church historians.
11. *Monthly Review*, 62 (May 1780) 337–41, by John Gillies; *Critical Review*, 49 (March 1780), 202–7.
12. Murray to John Bell, 15 July 1780, Murray's Copybooks.
13. Murray to John Bell, 15 June 1782, Murray's Copybooks.
14. Murray to Stuart, 1 Jan 1780, Murray's Copybooks.
15. Murray to Stuart, 9 June 1780, Murray's Copybooks. That Murray himself was a member of the High Holborn Protestant Association and Committee is confirmed by a letter to him from the secretary Joshua Bangs, 4 Oct. 1780, Murray Archive.
16. Dickens, *Barnaby Rudge* (first published 1841), ch. 67.
17. *Monthly Review*, 67 (Dec. 1782), 467, in a review of a *Sketch of a Conference with the Earl of Shelburne*.
18. By 'propriety' Stuart meant justness and truth.
19. Michael Lynch, *Edinburgh and the Reformation* (Edinburgh, 1981), cites numerous instances of religious rioting: pp. 19, 73, 75, 85, 107–8, 113 and 160–1.
20. Murray to Hugo Arnot, 9 Feb. 1779, Murray's Copybooks.
21. In a review of the *Letters and Journals of Robert Baillie, D.D.*
22. The Elder Seneca, *Controversiae et Suasoriae*, 6.2.1. Loeb Classics, II, 584, translated by Michael Winterbottom.
23. Ronald Syme, *Tacitus*, 2 vols (Oxford, 1958) remarks in this context:

> The commemoration of deaths, gives the historian scope for epigram, for praise or blame without subsequent appeal (I, 312–13). With full freedom to choose and arrange, the author unobtrusively suggests lessons of conduct, paradoxes of survival, the gap between past and present (I, 313).The historian, however impersonal his manner, could not fail to

leave the imprint of his own judgement (I, 314).

24. However, a writer for the *Critical Review*, 49 (March 1780), 206–7, 'condemned such poetical phrases as ['the gloomy Protestant walked over its ruins'] being unsuitable to the gravity of history'.

25. In the EMR, II, 692 ('Anecdotes of Eminent Persons of Scottish Extraction'), Stuart drew a short character portrait of the queen in which he wrote, 'she was as engaging as a woman, as she was awful as a queen'.

26. ER, 5 (March 1785), 213, in an article on the second edition of the *History of Mary Queen of Scots*.

27. Somerville, *My own Life and Times*, pp. 275–6.

28. For a useful account of the topic see Laurence L. Bongie, 'The Eighteenth-Century Marian Controversy and an Unpublished Letter by David Hume', in *Studies in Scottish Literature*, I (1964), 236–52.

29. James Phillips, *Images of a Queen: Mary Stuart in Sixteenth-Century Literature* (Berkeley, 1964), p. 7.

30. I. B. Cowan in *The Enigma of Mary Stuart* (London, 1971), p. 19, notes that the Popish plot of 1681 brought to an end the refurbishing of her image.

31. *Gentleman's Magazine*, 30 (Oct. 1760), 453; in a review of [William Tytler], *An Historical and Critical Enquiry into the Evidence Produced ... against Mary Queen of Scots ...* (Edinburgh, 1760). The title of Tytler's work was altered slightly in later editions.

32. Chalmers, *The Life of Thomas Ruddiman*, p. 226.

33. Two examples are James Anderson's *Collections relating to the History of Mary Queen of Scotland. Containing a Great Number of Original Papers Never Before Printed*, 4 vols (Edinburgh, 1727–8); and William Murdin's *Collection of State Papers left by William Cecil* (London, 1740–59).

34. Walter Goodall, *Examination*, 2 vols (Edinburgh, 1754) I, xxviii.

35. George Paton to Richard Gough, 15 June 1782, NLS, Adv. MS 29.5.7 (iii), f. 190.

36. Sher, *Church and University*, p. 102.

37. David Hume to Hugh Blair, 25 March 1766, *The Letters of David Hume*, II, 31 (Letter 314). For the attribution of a review of Robertson's *History* to Hume (*Critical Review*, 7 (Feb. 1759), 89–103) see David Raynor, 'Hume and Robertson's History of Scotland', in the *British Journal for Eighteenth-Century Studies*, 10 (Spring 1987), 59–63.

38 Mossner, *The Life of David Hume*, second edition (Oxford, 1980), pp. 397–8.

39. David Hume to Lord Elibank, 14 Aug. 1764, in 'New Hume Letters to Lord Elibank, 1748–1776', edited by Ernest Mossner in *Texas Studies in Literature and Language*, IV (1962), 456.

40. Ernest Mossner, *The Life of David Hume*, p. 413.

41. Hume, History of England, V, 394–5 (note M). For a study of Tytler see Clair Lamont, 'William Tytler, his Son Alexander Tytler (Lord Woodhouselee), and the Encouragement of Literature in Late Eighteenth-Century Edinburgh' (unpublished B.Litt. thesis, Oxford University, 1968).

42. William Robertson to David Dalrymple, 10 April 1783, NLS, Newhailes Papers, Acc. 7228/25, f. 117.

43. Stuart to the Earl of Buchan, 10 April 1783, printed in MQS, II, Appendix II, Letter II. Original in EUL, Dc. 1.24, f. 18..

44. Jeffrey Smitten, 'Robertson's *History of Scotland*: Narrative Structure

and the Sense of Reality', in *Clio*, 11: 1 (1981), 35.

45. This is a translation from Tacitus' *Germania*.
46. Gordon Donaldson confirms this opinion in *Scotland: James V to James VII* (Edinburgh, 1965), p. 121.
47. Hume, *History of England*, IV, 396–7 (note S).
48. Robertson, *History of Scotland*, II, 243.
49. Hume, *History of England*, IV, 353 and 236.
50. Robertson, *History of Scotland*, II, 245.
51. A scan through each book's table of contents, which corresponds with the marginal notes, shows the frequent use of such descriptive terms.
52. Hume, *History of England*, IV, 91–2; Robertson, *History of Scotland*, I, 359; Donaldson, *Scotland*, p. 113.
53. The phrase 'virtue in distress' is borrowed from R. F. Brissenden's *Virtue in Distress: Studies in the Novel of Sentiment from Richardson to Sade* (London, 1974). It is also the title of a pamphlet (London, 1749) about the Young Pretender after Culloden.
54. Another popular novel which recalls Mary's plight and ends in similar despair is Frances Sheridan's *Memoirs of Miss Sydney Biddulph* (1761). This point was made by Geoffrey Carnall, 'Historical Writing in the Later Eighteenth Century', in *The History of Scottish Literature*, Vol. 2, edited by Andrew Hook (Aberdeen, 1987), p. 216.
55. Hume, *History of England*, IV, 114. It was this very argument (or inference) to which William Tytler took exception. See the Postscript to Tytler's *Enquiry*, third edition (Edinburgh, 1772), pp. 376–8.
56. Robertson, *History of Scotland*, I, 371 and 'Dissertation', II, 317-30.
57. Donaldson, *Scotland*, p. 128. For other interesting views on this subject see: M. H. A. Davidson, *The Casket Letters: A Solution to the Mystery of Mary Queen of Scots and the Murder of Darnley* (London, 1965); and Jenny Wormald, *Mary Queen of Scots: a Study in Failure* (London, 1988), who attempts to revive the issue as a whole.
58. Donaldson, *Scotland*, p. 123, agrees that Mary entered into such an association for 'sound political reasons', but concludes that 'her relations with Bothwell, sometime before the death of Darnley, were not innocent'.
59. Hume, *History of England*, IV, 84.
60. Robertson, *History of Scotland*, I, 320.
61. Ibid.
62. Brissenden, *Virtue in Distress*, p. 29.
63. Stuart to the Earl of Buchan (Buchan's copy), 5 Jan. 1783, Glasgow University Library, MS Murray 502/70.
64. *Critical Review*, 54 (Sept. 1782), 214. The documents in question may have been the two volumes of 'State Papers' which Stuart had borrowed from Sir Alexander Dick of Prestonfield while writing the work. There are references to these in relation to the Babington affair (MQS, II, 289n).
65. Stuart to the Earl of Buchan, 10 April 1783, printed in MQS, II, Appendix II, Letter II.
66. *Encyclopaedia Britannica*, 10 vols (Edinburgh, 1778–83), IX, 6988–7174 [misnumbered 8074]. William Smellie did not edit this edition.
67. *Decisions of the Court of Session*, 25 June 1785 (No. CCXVI), pp. 340–1. Accounts were given in the *Daily Universal Register*, 30, June 1785; in more detail in the *Edinburgh Evening Courant*, 25 June 1785; in the *Caledonian Mercury*, 25 June 1785; and in the *Scots Magazine*, 47 (June 1785), 308. The defendants presented a reclaiming petition but were

unsuccessful (*Scots Magazine*, 47 (Aug. 1785), 411).

68. Most notable among those who followed Stuart's pro-Marian position were John Whitaker who wrote *Mary Queen of Scots Vindicated*, 3 vols (London, 1787) and the *Additions and Corrections Made in the Second Edition of Mary Queen of Scots Vindicated* (London, 1789); and George Chalmers, *The Life of Mary, Queen of Scots Drawn from the State Papers. With Six Subsidiary Memoirs*, 2 vols (London, 1818). An example of a work written after Stuart which took the opposite view is Thomas Robertson's *History of Mary Queen of Scots* (Edinburgh, 1793).

69. John Wesley, 5 Feb. 1786, *The Journal of John Wesley*, 8 vols, edited by N. Curnock (London, 1909–16), VII, 139–40.

70. For reviews in 1782 see *Critical Review*, 54 (July), 28–36 and (Sept.), 212–18; *Monthly Review*, 67 (Sept.), 208–21 and (Sept.), 477–9, and (Oct.), 277–85; *Scots Magazine*, 44 (Aug.), 421–4 , (Oct), 587–9; *European Magazine*, I (April), 278–83 and (May), 349–52 and *New Annual Register*, III, 225.

71. *Morning Chronicle*, 1 May 1782. Stuart's letter to Sir James Cummyng, Secretary to the Society of Antiquaries, was reprinted in the *Gentlemen's Magazine*, 52 (April 1782), 167–8 and MQS, II, Appendix II, Letter I. In the *History* Stuart had said in a similar vein of the earls of Moray and Morton concerning the murder of Darnley: 'They declined, however, to enter the lists; and ... this neglect or prudence exposed not only their courage to some suspicion, but served to confirm the opinion of their criminality' (MQS, I, 410).

72. Ibid.

73. Ibid.

74. The *Critical Observations* were reviewed in the *European Magazine*, 1 (Aug. 1782), 131–2.

75. *Edinburgh Evening Courant*, 5 Aug. 1782.

76. Sher, *Church and University*, p. 99, comments that 'what made Robertson's aloofness feasible was the fact that several of his Moderate friends were happy to handle the party's "dirty work" for him'.

77. George Stuart to the Earl of Buchan, 14 April 1783, EUL, Dc. 1. 24, f.9.

78. Stuart to the Earl of Buchan, 10 April 1783, printed in MQS, II, Appendix II, Letter II.

79. Stuart to the Earl of Buchan (Buchan's copy), 5 Jan. 1783, Glasgow University Library, MS Murray, 502/70.

80. Stuart to the Earl of Buchan, 10 April 1783, printed in MQS, II, Appendix, II, Letter II.

81. The Earl of Buchan to Stuart, 18 April 1783, printed in MQS, II, Appendix, II, Letter III.

82. [William Thomson], *The Man in the Moon; or Travels into the Lunar Regions*, 2 vols (London, 1783), II, 197. This work is a satire on Charles James Fox.

83. Two useful accounts of the events surrounding the charter application are: Roger Emerson, 'The Scottish Enlightenment and the End of the Philosophical Society of Edinburgh', in the *British Journal of the History of Science*, 21 (1988), 33–66; and Stephen Shapin, 'Property, Patronage, and the Politics of Science: The Founding of the Royal Society of Edinburgh', in the *British Journal of the History of Science*, 7 (1974), 1–41. See also Kerr, *Life of Smellie*, I, 333–4 and II, 88–9.

84. EUL, Senatus Minutes, 30 Dec. 1782. Da. 1, ff. 306–15. The Memorial was revised at meetings on 2 Dec. and 10 Feb. 1783. The final copy, as

it was sent to Dundas, is in the NLS, MS 2617, f. 58.

85. Boswell, *Applause of the Jury*, p. 58 (8 Feb. 1783). The vote in the Faculty was eleven against opposing Buchan and thirty-seven for opposing.

86. Emerson, 'The Scottish Enlightenment and the End of the Philosophical Society of Edinburgh', remarks that at this time there was 'an implicit recognition of the need to further specialize their scientific society and to purge it of such extraneous interests as history and antiquities' (p. 44). He extends his analysis to suggest that the founding of the Royal Society of Edinburgh in 1783 'signalled the end of one phase of the Scottish Enlightenment' (p. 61).

87. Minutes of the Society of Antiquaries of Scotland, 14 Nov. 1780 Society's Library at Edinburgh.

88. Ibid., 15 Nov. 1784.

89. Stuart to the Earl of Buchan, 24 April 1783, NLS, 585, f. 1057.

Chapter 6

1. Stuart to the Earl of Buchan, 5 Jan. 1783, Glasgow University Library, MS Murray, 502/70.

2. Ibid.

3. John Logan to Alexander Carlyle, 12 April 1786, EUL, La. II. 419/8.

4. *Gentleman's Magazine*, 56 (Dec. 1786), 1021. The author was John Pinkerton.

5. Stuart to David Dalrymple, 4 Nov. 1784, NLS, Newhailes Papers, Acc. 7228/25, ff. 10–11. Buchan's own contributions to the 'Biographia Caledoniead' were *An Account of the Life, Writings, and Inventions of John Napier of Merchiston* (Perth, 1787) and the *Essays on the Lives and Writings of Fletcher of Saltoun and the Poet Thomson* (London, 1792).

6. Stuart to the Earl of Buchan, 10 April 1783, MQS, II, Appendix II, Letter II.

7. *Monthly Review*, 67 (Nov. 1782), 345.

8. Murray to William Thomson, 27 June 1785, Murray's Copybooks.

9. Samuel Smiles, *A Publisher and his Friends*, 2 vols (London, 1891), I, 25.

10. Boswell, *Applause of the Jury*, p. 119 (28 April 1783).

11. *The Patriad, an Heroic Poem* (London, 1786), pp. 30–1.

12. Murray's letters to: Thomas Holcroft, 10 June 1783; to Robert Liston, 8 Nov. 1782; to John Logan, 5 Nov. 1782; to John Whitaker, 11 June 1784; to Alexander Hamilton, 11 Jan. 1783; to Thomas Beddoes, 25 Dec. 1783; to John Hellins, 31 Jan. 1785; and to William Godwin, 30 Nov. 1786. These letters are in Murray's Copybooks. For an account of Godwin's contribution see St Clair, *The Godwins and the Shelleys*, pp. 27–8.

13. Murray to John Logan, 5 Nov. 1782, Murray's Copybooks.

14. Murray to William Godwin, 30 Nov. 1786, Murray's Copybooks.

15. Murray to William Thomson, 28 Aug. 1786, Murray's Copybooks.

16. *Gentleman's Magazine*, 57 (April 1787), 296. Even Walter Scott, writing as late as 1808, believed Stuart conducted the *English Review*. Walter Scott to William Gifford, [25 Oct. 1808], *Letters of Sir Walter Scott*, 12 vols, edited by H. J. C. Grierson (London, 1932–6), II, 106.

17. John Logan to Stuart, 8 March 1783, EUL, La. II. 419/1. Also printed in Kerr's *Life of Smellie*, II, 10–12.

18. Logan referred to the review when he wrote to Alexander Carlyle: 'In … the next *English Review* … there is a compliment to Dr. Blair, to

make some attonement [sic] for the freedom with which he was treated formerly' (12 April 1786, EUL, La. II. 419/8).

19. Gunn, *Beyond Liberty and Property*, pp. 86–8 and pp. 284–8, elaborates on 'the Public Spirit' of the political views expressed in the *English Review* from 1783 until 1790.
20. I. R. Chirstie, *Wilkes, Wyvill and Reform. The Parliamentary Reform Movement in British Politics 1760–1785* (London, 1962), pp. 160–1.
21. For accounts of this committee see Christie, *Wilkes, Wyvill and Reform*, pp. 173–4 and 190; and Black, *The Association*, p. 123.
22. [Thomas MacGrugar], *Letters of Zeno* second edition (Edinburgh, 1783), p. 29
23. Christopher Wyvill to Stuart, 14 Nov. 1782, EUL, Gen. 1736, f. 15.
24. Stuart to Christopher Wyvill, 28 Nov. 1782, Yorkshire County Record Office, ZFW, 7/2/28/19.
25. Stuart to the Earl of Buchan, 28 Nov. 1782, EUL, Dc. 1. 24, f. 17.
26. Gunn, *Beyond Liberty and Property*, p. 72.
27. In the annotated Bodleian Library copy Adam Smith is credited with writing a 'Character of the Right Honourable Charles James Fox' (PH, II, 36). A printed note to the piece states that 'this character of Mr. Fox made its appearance at Edinburgh, and is supposed to be written by a very eminent author, whose genius has illustrated the most important points of political oeconomy'.
28. Stuart to the Earl of Buchan, 25 July 1785, NLS, 967, f. 211.
29. Ibid.
30. St Clair, *The Godwins and the Shelleys*, p. 36.
31. Buchan's Address to the Society of Antiquaries, *Gentleman's Magazine*, 56 (Oct. 1786), 906. The address also appeared in the *Morning Chronicle* on 9 Oct. 1786.
32. *Gentleman's Magazine*, 56 (Oct. 1786), 906.
33. Ibid., 905–6. Privately Buchan remarked that Dundas, Robertson and their supporters 'goaded poor Stuart … to madness' (marginal note on the back leaf of Stuart's letter to Buchan, 26 Aug. 1783, EUL, Dc. 1. 24, f. 20).
34. *Gentleman's Magazine*, 56 (Oct. 1786), 905
35. Murray to George Stuart, 14 March 1786, Murray's Copybooks.
36. Ibid.
37. Murray to George Stuart, 24 April 1786, Murray's Copybooks.
38. Murray to George Stuart, 14 March 1786, Murray's Copybooks.
39. John Logan to Alexander Carlyle, 4 March, 1776, EUL, La. II, 419/7.
40. Murray to Stuart, 5 Aug. 1786, Murray's Copybooks.
41. *Annual Biography for 1818*, II, 101, in an article on William Thomson.
42. Kerr, Life of *Smellie*, II, 2.
43. Murray to John Millar, 7 Sept. 1786, Murray's Copybooks.
44. George Stuart to the Earl of Buchan, 13 Aug. 1786, EUL, Dc. 1. 24, f. 15.
45. *Daily Universal Register*, 21 Aug. and 2 Sept. 1786.
46. *Gentleman's Magazine*, 56 (Aug. 1786), 716.
47. *Gentleman's Magazine*, 56 (Sept. 1786), 808. The poem was written by George Little, a friend of George Stuart. There is a manuscript copy: EUL, Dc. 1. 24, f. 15.
48. *Edinburgh Evening Courant*, 19 Dec. 1795.

Bibliography of Works by Gilbert Stuart[†]

> He was one of those who indulge in the comfortable
> consciousness, that any comparison between their own genius
> and that of any other given person is supremely ludicrous;
> and as someone said of La Harpe, it might have proved a good
> speculation to buy him at what he was worth, and sell him at
> his own estimate of his value.
>
> John Hill Burton, *Life and Correspondence of David Hume*
> (Edinburgh, 1846), II, 468

Note: An asterisk indicates that the work has not previously been attributed to Stuart.

1768

An Historical Dissertation concerning the Antiquity of the English Constitution. Edinburgh: Printed for A. Kincaid & J. Bell; and for W. Sanby, J. Dodsley, E. Dilly, and T. Cadell, London, 1768. xii, 291p.

Second Edition Corrected. London: Printed for T. Cadell, Successor to Mr Millar; and A. Kincaid and J. Bell, Edinburgh, 1770. xvi, 291p.

Second Edition Corrected. London: Printed for T. Cadell; and A. Kincaid and W. Creech, Edinburgh, 1771. xvi, 291p.

Historische Abhandlung von dem Alterhum der Englischen Staatsverfassung von Gilbert Stuart, L.L.D. Nach der zweiten Englischen Ausgabe übersetzt. Lübeck: 1779 bey Christian Gottfried Donatius. vii, 246p.

Dissertation Historique sur L'Ancienne Constitution des Germains, Saxons, et Habitans de la Grande-Bretagne; Ouvrage contenant des Recherches sur l'ancienneté; des Jurés & des Délibérations des Communes: Traduite de seu Gilbert Stuart; Par A. M. H. B.[oulard] Paris, Chez Maradan, Libraire, rue du Cimetière-Saint-André, n°. 9. An 2, 4ᵉ mois, (vieux style 1794). [iv], 254p.

†A more bibliographically detailed checklist of Stuart's works appeared in the *Book Collector*, 37 (Winter 1988), 537–46, 'Some Uncollected Authors LV'.

1771

*[Part-Translated] *Elements of the History of England, from the Invasion of the Romans to the Reign of George II.* Translated from the French of Abbé Millot by Mr. Kenrick. London: Printed for J. Johnson, and W. Nicoll, in St. Paul's Church-yard; and J. Murray, at No. 32, Fleet-street, 1771. Vol. 1: xxxii, 388p; Vol. 2: [i], 456p.

[Prepared for the Press] *The Roman History, from the Building of Rome to the Ruin of the Commonwealth.* Vol. IV. By N[athaniel] Hooke, Esq. London: Printed for G. Hawkins, W. Strahan, J. and F. Rivington, W. Johnston, T. Longman, T. Cadell, and R. Baldwin, 1771. Engraved frontispiece and map; vii, 464, [lxxv] p.

1773

*[Prepared for the Press] *A History of the Island of Man; from the Earliest Accounts to the Present Time.* Compiled from the Public Archives of the Island, and other Authentic Materials by the late Mr. Richard Rolt. London: Printed for W. Nicoll, 1773. [iv], 152, [xxiv]p.

Animadversions on Mr Adam's Latin and English Grammar; Being An Exhibition of its Defects: And an Illustration of the Danger of Introducing it into Schools. By John Richard Busby, Master of Arts. Sold by all the Booksellers of Edinburgh and Scotland [Edinburgh: John Bell], 1773. 63p.

**An Address to the Citizens of Edinburgh, Relative to the Management of George Heriot's Hospital.* By a Free Burgess of Edinburgh. [Edinburgh]: 1773. 19p.

[Second Edition] *Considerations on the Management of George Heriot's Hospital.* Dedicated to the Most Impudent Man Alive. Edinburgh: Printed for C. Elliot; and Cadell, Dodsley, and Murray, London [1774]. Price One Shilling. vi, 20p.

1775

*[Translation] *The Constitution of England, or an Account of the English Government; in which it is compared with the Republican Form of Government, and occasionally with the other Monarchies in Europe.* By J. L. De Lolme. Advocate, Citizen of Geneva. London: Printed by T. Spilsbury, in Cook's Court, Carey Street; and sold by G. Kearsley, in Fleet Street, 1775. vii, 448p.

1776

'A Discourse concerning the Laws and Government of England'.

in *Lectures on the Constitution and Laws of England: with a Commentary on Magna Charta, and Illustrations of Many of the English Statutes*. by the late Francis Stoughton Sullivan, LL.D. Royal Professor of Common Law in the University of Dublin. The Second Edition. To which authorities are added, and a Discourse is prefixed, concerning the Laws and Government of England. By Gilbert Stuart, LL.D.. London: Printed for Edward and Charles Dilly in the Poultry; and Joseph Johnson in St. Paul's Church-yard, 1776. xvi, xxxii, 415p.

Dublin: Printed by Graisberry and Campbell, for William Jones. No 86. Dame-Street, 1790. xx, xiiii, 570p.

Portland, Maine; Printed by Thomas B. Wait and Co., 1805. Vol. 1: lvi, 57–325p; Vol. 2: vii, 9–327p.

*'A Short Account of the Life and Writings of Mr Gray'.

in *Poems by Mr. Gray*. A New Edition. London: Printed for J. Murray. No. 32. Fleet Street and C. Elliot, Edinburgh, 1776. [i], xviii, 146p. Two engravings and title-page vignette.

London: Murray, 1778. [v], xxxix, [41]–158p. Three engravings and title-page vignette.

London: Murray, 1786. xxxix, [43]–178p. Three engravings and title-page vignette.

London: Murray, 1790. [i], xxxix, [41]–178p. Six engravings.

Parma: Bodoni, 1793. [vi], xxvi, 109p.

1778

Faction Displayed or, a Genuine Relation of the Representation of the Trades, and of the late Political Contentions in the City of Edinburgh [Edinburgh: 1778]. 25p.

A View of Society in Europe, in its Progress from Rudeness to Refinement: or, Inquiries concerning the History of Law, Government, and Manners. Edinburgh: Printed for John Bell; and J. Murray London, 1778. xx, 435p.

Dublin: W. Witestone, W. Colles, J. Hoey, Wilson, J. Williams, T. Walker, C. Jenkin, L. L. Flin, G. Burnet, L. White, J. Beatty, and J. Exshaw, 1778. [ii], xvi, 445p.

Gilbert Stuarts *Abriss des gesellschaftlichen Zustandes in Europa, in seimen Fortgange von Rohigkeit zu Ferfeinerung. Oder*

Untersuchungen, die Geschichte des Gesetze, der Regierungsform, und der Sitten betreffend. Aus dem Englischen übersetzt, und mit einigen Anmerkungen begleitet. Leipzig: bey N. G. Weidmanns, Erben und Reich. 1779 [Translated by Christian Friedrich von Blankenburg]. xvi, 414p.

Second Edition. London: Murray, 1782. xx, 435p.

Second Edition. London: Murray, 1783. xx, 435p.

Tableau des Progrès de la Société en Europe, Traduit de l'Anglois de Gilbert Stuart. Ouvrage contenant des Recherches sur l'Origine des Gouvernments, les Variations des Moeurs, & du Système Féudal. Paris: Chez Maradan Libraire, Hôtel de Château-vieux, rue Saint André-des-Arcs, 1789. Tome Premier: [3], xvi, 280p; Tome Second: [8], 200p

New Edition. Basil: J. J. Tourneisen, 1797. xii, 315p.

London: Printed for Longman, Hurst, Rees, Orme, and Brown; and for Bell & Bradfute, Edinburgh, 1813. xv, 351p.

1779

*Character of a certain Popular Historian, now Ministerial Agent, for Reconciling our Complaisant Clergy to the Church of Rome. From the Writings of a Celebrated Philosopher, now Deceased. [Edinburgh: 1779]. Single-sided broadsheet.

Observations concerning the Public Law, and the Constitutional History of Scotland: with Occasional Remarks concerning English Antiquity Edinburgh: Printed for William Creech; and John Murray, London, 1779. xxiii, 395p.

Second edition. Appended to the second edition of the *History of Scotland, from the Establishment of the Reformation, till the Death of Queen Mary* (see below, 1782).

1780

The History of the Establishment of the Reformation of Religion in Scotland. London: Printed for J. Murray, No. 32 Fleet-Street; and J. Bell at Edinburgh, 1780. Engraved portrait of Stuart; viii, 268p.

Gilbert Stuarts Doctors der Rechte und Mitgleids der Gesellschaft der Alterthumsforscher in Edinburg. *Geschichte der Reformation in Schottland.* Aus dem Englischen. Altenburg: in der richterschen Buchhandlung, 1786 [Translated by Leopold Ludwig Wilhelm Brunn]. 16, 424, 76p.

New Edition. Edinburgh: Printed by Robert Allan, 1805. Portrait; [vi], vii, 395p.

New Edition. Greenock: Printed for William Scott, 1810. Portrait [iv], vii, 395p.

1782

The History of Scotland, from the Establishment of the Reformation, till the Death of Queen Mary London: Printed for J. Murray, N° 32, Fleet-Street, 1782. Vol. 1: [xii], 448p; Vol. 2: [x], 410p.

London: Printed for J. Murray, N° 32, Fleet-Street; and John Bell at Edinburgh, 1782. Vol. 1: [xii], 448p; Vol. 2: [x], 410p.

Dublin: W. Gilbert, T. Walker, J. Beatty, R. Burton, J. Exshaw, P. Byrne, & J. Cash, 1782, Vol. 1: [xix], 489p; Vol. 2: [xv], 448p.

New Edition. London: C. Dilly, 1782. Vol. 1: [xix,] 489p; Vol. 2: [xv], 448p

Second Edition. To which are Annexed, *Observations concerning the Public Law and the Constitution of Scotland.* London: Printed for J. Murray and G. Robinson, 1783–84. Vol. 1: Portrait of Mary; xxiv, 476p; Vol. 2: [i], 312, iv, [5]–159 [xxxii]p.

Second Edition. London: J. Murray and G. Robinson, 1784. Vol. 1: Portrait of Mary (reversed and different engraver). [xxiv], 476p; Vol. 2: [i], 312, iv, [5]–159, [xxii]p

Critical Observations concerning the Scottish Historians Hume, Stuart, and Robertson: including an Idea of the Reign of Mary Queen of Scots, as a Portion of History; Specimens of the Histories of this Princess, by Dr. Stuart and Dr. Robertson; and a Comparative View of the Merits of these Rival Historians: with A Literary Picture of Dr. Robertson, In a contrasted Opposition with the celebrated Mr. Hume. London: Printed for T. Evans, Pater-Noster-Row, 1782. [i], 53p.

Index

Adam, Alexander, 88-90
Allibone, Austin, xi
'Anecdotes of Laura and Petrarque', 91-2
appendices in Stuart's works, 99, 168-9
Aristotle, 21
Armstrong, John, 36
Arniston, Lord *see* Dundas, Robert
Arnot, Hugo, 61, 85, 111
Atholl, Duke of, 4, 5, 48-54

Babington Conspiracy, 161-2
Bacon, Francis, 14
Balfour, James, 33, 34, 105-6
Baron, William, 64
Beattie, James, 64, 71, 74
Beckford, William, 139
Beddoes, Thomas, 175
Bell, John
    and *English Constitution*, 10
    and *History of the Reformation*, 134
    and *Public Law of Scotland*, 120
    and *View of Society*, 96, 112
birth of Stuart, 1
Blacklock, Thomas, 64
Blackstone, Sir William, 99
Blair, Hugh, 47, 74, 147
    Stuart's comments on, 175-6
Bolingbroke, Henry St. John, 14
Boswell, James, 174, 177
    education of, 5, 9
    'Journal of my Jaunt', 40
    London Magazine, 44-5, 57, 69
    political views of, 103-4, 125, 126, 127-9
    Robertson, comments on, 170
    Stuart, comments on, xiv
Bothwell, Earl of, 149, 152-8
Boucé, P.G., 55
Boulard, Antoine, 112
Brady, Robert, 25, 116

Brooke, Frances, 58
Brougham, Henry, 107, 123-4
Brown, Dr John, 35, 108
Bruce, Alexander, 185
Bruce, John, 86
Brutus, Lucius Junius, 85, 180
Buccleuch, Duke of, 125, 129
    Stuart's attacks on, 108-10, 178-9
Buchan, Earl of
    'Biographia Caledoniead', 172, 173
    and Dundas, Henry, 181, 182-3
    and Edinburgh Committee, 178
    and *History of Mary Queen of Scots*, 168
    and Moray, Earl of, 160
    as patron, 4
    and Robertson, William, 169
    and Royal Society, 170-1
    and Society of Antiquaries of Scotland, 166, 182
    and Stuart's death, 185-6
Buchanan, George
    and Casket Letters, 155-6
    influence of, 89, 138, 170
    and Ruddiman, Thomas, 2, 143-4
    Stuart's comments on, 127, 144-5, 149, 185
Burke, Edmund, xiii, 181
Burnett, James *see* Monboddo, Lord
Burns, Robert, 38
Busby, John Richard, 88
Bute, Earl of, 7, 66

Caesar, 24, 28
Caledonian Mercury, 2, 87
    advertisements in, 60, 70, 114
Campbell, Ilay, 129, 179
Carlyle, Reverend Alexander
    and *Edinburgh Magazine and Review*, 64
    and Mary Queen of Scots, 172

and religion, 74
Robertson, comments on, 104, 106
Scots militia, comments on, 125-6
and Stuart: comments on, 121;
    death of, 184, 186
Carlyle, Thomas, 31
Cartwright, Edmund, 175
Casket Letters, 146, 154, 155-6
Chalmers, George, 104-5, 121
Cicero, 47
Cockburn, Henry, 127
Coleridge, Samuel Taylor, 31
conjectural history, 11-16, 22, 32
Craig, James, 84
Craig, Thomas, 172
Creech, William
    as buyer for Stuart's works, 60, 114,
        120-2
    and *Edinburgh Magazine and Review*,
        63, 70
    and Monboddo, Lord, 94, 95
critical notes, 24, 25
Critical Observations, 13-14, 55, 166-7
Critical Review, 69, 79
    Stuart's contributions to, 45, 80-1
    Stuart's works, reviews of, 31, 48,
        111, 121, 162
Cullen, Dr William, 42
Cumming, Reverend Patrick, 1
Cummins, R., 186
Currie, James, 175

D'Israeli, Isaac, xi, 77-8
Daily Universal Register, 9, 186
Dalrymple, David, 4, 100, 147
    Annals of Scotland, 42, 73
    Stuart's correspondence with, 95,
        113, 123, 173
Dalrymple, John, 14, 15, 32, 101
Dalzel, Andrew, 37
Darnley, Lord, 149
    murder of, 146, 151-4, 146, 158, 161
De Lolme , J . L., 58-9 , 73
death of Stuart, 182-7
Dickens, Charles, 134
Donaldson, Alexander, 94
Donaldson, Gordon, 155
Donaldson, John, 132, 168
Douglas, Gavin, 2
Drummond, William, 2
Duncanson, James, 4
Duncanson, Jean *see* Stuart, Jean Dun-
    canson
Dundas, Henry

Boswell's comments on, 128-9
    and chair of Public Law, 34, 107
    as Lord Advocate , 83 , 170
    and patronage, 4, 60
    political career of, 117, 125, 169,
        179, 181-2
    Stuart's opposition to, xiii, 108-10,
        168, 178, 187
Dundas, Sir Laurence
    as patron, 4
    political career of, 66, 75
    Stuart's opposition to, 83, 85-6, 108-
        11
Dundas, Robert (Lord Arniston), 3

Edinburgh, Stuart's history of, 60-1
Edinburgh Advertiser, 7
*Edinburgh Amusement see Weekly
    Magazine*
Edinburgh Magazine and Review, 63-95,
    187
    criticism of, 41
    establishment of, xiii, 7, 45
    and Smollett, Tobias, 56
    Stuart as editor of, xii, 54, 105, 108
    Stuart's comments in, 9, 49, 59, 125,
        136-7
Edinburgh Review
    of 1755-6, 66-8
    of 1802, 13, 64, 65, 66, 73
Edinburgh University, 1-3, 9-10, 33-4,
    107-8
education of Stuart, 6-7
Elizabeth I, 170
    in *History of Mary Queen of Scots*,
        149-53, 159-63, 169
    in *History of the Reformation*, 140-1
Elliot, Gilbert (Lord Minto), 2-4
Elliot, Gilbert (3rd Baronet)
    and *English Constitution*, 20
    and Stuart, George, 6-8, 10, 33-4
    and Stuart, Gilbert, 39-40, 125
Encyclopaedia Britannica, 35, 165
English Analytical Review, 174
English Constitution, xiii-xiv, 10-11, 14-
    35, 39
    and Hume, David, 59, 187
    and Millar, John, 43
    and Murray, John, 41
    and politics , 51, 81, 97 , 115 , 116
    and Robertson, William, 44
    and *View of Society*, 101, 113
English Review xiv 173-80
Erskine, David Steuart *see* Buchan,

Earl of
Erskine, Henry, 38, 169, 178-9
Erskine, John, 87
European Magazine, 106, 112
Evans, Thomas, 55

Faction Displayed, 109-10
Ferguson, Adam, 33, 74, 101, 119
    Essay on the History of Civil Society,
        12, 27
    History of the Roman Republic, 13
    Stuart, influence on, 7, 25, 86
Ferguson, Walter, 84
Fergusson, Robert, 71
Fletcher, Andrew, 125
footnotes in Stuart's works, 24-5, 99,
    114-15, 122
Fox, Charles, James, xiii, 176-7, 178-9

Garrick, David, 56
Gentleman's Magazine, 69, 186
Germany, parallels with Britain, 28, 31,
    60
Gibbon, Edward, 15, 130, 164
    Decline and Fall of the Roman Empire,
        13, 64, 72, 103, 148
Gillies, Reverend Alexander, 64, 68, 70
Gillies, John, 111
Godwin, William
    and *English Review*, 175
    and *Political Herald*, 179-80, 182-3
    and Stuart, xi-xii, 26, 188
Goodall, Walter, 145-8, 154, 155
Gordon, Lord George, 119, 134
Grant, Reverend Donald, 37
Gray, Thomas, 57
Gregory, Dr James, 186
Grenville, George, 50-1, 53
Griffiths, Ralph, 45, 173

Hailes, Lord *see* Dalrymple, David
Hamilton, Alexander, 175
Hamilton, Archibald, 45, 69, 79
    and *History of the Reformation*, 131
Hawkesworth, John, 87
Hayley, William, 26
Hellins, John, 175
Henry, Robert, 75, 77-81, 82, 83
Heriot's Hospital, 83-5
history of Edinburgh, 60-1
History of Mary Queen of Scots, xii-xiii,
    130, 141-73
    and religion, 76
    review of, 186

style of, 13, 34
success of, 124
History of the Reformation in Scotland,
    13, 130, 131-42
'History' section of *Edinburgh
    Magazine and Review*, 71-2, 84
Holcroft, Thomas, 175, 188
Home, Henry *see* Kames, Lord
Homer, 24
Hooke, Nathaniel, 47
Horace, 114
Hume, David
    and *Edinburgh Magazine and
        Review*, 64, 73-4, 77-80, 95
    and Elizabeth I, 152
    and Elliot, Gilbert, 3
    and *English Constitution*, 25, 26, 27,
        32, 59, 187
    and *History of England*, 30, 43, 99-
        100, 135, 143
    and MacPherson, James, 22
    and Mary Queen of Scots, xii-xiii,
        145, 147-9, 153-4, 156, 162
    and Millar, John, 42
    and Monboddo, Lord, 93
    and Moray, Earl of, 159
    and patronage, 4, 39-40
    and politics, 18-21
    and *Public Law of Scotland*, 116
    and religion, 119, 121
    and Stuart: attacks by, 81, 82-3;
        correspondence with, 41;
        influence on, 46, 167
    style of, 11-14, 112-13, 130, 139, 164
    success of, 63
Hunter, Professor William, 88-9

James V, 136-7
James VI of Scotland (James I of
    England), 160-1, 163
Jeffrey, Francis, 13, 64-8, 73
Johnson, Dr Samuel, 81, 103, 174
    and politics, 17, 126, 143-4
    writings of, 46-7, 70, 72, 86
Jones, William, 129-30
Junius, 41, 47, 53
Justamond, J.O., 175

Kames, Lord, 25, 32, 101
    Historical Law Tracts, 14, 15, 21
    Sketches of the History of Man, 12, 73,
        99
    Stuart's comments on, 23, 100, 115
Kenrick, William, 57-8

Kerr, Robert, 34, 64
Kincaid, Alexander, 10, 61
Kinoull, Earl of, 84
Knox, John, 156, 172
  in *Edinburgh Magazine and Review*, 76-7
  in *History of Mary Queen of Scots*, 149, 150, 157
  in *History of the Reformation*, 132, 136, 139

Langhorne, John, 57
Laurie, Gilbert, 75, 83, 85
Lennox, Earl of, 137, 161
'Letters of Junius', 17
Liston, Robert, 58, 175
Livy, 115
Locke, John, 46
Logan, Reverend John, 172, 175-6, 184
London Magazine, 44, 89

MacDonald, Sir Alexander, 103
MacGrugar, Thomas, 177
Mackenzie, Henry, 8, 46, 80
Mackenzie, John (of Delvine), 8, 32, 54-5, 100
  and 'Memoirs of the Isle of Man', 48-9, 51-3
Mackie, Charles, 3
MacMillan, John, 44, 69, 89
Maconochie, Allan, 107
MacPherson, James, 22
MacQueen, Reverend Daniel, 74, 79
MacQueen, Robert, 82
'Magazine' section of *Edinburgh Magazine and Review*, 69, 70, 91, 92
Maitland, William, 60
Mandeville, Bernard, 36
Mansfield, Lord, 4, 32
Mary Queen of Scots, xiv, 2, 14, 187
  in *History of the Reformation*, 132-3, 136, 137-8, 140
  see also *History of Mary Queen of Scots*
Mason, Janet, 4
Mason, William, 57
'Memoirs of the Isle of Man', 13, 48-54, 187
Millar, John, 100, 108, 112, 119, 185
  Observations concerning Ranks, 12, 42-3, 96
Millot, 58
Minto, Lord *see* Elliot, Gilbert

Monboddo, Lord, 12, 73, 93-5, 173
Montesquieu, 14, 32, 46, 101
  Stuart, influence on, 15, 25, 26, 28, 31
Montgomery, James, 33
Monthly Review, 69 , 79, 111
  articles by Stuart, 8, 45-8, 58, 60, 61, 173
  articles on Stuart, 31, 121
Moore, John, 56, 175
Moray, Earl of (James Stuart), 140, 170
  in *History of Mary Queen of Scots*, 149, 153, 155-6, 158-60
Morton, Earl of, 155, 160-1
Mossner, Ernest, xi, 77-8
Mountstuart, Lord, 114, 125
Murdoch, John, 6
Mundell, James, 6
Murray, John
  and De Lolme, 58-9
  and *Edinburgh Magazine and Review*, 63, 70-3, 83, 85, 92, 95
  and *Encyclopaedia Britannica,* 165
  and *English Review*, 171, 173-5, 179
  and *Faction Displayed*, 110
  and Hawkesworth, John, 87
  and Henry, Robert, 80
  and *History of Mary Queen of Scots*, 166, 168
  and *History of the Reformation*, 131-4, 136
  and Hume, David, 79
  and Monboddo, Lord, 94
  and narrative history, 13
  and *Poems of Mr. Gray*, 57
  and *Public Law of Scotland*, 114, 119-21
  and Smollett, Tobias, 54, 56
  and Stuart, 41-2, 45, 60-2, 106, 108: correspondence with, 37, 67, 75, 89-91; death of, 38, 183-4, 185
  and *View of Society*, 96, 100-1, 111-12
  and Whitaker, John, 81-2

narrative history, 12-14, 19, 22
Newton, Isaac, 14
Newton, Lord, 38
Nimmo, William, 70
North, Lord, 4, 16, 60, 176-9, 181
notes in Stuart 's works, 24-5, 99, 114-15, 122

Phillips, James, 143

Pinkerton, John, 26
Pitcairne, Archibald, 2
Pitt, William, xiii, 177, 179, 180-1, 182
Political Herald, 179-84, 187-8
    articles by Stuart, 62, 119, 128-9
Price, Richard, 86
Priestley, Joseph, 72-3, 86
Pringle, John, 108
Public Law of Scotland, xiv, 113-29, 133,
    134, 149, 187
    and *History of Mary Queen of Scots*,
        169
    notes in, 24
    review of, 177
    and Robertson, William, 142, 148,
        167
    style of, 12, 32

Ramsay, John, 5
reference notes, 24-5
*Repository: or Treasury of Politics and
    Literature for MDCCLXX, The*,
    41-2
'Review' section of *Edinburgh Magazine
    and Review*, 69, 72
Richardson, John, 111
Richardson, Samuel, 154-5
Richardson, William, 56, 64
Robertson, William
    and Blair, Hugh, 176
    and Boswell, James, 128
    and *Critical Observations*, 166-72
    and Elliot, Gilbert, 3
    and *History of America*, 99
    and *History of Charles V*, 96, 101-2
    and *History of Mary Queen of Scots*,
        145-9, 152-6, 162
    and *History of Scotland*, 44-5, 77,
        126, 143
    and *History of the Reformation*, 142
    and Hume, David, 78-9
    and Millar, John, 42
    and Murray, John, 131
    and *Public Law of Scotland*, 116, 118-
        24, 129-30
    and religion, 74
    and Stuart, 39, 104, 185-7: attacks
        by, 81, 83, 90, 100, 110-14, 179;
        support from, xii, 47-8, 75
    style of, 13, 139, 164
    and *View of Society*, 105-8
Rolt, Richard, 48
Roper, Derek, 64
Ruddiman, Thomas, 1-3, 5, 88-9, 143-4

style of, 32, 146
Ruddiman, Walter, 1, 2, 69

Sandby, William, 10, 41
Scots Magazine, 69
Sheridan, Richard Brinsley, xiii, 179
Sheridan, Thomas, 7
Sibbald, Robert, 2
Smellie, William, 34-5, 36, 38, 108, 186
    and *Edinburgh Magazine and
        Review*, 63-4, 70-3
    and Henry, Robert, 75, 80
    and Hume, David, 78
    and Monboddo, Lord, 93, 94-5
Smiles, Samuel, 174
Smith, Adam, 11, 12, 14, 93, 101, 119
    and *Edinburgh Review*, 66, 67
    and Robertson, William, 104-5
Smith, Sydney, 65
Smith, William, 48
Smollett, James, 4, 54
Smollett, Tobias, 2, 4, 45, 69
    Stuart's biography of, 54-6
Somerville, Thomas, 40, 44, 104, 144
Sophocles, 24
Stewart, Dugald, 11-12, 104
Stockdale, Percival, 45
Stoddart, James, 83, 109
Stuart, George, 1-10, 88-9, 99, 183-6
    and Elliot, Gilbert, 33-4
    and Mackenzie, John, 55
    and Robertson, William, 39
Stuart, Gilbert
    birth of, 1
    death of, 182-7
    as editor, 47, 48, 54, 59
    education of, 6-7
    as translator, 57-9
    see also titles of works
Stuart, James *see* Moray, Earl of
Stuart , Jean Duncanson , 1, 4, 55, 184
Stuart, Walter, 1, 61-2
Sullivan, Francis, 59-60, 81
Swift, Jonathan, 17

Tacitus, 15, 22, 151
    Stuart, influence of Tacitus on, 24,
        28, 31, 137
Temple, William, 57
Thomson, William, 38, 169, 184
    and *English Review*, 175
    and *Political Herald*, 179-80
    and *View of Society*, 106, 112
translations by Stuart, 57-9

Tytler, Alexander Fraser, 108
Tytler, William, 147-8, 154

View of Society, xiv, 12, 87-8, 133
 and Hume, David, 20
 notes in, 24
 and politics, 36, 43
 and religion, 75-6
 and Robertson, William, 44, 119
 style of, 32, 115
 success of, 111-13, 187
Virgil, 24
von Blankenburg, Friedrich, 112
Voltaire, 104

Waaggstaffe, Walter, 110
Wallace, William, 7
Walpole, Horace, 139
Wedderburn, Alexander, 66, 67-8
Weekly Magazine, 69, 74
Wesley, John, 165-6
Whitaker, John, 81-3, 175
Wilkes, John, 41, 53, 56, 62
Witherspoon, John, 87
Wyvill, Reverend Christopher, 178

Yorkshire Association, 178

28 DAYS

DATE DUE

NOV 1 1 1995		
DEC 6 1995		
JAN 2 3 1996		
APR 4 1996		
APR 1 9 1996		
MAY 2 3 1996		
AUG 9 1996		
SEP 7 1996		
NOV 1 3 1996		
DEC 9 1996		
FEB 1 5 2003		
NOV 2 1 2003		